MAP OF NETHERLANDS
MODERN DAY

THE DUTCH FISHING VILLAGES, WHOSE JERSEYS ARE INCLUDED IN THIS BOOK

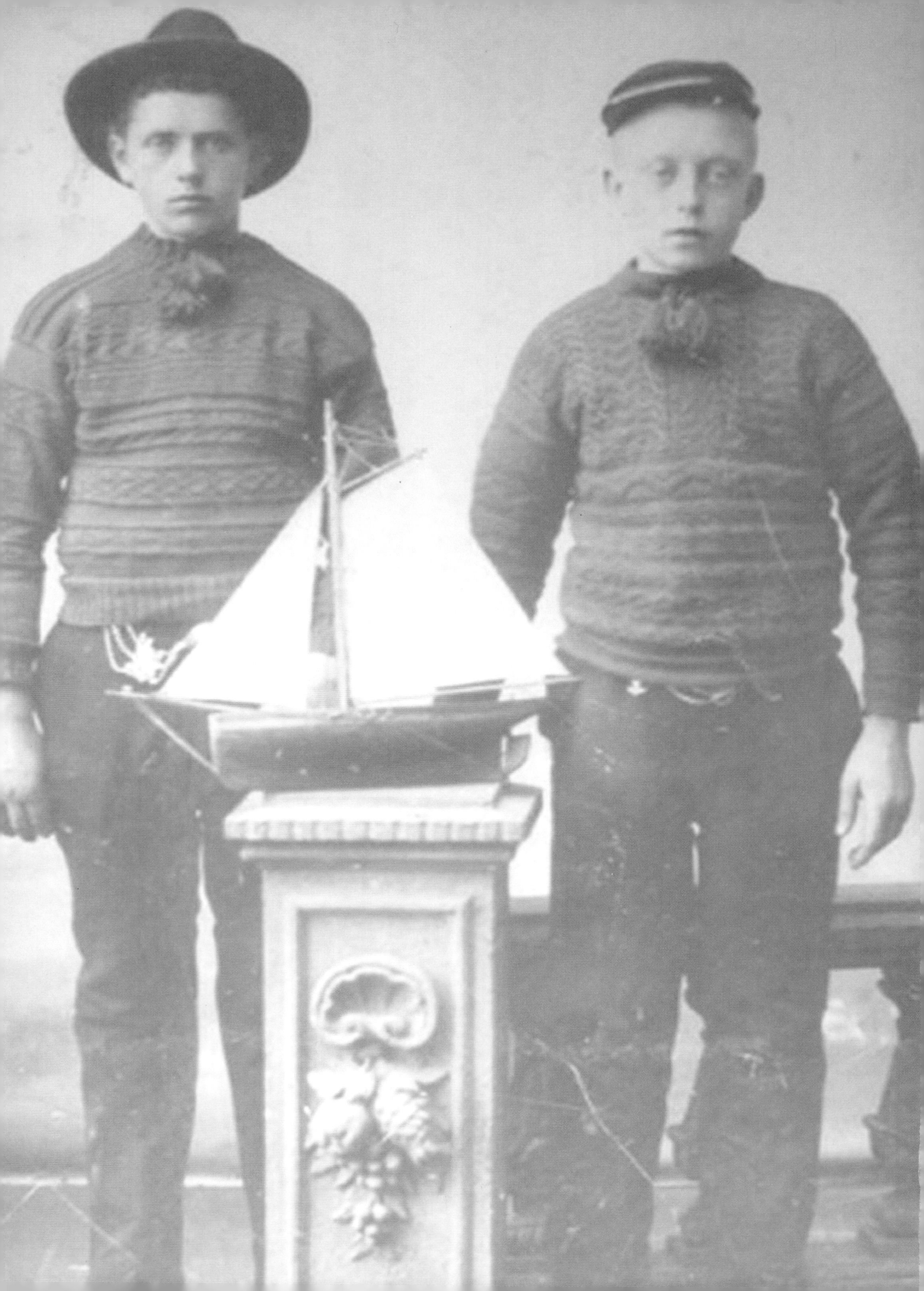

STELLA RUHE

MORE TRADITIONAL DUTCH GANSEYS

65 CLASSIC SWEATERS TO KNIT
FROM 55 FISHING VILLAGES

SEARCH PRESS

CONTENTS

FOREWORD	**4**

1. HISTORIC OVERVIEW — 6

Corrections	7
Ganseys	8
Knitting	9
Sweater	10
Hand-knit & machine-knit sweaters	11
Work gear	12
Practical sweaters	12
Sea fishing	14
Herring fishing	14
Shetland Islands	17
Dialects	17
Religion	20
Scotland, England & Ireland	21
Herring girls	21
Scottish & English ganseys	22
Other countries fishing for herring	25
Germany	25
Belgium and France	26
Fishing for fresh fish	26
River or inland fishing	27
Disasters: a high price to pay for fish	28

2. FISHING CULTURE AROUND 1900 — 30

Shipping companies	32
Vessels	32
Signing on	34
Crew	34
Wages	37
Stop box & clothing	37
On board	37
Provisions	38
Navigation	41
Lack of wind	42
Signalling & fishing system	42
Fishermen's wives	43

3. KNITTING — 44

Sajet	46
Yarn types	47
Needles & tools	48
Technique	48
Sizes	48
Stitches	49
Swatch & stitch count	49
Motifs and patterns	50
Basic sizes	52
Patterns & charts	53
How to start a gansey	54
General knitting instructions	
Knitting in a round	54
Front and back of the sweater	54
Collar	55
Sleeves	55
Finishing	55
Flat knitting	55
General information	55
Other models	55

4. NORTH SEA COAST — 56

North Holland	
Den Helder & Huisduinen	58
Petten	65
Egmond aan Zee	67
IJmuiden and Velsen	69
Zandvoort	71
South Holland	
Katwijk	73
Scheveningen	78
Pernis	81
Vlaardingen	84
Zwartewaal, Voorne-Putten	91
Middelharnis, Goeree-Overflakkee	95
Stellendam, Goeree-Overflakkee	97
Goedereede-Havenhoofd, Goeree-Overflakkee	99
Ouddorp, Goeree-Overflakkee	102
Zeeland	
Colijnsplaat, Noord-Beveland	105
Breskens, Zeeuws-Vlaanderen	106

5. MAJOR RIVERS 110

South Holland: Charlois 112
North Brabant
    Woudrichem 114
    Willemstad 118

6. WADDEN SEA COAST 120

North Holland: Oosterend, Texel 122
Friesland: Wierum 127

7. ZUIDERZEE COAST 130

North Holland
    Wervershoof & Medemblik 132
    Enkhuizen 135
    Hoorn 138
    Volendam 140
    Marken 143
    Huizen 145
Utrecht: Bunschoten-Spakenburg 148
Gelderland
    Harderwijk 152
    Elburg 155
Overijssel: Genemuiden 158
Flevoland: Urk 160
Friesland
    Lemmer 164
    Hindeloopen 168

8. MODERN INTERPRETATIONS 170

WORD OF THANKS 173

ACKNOWLEDGEMENTS 174

UNKNOWN COUPLE FROM ARNEMUIDEN/VLISSINGEN, CA. 1900. VLISSINGEN CITY ARCHIVES

FOREWORD

In September 2013, I published my book *Visserstruien uit 40 Nederlandse vissersplaatsen* (published in November 2013 in English as *Dutch Traditional Ganseys*), about the sweaters worn by fishermen in the Netherlands between approximately 1880 and 1950. I wrote this book after discovering that, in a lot of fishing villages, the knowledge about traditional ganseys had been lost – many people had even denied that they were ever worn. The idea that the knowledge of this special part of Dutch heritage would soon disappear altogether made me brush aside my initial hesitation to write about this subject. My book created quite a stir, both in the Netherlands and abroad. After attending my lectures and the travelling exhibition of the reknit sweaters, people dived into archives and looked up photo albums only to discover that they did have photos of their grandfathers or great-grandfathers, who were fishermen, wearing a gansey. Nowadays it is quite normal to see a man in a sweater, but back then fishermen were the only men wearing sweaters, which they wore as *bovengoed* – or outerwear. The other men wore a suit or a *kiel*, meaning a frock. Lots of people and organisations sent me old photographs of fishermen in ganseys, such as the City Archives of Vlaardingen. These included photos I already knew about, described in the book *Nederlandse visserstruien* by Henriëtte van der Klift in 1983 (published in English in 1985 as *Knitting from the Netherlands: Traditional Dutch Fishermen's Sweaters*), and they have been included here to complete the picture of the ganseys worn in the Netherlands. I also received amazing photos from the KNRM archives (Royal Dutch Lifeboat Society) in Den Helder, confirming the rumours that ganseys with block patterns were worn in Den Helder. To my great surprise, the photos also showed natural-coloured ganseys, and even a sideways knit gansey. I received special photographs from new fishing villages, where people had also thought no ganseys were worn, such as Huisduinen, Petten, Colijnsplaat, Breskens, Oosterend, Wervershoof/Medemblik, Hoorn, Huizen, Genemuiden, Lemmer, and river towns, such as Rotterdam Charlois, and the towns of Willemstad and Woudrichem in Brabant! From towns with known ganseys I received more photographs, showing even more ganseys, confirming that different sweaters were worn side by side in many fishing villages: women would knit what they liked, but were also inspired by the work of other knitters. The ganseys from the first book, which were reknit later, and those from towns where no new ganseys were found, can be seen on the fly leaves at the back of the book. For the charts, I refer to *Dutch Traditional Ganseys*.

Not only fishermen fishing for herring, flatfish and roundfish wore ganseys, but also the fishermen on the big rivers fishing for salmon, sturgeon and eel. Especially along those rivers, there may still be quite a number of ganseys yet to be discovered. A possible future mission!

The amazing stories, the new facts, the photos that we discovered during and after the lectures, the finds on photos of ganseys from the first book which we were not able include there, the additional information I found in various books and on many websites, as well as a number of visits to the English East coast and the Shetland Islands, have all contributed to an increased insight into the history of the ganseys – which was surprisingly varied – and their uses. This new information was the reason to continue with research, and publish this second book, with 65 new ganseys – naturally with charts which, again, were reknit following the original T-shape. To secure the ganseys as part of our Dutch heritage, the same formula has been used as for the first book: the sweaters are knit in available yarns, varying from thin to thick yarn, in a colour palette that was typical of ganseys, from more natural tones such as Nassau-beige and grey, to countless shades of blue and black. Again, no step-by-step instructions are given for the ganseys. Not only would they be insufficient and more importantly too restrictive, but because the basis of all ganseys is the same. What we do specify is how the knitter worked, which serves as a guideline for knitting your own sweater.

Before you start knitting a sweater, read the chapter 'Knitting' and the extensive, general knitting instructions on pages 54 and 55. These instructions apply to all ganseys, irrespective of size and yarn used. The chest measurements always determine the size of a gansey, and the gauge determines how often the stitches and rows of the motif have to be repeated. This makes it possible to knit a gansey for a man, woman or child, in any type of yarn. If you are not an experienced knitter, start with a simple sweater before casting on a complicated design. Practice makes perfect!

Again, the sweaters in this book were knit by talented knitters from all over the country. They were instructed to simply follow the patterns, but they also had the freedom to adjust their ganseys on the basis of the material used – as the fishermen's wives would have done. These ganseys now form part of a large exhibition that has been travelling around the Netherlands since 2015, with all the ganseys from the two books. More and more, we are getting a complete picture of the ganseys worn in the country. There were approximately 240 fishing towns and villages in the Netherlands around 1900. Still very little is known about the ganseys that were worn in other countries around the North Sea. Some information is now coming to light, but there is still plenty of work to be done.

One of the starting points for the social-historical part of the book is the fishing culture: these include the voyages a fisherman made every season (mainly herring) to the fishing grounds, what he needed and brought with him, what he ate and what he did on board, for example, when there was no wind. Another starting point is the connection with the English and Scottish fishermen: what they thought of the Dutch as they arrived in England and Scotland, and how they did not quite understand why the Dutch were so good at herring fishing.

To not only make this special part of Dutch heritage come alive, but also to make it 'fashionable' again, the motifs and patterns used in the ganseys – in addition to the T-shape – have been used as the inspiration for some contemporary designs, with different types of sleeves, such as raglan, cuffs and collars. Again, there is no extensive description given, because that would simply take up too much space.

Just knit and combine the motifs and patterns as you like, as the women once did. You can make your own tribute to the countless, anonymous women and girls who made the most beautiful creations with their skills and creativity in simple knit and purl stitches, with the odd cable.

Stella Ruhe
Amsterdam 2015

GROUP OF FISHERMEN FROM VLAARDINGEN. FROM LEFT TO RIGHT: ARIE KEMP, MAARTEN BOT, JOHANNES VAN DER LUGT, VAN EMBDEN (?) AND KLAAS VAN DORP, CA. 1905. VLAARDINGEN CITY ARCHIVES

1 HISTORIC OVERVIEW

THE VL 112 *ADRIAAN* FROM THE SHIPPING COMPANY IJZERMANS, CA 1922. COPYRIGHT J. BORSBOOM. VLAARDINGEN CITY ARCHIVES

Dutch Traditional Ganseys (2013) gives an extensive explanation of the origin and the use of ganseys, the associated developments in the fishing industry in the second half of the nineteenth century – in particular herring fishing, which was crucial for the wearing and dissemination of the gansey – and the poor living conditions of the fishermen and their families around 1900. We found and recorded some beautiful stories in my previous book. Here, I shall give a summary of the origin and use of the gansey, and explain a bit more about herring fishing and the life of fishermen at sea. I add some interesting facts and details which were not known to me when I wrote the first book, and which have, in some cases, led to different insights. These insights are also based on new information about the Scottish and English ganseys, which partly form the basis for the Dutch ganseys.

CORRECTIONS

As in the previous book, a number of photographs are listed under the location where they were found, as are the names of the people wearing the ganseys. During my lectures, I met people who recognised the fishermen in those pictures as their grandfather (or great-grandfather), or who knew the exact names of the fishermen. For example, Babs van Dongen recognised the man in the Ouddorp photo as her grandfather, sailor Johannis van Dongen (1877– 1912) from Middelharnis. He perished when the MD 3 *Anna* sank in 1912. The motif of the gansey was often seen in Ouddorp, but the front placket in

1 JOHANNIS VAN DONGEN FROM MIDDELHARNIS. VAN DONGEN FAMILY COLLECTION

2 FISHERMEN FROM ZOUTKAMP, MUSEUM 'T FISKERHÚSKE PAESENS-MODDERGAT AND ZOUTKAMP FISHING MUSEUM

the gansey is typical for ganseys from Middelharnis (Fig. 1).

The group photograph on page 126 of *Dutch Traditional Ganseys*, provided by Museum 't Fiskershúske in Paesens-Moddergat, on which sweater 3 from Paesens-Moddergat is based, caught the eye of Berend Zwart from the Fishing Museum in Zoutkamp, who believed it came from Zoutkamp. All the names of the fishermen are now known – from left to right, standing: Jacob Buitjes, Ties Bos, Jan Benes, Jans Rispens, Jan Faber (nickname Jan Abraham), Geert Buitjes and Hendrik Bol. The last man was nicknamed 'Hennerk Houd' because of the fact that he always wore a hat (*houd* meaning 'hat' in Groningen dialect). Because he also had a bald head, he got a second nickname: 'Blode kont ien houd', again in the Groningen dialect and meaning 'Naked bum in hat'. In Fig. 2, all of the men are seen to be wearing knitted hats – in the front row, from left to right: Lammert Groefsema, an unknown man, Benes, Jacob Kamstra, Allert Frik and Willem Ritsema. This means that not just the men from Paesens-Moddergat but also those from Zoutkamp wore Scottish-inspired, knitted tams. This book now includes these ganseys, where they rightfully belong.

GANSEYS

Ganseys – not to be confused with the sweaters with a zip that were worn by river and freight captains after the Second World War, which were inspired by the then hugely popular English navy sweaters – were worn between approximately 1875/80 and 1940/50 (i.e. before the Second World War) as work gear by fishermen and other sailors, such as life-boat crews, pilots, crews of ferries, cane cutters and life guards. Because the ganseys were just work gear and made by women, nothing was recorded. Photographs are practically the only source for finding ganseys, because there are only a few ganseys in museums, all of which are of a more recent date. Usually, ganseys ended up as deck mops, which means that very few have survived (Fig. 3).

The photographs of fishermen before 1920 are the best and the sharpest, because photographers used glass plate negatives and the daylight collodion-silver print method (a technique used until 1940). Photographs were expensive, and individual fishermen could only afford to have their

3 GANSEY FROM SCHEVENINGEN CA. 1945, MUZEE SCHEVENINGEN

picture taken when they had had a good catch and earned a bit more money than usual – they were paid on the basis of a percentage of the proceeds. Around 1900, at the height of the fishing industry, ship owners would often have photographs taken of their crews. The oldest photos of Dutch fishermen in ganseys date from the 1880s (Fig. 4). That is why it is difficult to determine when the first ganseys were worn in the Netherlands. In addition, because of the long-term contacts with fishermen from Shetland, Scotland and England, dating from the fifteenth/sixteenth century, who already wore ganseys as sweaters around 1830 (see box, Fig. 5), it is quite possible that the Dutch fishermen also wore ganseys much earlier. However, again, because of the high cost and rarity of photographs (invented around 1820) during that early period, there is no photographic – or any other – evidence.

4 TWO FISHERMEN FROM HARDERWIJK OR URK, CA. 1881, MUSEUM OF HARDERWIJK

5 Detail from a painting from 1829 by Joseph Stannard (Norwich, 1797–1830), Cromer Museum in Norfolk on the English East Coast. It shows a fisherman in a knit gansey, which, oddly, is red.

When people became more prosperous after the Second World War and could buy clothes instead of making them themselves, the gansey gradually disappeared. Not because the men no longer wanted to wear them, but because the women no longer wanted to knit them. In areas where the traditional costume managed to stand ground, the gansey was also worn a lot longer.

Knitting

Knitting is one of the oldest textile techniques (Fig. 6). It is a so-called one-thread system (like, for example, crochet, filet knotting and spool knitting), and is dissimilar to weaving, which requires two threads, a warp and a weft. In northern areas such as Iceland and Scandinavia, people were already knitting sweaters in the fifteenth century to offer fishermen added protection against the harsh weather. These knits were characterised by the fact that they were in two or more colours, because the extra threads carried along at the back made the sweater warmer. Usually, the sweaters were knit a lot bigger and then fulled (a controlled method of felting) to make them extra sturdy. These processes made the sweaters less soft and supple. The picture (Fig. 7) taken around 1920 on the Faroe Islands shows a fisherman wearing a gansey in one colour, like the ones in this book, and the other (Fig. 8) shows several multicoloured sweaters with a circle motif.

The hand-knit sweaters, such as the ganseys and sweaters now worn in the Netherlands, originally come from the English Channel islands of Guernsey and Jersey. From the sixteenth century onwards, men would knit sweaters for export and to have something more useful to do than smuggling and piracy, which before then were their major sources of income. This was the start of the sweater tradition along the British coasts, as the gansey was easier and warmer to work in than the smocked frocks they originally wore. From Scotland, the so-called 'herring girls' disseminated patterns along the English coastline to the south from around 1840 (see page 21).

In the Netherlands, fishermen were the first to wear hand-knit sweaters as outerwear. Knitting was common in the Netherlands. In fact, the Dutch had been famous for their knitting since the Middle Ages, when guilds of (male) *breiders* ('knitters') were set up, who hand-knit the most beautiful silk stockings and shirts for

6 ALTARPIECE IN BUXTEHUDE NEAR HAMBURG WITH EARLIEST DEPICTION OF KNITTING, CA. 1390

7 OLD FISHERMAN FROM THE FAROE ISLANDS, DENMARK

European royals and nobles. Sweaters were actually worn as underwear, under frocks and other woven items of clothing (Fig. 9); the body and sleeves were always knit circularly, like a tube. Mothers taught their daughters how to knit at a very early age, and there were so-called knitting and sewing schools.

The ganseys were knit circularly in the same way, on four or five thin needles, using *sajet* or 'sagathy' (fine, twill, worsted wool from Texelaar sheep, see page 46), according to the same tube system. They would add 4–6cm (1½–2⅜in) to the chest measurements (measured under the armpits, around the chest). All sizes and numbers were then divided by three. A third of the number of stitches was for the one shoulder, one third for the neck opening – which was not rounded initially, and ran in a simple straight line over the shoulders – and one third for the other shoulder. At the height of the armholes, which formed one third of the length of the overall gansey – the body made up the other two thirds – the work was divided into two parts, and the back and front were worked separately on two needles. The shoulder seams were closed with a knit bind-off, creating the armholes. Stitches were then picked up around the armhole to knit the sleeve, decreasing the number of stitches towards the wrist. There were no seams to sew, making the ganseys totally seamless.

It wasn't until the 1920s when Coco Chanel – inspired by the sweaters worn by fishermen from Brittany – introduced the sweater as outerwear for everyone. While the fishing ganseys were developed and knit based on the skills and oral traditions of knitters, the new fashionable sweaters were designed from a tailor's perspective. They were published in knitting magazines of yarn manufacturers with patterns and clear instructions. It can be said with great certainty that the men wearing the ganseys on photos before the 1920s are fishermen. The sweaters they are wearing all have the same knitted tube form, of a T-shape with sleeves knit from the armhole down. The motifs, in knit and purl stitches, in just one colour, sometimes with cables or openwork motifs, dictated the structure. Per location, these motifs could differ greatly; the most simple ganseys are found in Zeeland, while the most elaborate are found on the islands in Zuid-Holland. More about this later.

Although some people assume that sailors and sportsmen like golfers and cyclists from that period also wore sweaters, these were quite different: they were usually completely smooth jerseys, often machine-knit. Examples of these from the period post 1910 can be found on the Internet.

9 WOOL, LONG-SLEEVED VEST IN T-MODEL. THE SEAMS UNDER THE ARMS ARE LEFT OPEN. SHETLAND MUSEUM, LERWICK, SHETLAND ISLANDS

Sweater

The Dutch word for sweater, *trui*, is possibly related to the Estonian word *troi* and the Danish *troje*. The word in Low German is similar: *tröje*. Other similar words are found in Middle Dutch (*troye*,

8 FISHERMEN FROM THE FAROE ISLANDS IN TRADITIONAL COLOURFUL AND PLAIN KNIT SWEATERS, CA. 1915

troie), Old Norse (*treyyja*, meaning 'frock under the breast harness') and possibly Latin (*troga*, meaning 'monk's shirt made of horsehair'). In the Egmond dialect, the Derpers, the word *trooi* is still used. In the Dutch language, the word trui was first recorded in the Leeuwarder Courant of 1837: '(...) dressed in a blue overcoat, blue striped vest and colourful trui (...).' The sailors that went to the Baltic Sea may have spread the name for this garment.

The English word for the fishing sweater is 'guernsey' or 'gansey'. There is a lot of discussion about the origin of the word: a dialectical derivation of the word Guernsey, after the island of Guernsey, where the first sweaters came from (sixteenth century) or of the Gaelic word *geansaidh* or Norwegian *genser*, which also mean 'sweater'. As there is a link to herring fishing in that time, this last explanation makes more sense. Another English word for sweater, 'frock' or *froke*, is still recognisable in the dialect in Katwijk, where they still talk of a *frok*, or in Middelharnis, where *vrok* means gansey.

Hand-knit & machine-knit sweaters

The ganseys were knit by hand, were worn collectively by fishermen and are comparable to work jeans or overalls today. With the exception of Volendam, the sweater was not part of the official costume; as a result of which there are no written records, meaning that we know little to nothing about them.

As fishing communities were often very close-knit and isolated – the women, in particular, had little contact with people outside their own village or community – sweaters with their own motifs were developed. These were based on daily life, faith, the sea, the beach, the weather, the vessels and the fishing tradition. The motifs all had their own meaning, often to ward off danger and disaster (see pages 50–52). The women would find their inspiration in what others were knitting. In all villages, many variations on local patterns can be found. When a woman moved to another village after marrying, she would introduce new motifs and patterns as they were passed on from mother to daughter. She would often make her own versions based on the patterns she was taught, in order to reflect the fashion of the day, but still create something a bit different. This not only happened here in the Netherlands but elsewhere, as I discovered in the UK. There, the Scottish

10 SCHOOL CLASS FROM ARNEMUIDEN, CA. 1895. THE PHOTOGRAPH SHOWS THREE BOYS (BOTTOM LEFT) WEARING DIFFERENT TYPES OF GANSEY. ARNEMUIDEN HISTORICAL ARCHIVES

'herring girls', who followed the fishing fleet, were the source of inspiration (see page 21). This meant that the sweater could, in some cases, be used as a means of identification when a drowned fisherman washed ashore, as in those days people did not have passports. This is one of the possible myths about the ganseys, as no proof of this has been found, although in Urk I was told that a fisherman from there, who washed up at Egmond, had been identified by his sweater. Sometimes sweaters combined different motifs (Fig. 10, 11). Another myth is that the women, when knitting a gansey for their fiancée for the first time, would knit some of their long hairs into the design, as a sign

11 GANSEY COMBINING BLOCK AND SNAKE MOTIFS, WHICH ORIGINATE FROM ARNEMUIDEN. HOLLAND OPEN AIR MUSEUM, ARNHEM

12 PLAIN, ENGLISH, MACHINE-KNIT GANSEY FOR THE DUTCH MARKET, WITH THE EYE OF GOD ON THE CHEST

of their love and to protect their beloved against the dangers at sea. This might well be possible, because superstition played a major role in those communities. However, no proof of this has been found in the ganseys that have survived.

All over the country, in addition to the home-knit sweaters, people also wore machine-knit English sweaters, specifically made for the Dutch market: 'smooth' jerseys, with the eye of God on the chest (Fig. 12). These sweaters, which I initially thought were cheaper to buy than the sajet for a home-knit sweater, were actually a status symbol. If you could buy a jersey, that meant that you were well-off. However, if a dead fisherman washed ashore wearing such a sweater, there was no way of telling where he came from. In England, both those smooth jerseys and sweaters with motifs were machine-knit. I found one example of such a sweater on a fisherman, in a photograph of the crew of a Katwijk lugger (Fig. 13); the sweater may possibly have been bought in the fishing village of Cromer, Norfolk, on the east coast of England. There were several knitting factories in that area, and Dutch fishermen would regularly go ashore to buy clean water and salt for gutting.

Work gear

We have to make a great deal of speculation about the ganseys, and base our insights on stories and

13 CREW OF THE KW 97, WITH FISHERMN WEARING A MACHINE-KNIT GANSEY WITH ZIGZAG MOTIF FROM CROMER (CENTRE), CA. 1914. MUSEUM KATWIJKS

the consolidation of the available information. Apparently, people were very proud of their home-knit ganseys, because many fishermen had photographs taken of themselves wearing them. The majority of fishermen would generally only have one work sweater, in addition to their Sunday sweater. Although the work sweater would start as a Sunday sweater, which was sometimes also worn at weddings, it would usually end up as a deck mop or polishing rag, after having been endlessly made

14 BRIDE AND GROOM ABRAHAM DIERMEN (1904–1980) AND REINTJE HARTOG (1907–1980) FROM SPAKENBURG, CA. 1924. PHOTOGRAPH OF BERTINE RUIZENDAAL-BAAS, BUNSCHOTEN-SPAKENBURG

longer, mended and patched up. The Sunday sweater would then become the work sweater, and a new Sunday sweater was knit. In England, the distinction between the Sunday or wedding sweater and the work sweater is easier to see: the first would be knit in a significantly thinner yarn, 3-ply, on very thin needles, while the work gansey was knit with thicker 5-ply yarn on bigger needles.

Practical sweaters

Everything about the ganseys was practical:
- A gansey had no seams in order to make it wind- and waterproof. The sweater was knit circularly. The shoulder seams were also closed with a knit bind-off.
- The ganseys had a T-shape, making it easy to hang them up on a long stick through the sleeves in order to dry them when they got wet.
- They had little ease (chest + 4–6cm (1½–2⅜in)) and were tightly knit on much thinner needles than we would do now, to make them windproof. In some ganseys one shoulder would be left open and fastened with buttons (Fig. 16), or they would get a front placket (Middelharnis, Fig. 17) to make them easier to pull over the head. The sleeves were on the short side, to keep the hands

15 FISHERMAN FROM PERNIS, CA. 1910. VLAARDINGEN CITY ARCHIVES

16 YOUNG FISHERMAN, PROBABLY FROM WIERUM, CA. 1900. FRIES MUSEUM

17 KRIJN VAN GELDER, MIDDELHARNIS, CA. 1900. GOEREE-OVERFLAKKEE LOCAL ARCHIVES

18 MINISTER CORNELIS VAN DE GRUITER AS A YOUNG FISHERMAN, ARNEMUIDEN, 1900. ARNEMUIDEN HISTORICAL ARCHIVES

and forearms free during work. Often, sleeve protectors were worn. Fishermen also frequently had very nasty wounds called *mouwvreters* ('sleeve rippers') from the cuffs to their fingers, because they held their arms and hands in salt water whilst gutting herring with razor-sharp knives or with the hooks of the longliners (see the box on page 15, and also page 26). Not everyone had the money to buy good (waterproof) gloves. Some of the men would make mittens from an old blanket or sheet.

- The vulnerable cuffs, which wore a lot faster, were sometimes knit with the yarn held double.
- The turned cuff, visible on many photos, was not just made simply so that it was knit in the same thickness as the rest of the sweater; it was also a fashion statement and very practical: the cuffs were used to keep cigars, which were considered to be healthy in those days; boys would smoke therefore from a young age. When they came back from their first voyage, they were often given a box of cigars.
- There was no elastic band. With time, the collar would be loose and sag, and the cold and water could come in. Fishermen would then weave a cord through the holes in the collar to tighten it up. The cord would have tassels or pompons at the end (Fig. 18). They also had another function: if the herring fleet (see the box below) on the North Sea pulled up the nets and the herring was shaken out, there would also be quite a bit of by-catch, including jellyfish. These jellyfish would secrete poison, which could enter your eyes. The tassels or pompons were used then to wipe the eyes. The cords were typical for Dutch ganseys. For the cord to be woven in easily, a row of holes would be knit a few rows before the collar bind-off. I have also seen ganseys with the cord simply inserted through the ribbed collar.
- The ganseys were never washed and often not even take off. Hygiene played no significant role, and washing was done by simply wiping your face with the wet tip of your handkerchief. Besides, you wouldn't want to wash yourself with salt water. There was limited drinking water on board, which was only used for coffee, tea and cooking. The herring would be caught at night or early in the morning, as those were the periods when they swam to the surface. When fishing, fishermen would work four-hour shifts alternating with four hours off, so it made no sense to change clothes. As a result the ganseys were very dirty and greasy, but with the advantage that they also became water- and windproof. However, fishermen were sometimes so dirty that the clothing fused to the skin. If they had to go to hospital, they were first soaked in oil for two days before the clothing could be pulled off. Then, they would be washed and scrubbed with soap, after which they might die within days as their skin no longer kept out the germs.
- If the fishermen were very poor, which was usually the case, the sweaters would be knit in stocking/

The vleet
A vleet *was a long series of drift nets, sometimes 3 to 4 kilometres (1.86 to 2.5 miles) long, used for herring fishing. The* vleet *was kept afloat by floats, called* breels, *and weighted down at the bottom with leads, creating a type of sea curtain. The nets were attached to a thick hemp rope, the* reep, *with thinner ropes. The nets could be raised or lowered, depending on where the herring was.*

> **Dirty**
> In Paesens-Moddergat and Zoutkamp, I wrote down a story about hygiene: there were two women in Paesens-Moddergat who would lay out the dead, including fishermen who had perished at sea. After a while, one of the women said to the other, 'Do you want to take his socks off?' The woman answered, 'I already did!' His feet were so dirty that it seemed like the man was still wearing socks.

stockinette stitch for the largest section – from the bottom hem to the chest and the sleeves – with motifs for the part of the gansey that had to stay extra warm: the chest and lungs. This applied to both the front and the back. A motif requires more yarn than stocking/stockinette stitch and is therefore warmer.

- In contrast to the Scottish and English sweaters, only the very oldest ganseys had underarm gussets and shoulder straps (page 24, Fig. 35 and 37). These are no longer present in later ganseys. The gussets were knit to give the neckline more shape, which the knitter would bind off straight both front and back. This meant it did not matter which way was front or back. The underarm gussets would allow for a bit more space to move.
- The sweaters were forever patched up and reknit. The cuffs and elbows would wear first. Because the sleeves were knit from the armholes down, the sleeves could easily be ripped out to above the worn spot and reknit. Often, the old yarn was no longer available and the knitter would simply use the yarn at hand. This yarn might be of a different thickness and/or colour. Sweaters often had smooth sleeves or a motif above the elbows. If the elbows were worn, ripping out would have no effect on the motif. If the sweater could no longer be patched up and was totally worn and threadbare, it would be used as a deck mop or polishing rag.
- In some villages, such as Bunschoten-Spakenburg, Elburg and Urk, I was told that the sweaters were knit bigger than the intended size and then felted in boiling water. This made the sweater even more water- and windproof. The disadvantage of this was that worn sleeves could not be reknit. However, no photos were found to prove this.

SEA FISHING

Within the sea fishing industry, we distinguish between herring fishing and fishing for fresh fish. Fishing for herring was big business. Until 1857, only the villages of Vlaardingen and Maassluis were allowed to fish for herring; before that, Enkhuizen had the monopoly until 1704. Herring fishing was a type of test run for the expeditions to the East. The other villages along the coast would fish for fresh fish, such as flatfish and roundfish (plaice, sole, cod, haddock, mussels and shrimp).

Herring fishing

Without herring fishing there would be no ganseys. And without knowledge of the developments and history of the herring fishing industry in the second half of the nineteenth century, we would have no understanding of the creation and the use of the ganseys, which are both strongly connected to the industry. Between 1461 and 1861, the Dutch herring fishermen used large sailing ships, the so-called *haringbuizen* or 'herring buses', of which 800 to 1000 populated the North Sea around 1620 (Fig. 19). These vessels were usually owned by a few investors: the *partenrederij* ('part companies'). This organisation was also seen in the commercial sector and is considered as a precursor of the stock market shares system. Outside the herring season, the herring buses would fish for cod and also be used for freight, as they had a lot of available cargo space.

In those days, the Shetland Islands – where the herring migration approximately began – was already in use as a base during the herring season, which ran from June 24 (St. John's Day) until the end of November. This allowed the fishermen to be home for Sinterklaas, an annual winter celebration in the Netherlands that takes place the day before St. Nicholas' Day (December 6). From the islands, they followed the herring in international waters close to the Scottish and English south east coast, to the Channel/Straits of Dover. The relationship with the Shetland Islands were excellent from the beginning, and still are today. The contact with the English was more laborious, because the Dutch were rather successful at herring fishing.

> **Gutting ban**
> *In the seventeenth century, the States of Holland granted Vlaardingen, Maassluis and Enkhuizen, with their large ports, the exclusive right to gut herring, along with the lucrative herring export to Germany and France. A gutting ban was imposed on the other fishing towns, and landing gutted herring was strictly prohibited. These towns were forced to fish close to the shore for flatfish, roundfish, shrimp and mussels, which could only be kept fresh for a short time and had to be sold and eaten quickly.*

There were constant wars about, for instance, the rights to the herring grounds.

In the beginning, the villages of Vlaardingen, Schiedam, Maassluis and Delfshaven were the main ports for herring fishing. After the battle on the Zuiderzee in 1573, which in those days still had an open connection with the North Sea and was a spawning ground for the Zuiderzee herring, the herring fishing industry in Enkhuizen boomed. At that time, Enkhuizen had the largest herring fleet in Holland.

After a considerable dip in the eighteenth and beginning of the nineteenth century, the abolition of the gutting ban and arrival of the lugger (see page 33) resulted in an explosive growth in the size of the herring fleet in the second half of the nineteenth century (see box).

Other fish, such as haddock and cod, were caught early around Iceland and Greenland by fishermen from places such as Pernis and Zwartewaal. As a result, they may have been the first ones to come into contact with sweater-wearing fishermen from the North. At that time, they would also go on whaling expeditions in northern waters. At the end of the seventeenth century, England and the States of Holland waged a number of wars at sea for fishing rights and trade routes, which in those days were like highways for the transport of freight and fish. In 1704, Enkhuizen lost the largest part of its herring fleet in the wars with the English and in an attack by privateers from Dunkirk in the bay of Lerwick, Mainland (the largest of the Shetland islands). Enkhuizen never recovered from this loss and from then on the town focused on anchovy fishing on the Zuiderzee.

After a new Fisheries Act lifted the gutting ban in 1857, to aid the long-suffering fishing villages on the Zijde (the coastline between Den Helder and Hoek van Holland), and the development of a fast sailing lugger around 1866, all fishing villages were able to start lucrative herring fishing for ship owners and exporters.

Just like the fleets of Vlaardingen, Maassluis and Enkhuizen had already done, the other Dutch fleets decided to use the Shetland Islands as their base during the herring season. Lerwick, the main city on Mainland island, partially owes its existence to the Dutch fishermen. In Lerwick town hall, a stained-glass window from Amsterdam bears witness of this origin.

However, there was a problem. The fishing villages on the North Sea Coast between Den Helder and Hoek van Holland had no ports for their rapidly growing lugger fleets, which needed a port for mainly two reasons:

1. the required breakthrough in the dunes was technically impossible because of their keel
2. the government was terrified that enemy fleets would use those ports – in particular the port of Scheveningen, which was only three kilometres from The Hague – to quickly attack and overthrow The Hague.

In towns like Scheveningen, Katwijk and Noordwijk, Zandvoort, Petten, etc., fishermen would fish for fresh fish along the coast, traditionally with pinks and later with *bomschuiten* (see page 32, Fig. 54 and 55) – flatboats that could start

> **Gutting herring**
> *Gutting herring on land has been a custom since the twelfth century, as shown in archaeological finds in the Roskilde Fjord in Denmark. The technique of gutting at sea was developed around 1400 by Willem Beukelszoon from Biervliet. Using a sharp gutting knife, the gills, heart, stomach and gall bladder were removed, leaving the pancreatic tissue in the fish (with enzymes to mature the fish meat), after which the fish was cured in brine. Since the invention in Hoorn of the knit (filet-knotted) herring net in 1416, large numbers of Dutch fishermen started fishing for herring. As a result of the curing process, herring was the nation's favourite food until the Second World War: herring was cheap, nutritious, full of protein and could be kept for a fairly long time.*

19 HERRING BUS. ORIGIN UNKNOWN

Herring

Herring (Clupea harengus), also called silverback, grows up to 45 centimetres (17¾in) long, can weigh up to 1 kilograms (2.2 pounds) and can live for up to 22 years. The fish has a silver body with a grey-green or blue-green back. Herring make 'farting' noises by letting gas escape from their swim bladder. Herring live up to a depth of 200 metres (109.25 fathoms), but move closer to the surface in the morning to eat plankton. Schools of herring can contain millions of fish. That is also where the name herring comes from. In Old Dutch, herring was written as heering; the word is derived from the word heer, which means 'army'. It is therefore a fish that lives in large schools, or armies, in the North Sea. It migrates each year, following a set pattern. Irrespective of the circumstances and weather, herring always follow the same route. That makes it easy to predict where the fish will be. Herring is a fatty fish that is rich in omega-3 fatty acids. They can sometimes have herring worms, a parasite that can damage the stomach or intestinal wall in humans. To combat this worm, Dutch law prescribes that all herring for human consumption has to be frozen first.

Consumption

Herring is eaten in various forms. As matjes herring/ Hollandse nieuwe with a minimum of 16 per cent fat; as herring in brine/salt, as pickled herring and rollmops (rolled around a gherkin); as pan herring (unsalted fried herring); as smoked herring or kipper; and as surströmming – canned, Swedish fermented herring.

20 PICKLED HERRING

from and land on the beach. From 1857, they were also allowed to fish for herring. When, after 1866, the industry gradually started using the much more manoeuvrable and faster sailing luggers, the fleets of Scheveningen and Katwijk were moved to the ports of Vlaardingen and Maassluis. The other towns stayed true to their *bomschuiten* and did not build on their lugger fleets. Gradually, fishing would make way for tourism, a huge growth industry around 1900. IJmuiden only got a large fishing port at the end of the nineteenth century (in 1896), after the North Sea Canal was built in 1876. Scheveningen followed in 1904, but with a 'marine threshold' keeping enemy ships out of the port. Fishermen from all over the country would sign on in Vlaardingen, Maassluis and IJmuiden on the lugger fleets located there when their own fishing grounds were poor, for instance around the year 1900. This explains a few 'riddles' in photographs of fishing crews, showing ganseys from various towns and villages.

Most fishermen from the Northern coastal areas would go to the German port city of Emden – on foot – where a number of shipowners from Vlaardingen had built up herring fleets.

The fishing world was relatively small. People would not only meet each other on board of ships, on the Shetland Islands and in English ports, but also in the so-called shelter ports, where boats could take refuge against the bad weather. Most fishermen would know each other. By the end of the nineteenth century, the port of IJmuiden was used by fleets from villages on the Zuiderzee, such as Marken, Volendam, Huizen and Urk, to quickly access the North Sea and supply Amsterdam. Boats from, for example, Middelharnis (Fig. 21) and other towns

21 SLOOP FROM MIDDELHARNIS WITH CREW IN THE PORT OF IJMUIDEN, CA. 1900. GOEREE-OVERFLAKKEE LOCAL ARCHIVES

22 PORT OF LERWICK WITH DUTCH LUGGERS.
KATWIJKS MUSEUM

If the herring was not mature enough, or if there was no herring left, the fleet would sail along the English south coast to fish for other types of fish, such as mackerel.

When fishermen came into contact with the ganseys worn by fishermen as work gear on the Shetland Islands and in the English and Scottish coastal towns, they brought them with them to the Netherlands, either by smuggling them or by

would make use of this port, because their own ports had started to silt up. All these contacts between fishermen spread the practice of wearing a gansey as work gear, not just amongst herring fishermen but also those who fished on rivers. The gansey became part of every fisherman's attire.

Shetland Islands

Most Dutch fishing fleets chose Lerwick on the Shetland Islands as a base during their herring season, which started at the end of May (Fig. 22, 23, 27). It would take too long to sail all the way home, so they would load the barrels of gutted herring onto so-called jagers or carriers – ships from the same shipowner – which would transport the catch back to

Coopers
Gutted herring was stored in a wooden barrel, called kantje, made by a dry cooper. A barrel would have around 100 small or 400 large herrings. A load or last of herring would be 17 kantjes (Fig. 21). For heavily salted, gutted herring, one barrel of salt would be used for four barrels of herring. After settling, 12 to 14 kantjes of herring would be left. The so-called wet cooper would open up the barrels of settled herring on land and fill them up with more herring. The catches that would be brought ashore with bomschuiten were fresh, ungutted and only lightly salted herring (a barrel of salt for 12 barrels of herring) because of the gutting ban. This type of herring was also called 'green herring'.

exchanging them for tobacco and *jenever*, 'gin' (jugs of which can still be seen in some of the museums on the Shetland Islands). In the Netherlands, the women would copy these ganseys. Like most of the English and Scottish women they used one colour of wool, knitting motifs in knit and purl stitches, with cables and a bit of openwork here and there. This explains why the Dutch ganseys were knit in the indigenous Texelaar yarn, sajet (see also page 46). Sweaters by this time were already being knit and worn as vests, but never as outerwear (see also pages 9 to 10).

Dialects

The fact that fishermen would spend six months on the Shetland Islands and in England also explains why the dialects in Dutch fishing villages contain lots of pidgin English and differ from the dialects spoken in towns and villages close by. People from Egmond, Katwijk and Scheveningen could understand each other quite well, but in Alkmaar, less than ten kilometres from Egmond, people wouldn't be able to understand a word of what they were saying. Quite a

23 DUTCH FISHERMEN IN LERWICK. KATWIJKS MUSEUM

the Netherlands while the fleet could remain at the fishing grounds. The Dutch shipowners were the only ones who worked in this way, and it gave them a huge advantage over herring fishermen from other countries. This led to the herring race: the ships that brought in the first catch of herring had the honour of presenting a barrel to the king or queen.

Sea singing

Non-rhythmic chanting, or 'sea singing', is a way of singing whereby each note – usually a semibreve or whole note – is sung for the same duration. It is still used in traditional Dutch reformed churches. Churches often had bad acoustics, which meant that the notes would resonate too long to sing complicated tunes. Therefore, people started singing whole notes, as it was simply a lot easier to do. Psalms are often still sung in whole notes in traditional Dutch churches. Rhythmical singing is considered as too salacious and could be the start of other evil practices, like singing praise songs – or as they would say, 'It begins with rhythmic singing and it ends with hupsakee and tralala.' They were also of the opinion that singing at a slower pace and with semibreves was more devout, because there was more time to reflect on the text. However, there are no Biblical arguments for this. Sea singing, or *op het zeetje zingen*, was also purported to have developed from the chorals sung to the rhythmic sound of footsteps walking up to the temple in Jerusalem.

Loony Lugger

Life at sea was difficult and scary, with the high waves, mist and unpredictable, stormy weather. Strange phenomena would occur, such as *bramzijgers* – vapours rising up from the water, taking on ghostly, devilish shapes. In this context, a whole new world and belief system was created. The normal world and the spiritual world of the Heavens were separate entities, but both were real for the people of that time. Nobody ever doubted that a heavenly world existed.

On 3 August 1915, the crew of the Katwijk lugger KW 171 *Noordzee V* left the port of IJmuiden, not knowing that soon three brutal murders would be committed. The KW 171 would later be called the 'Loony Lugger'. The boat had a crew of 13. One of the sailors, Arie Vlieland, had visited sectarian group meetings in the First World War, and had had strange religious experiences. The year before, in September 1914, hundreds of bodies had washed up on the North Sea coast as a result of the war at sea. The mass funeral and burial at the Nieuwe Kerk in Katwijk drew a lot of attention and left a deep impression. A number of natural disasters had also taken place. Since the start of the war in 1914, Arie had received signs from above that the End of Times was nigh and that he had a major role to fulfil: when the world ended, he had to safely sail his ship to the New Jerusalem. During the lugger's second voyage of the season, Arie saw in a vision that it was time. In a thick fog, a huge image appeared which became bigger and bigger (this later turned out to be the Norwegian freighter *Joan Rein*). Skipper Nicholas de Haas went weak at the knees, and the delusional Arie Vlieland took charge. With his charisma, he convinced the rest of the crew that they were the chosen ones to set sail for the Heavenly Jerusalem. During the voyage, a number of 'miracles' occurred: Arie balanced a book on its side, and there were a number of apparitions (possibly *bramzijgers*) on board. However, not everyone believed Arie, and three members of the crew were brutally murdered because they were said to be possessed by the devil. On September 12, the lugger was towed into a Dutch port by the *Joan Rein*. The survivors were admitted to a psychiatric hospital for further examination. The events are a dark chapter in the history of Katwijk.

24 THE KATWIJKSE LUGGER KW 171 *NOORDZEE V*, OR THE 'LOONY LUGGER'. KATWIJKS MUSEUM

Developments in herring fishing

Deep-sea fishing or *de Grote Visserij* focused on herring, an industry that was both protected and very lucrative because of the gutting ban. This situation did not change until 1870. In old, unwieldy and heavy ships (herring busses, hookers and, after 1857, also bomschuiten), fishermen would take their *vleets* out to sea between June and November to fish for herring along the English east coast.
The rest of the year, they would fish closer to home, with longliners (see page 26), for flat fish and round fish.

A new type of *vleet*

At the Amsterdam Fisheries Exhibition of 1861, Dutch fishermen, who used hemp drift nets for heaving, saw that the English and French had cheaper and lighter cotton nets and had ice on board, which gave them a huge advantage. Cotton nets then were introduced in the Netherlands around 1865, and ice was used from 1875. The length of the vleet, the total of all nets used, increased to 3 to 4 kilometres (2 to 2.5 miles), with the nets being up to 30 metres (33 yards) high. The catch increased dramatically, but they could not be handled by the slow fishing boats. As a result, fishermen changed to lighter and faster luggers and the carrier system. Within a period of 20 years, the fleet of busses and hookers was obsolete and almost completely replaced by modern luggers. Between 1850 and 1900, the catch increased tenfold, and in 1856 the market was expanded by the completion of the Rhine railways to Germany. In 1916, the Dutch herring fleet, with 900 luggers, brought in a record catch which was much higher than in the Golden Age. Most of the new ships were sailing ships. Steamers were hardly used, because the ships were stationary during fishing. The first steam capstan was installed in 1895, to enable the vleet to be hauled in mechanically. In 1897 the first steam luggers appeared.

Trawlers

In 1989, the small fishing town of IJmuiden premièred the first steam trawler. From then on, things progressed

25 FLOOD OF 1916, DEVASTATION IN SPAKENBURG. STICHTING ZUIDERZEEAMBACHTEN ENKHUIZEN COLLECTION

quickly: in 1914, the Dutch trawler fleet numbered 155 ships. Trawlers were ships that would continue to sail during fishing, which meant that steam and engine power became important. The trawlers would drag their nets on both sides of the ship along the sea bed. A sailing ship would not be able to provide the power needed. Because of trawler fishing and the introduction of ice coolers on board, large quantities of fresh plaice, sole, cod and haddock could be landed. The new developments quickly resulted in the expansion of the fishing grounds, spanning the entire North Sea up to the Icelandic waters. The catch increased to record heights, which could easily be marketed. Although more than half of the trawler fish would go to the hinterland, the export of fresh fish grew by 100 per cent between 1900 and 1914; most of this went to Germany.

Changes on land

The emergence of IJmuiden, built near the mouth of the North Sea Canal, dug in 1876, not only had an impact on the sea, but also resulted in changes on land. In 1896, the National Fisheries Port was opened, which not only was a fine accommodation for the modern trawler fleet, but was also connected to the railway network in 1897. In 1899, the National Fish Auction followed, which in 1914 already achieved *a turnover of more than seven million guilders. The concentration of the supply of, and trade in, sea fish at the mouth of the North Sea Canal was to the detriment of other fishing villages, although the fishermen of places such as Maassluis and Vlaardingen partially moved their supply to IJmuiden, and Scheveningen got its own modern fishing port in 1904.*

Hard times
Middelharnis, Zwartewaal and Pernis, with their longline boats, were badly affected; they were suffering also because the ports had started to silt up. Some shipowners moved their ships to the port of IJmuiden. The fishing industry on the Zuiderzee and the Wadden Sea was also going through some rough times. On the south shores, fishing disappeared from Elburg and Harderwijk. Ports further north, such as Enkhuizen, Stavoren, Lemmer and Hindeloopen, managed to keep their heads above water, but their traditional fishing grounds were overfished.
The development of the Oranje Locks in Amsterdam, closing off the river IJ from the Zuiderzee, formed a huge obstacle for the Zuiderzee fishing industry. A number of fleets were moved to the new port of IJmuiden, fishing for herring on the North Sea, in order to be able to sustain some form of seasonal fishing on the Zuiderzee. While North Sea fishing was booming around the turn of the century, the future of the fishermen on the Zuiderzee looked bleak. Continuous flooding of the islands of Wieringen, Marken, Urk and Schokland, and the devastating flood disaster of February 1916 (Fig. 25, 26), resulted in the construction of the Afsluitdijk in 1932, as part of the Zuiderzee Works, which totally closed off the inland sea. The sea became a fresh-water lake, the IJsselmeer.

26 FLOOD DISTASTER OF 1916, DEVASTATION IN MARKEN. STICHTING ZUIDERZEE-AMBACHTEN ENKHUIZEN COLLECTION

MARKEN De Groote Watersnood van 1916

In het omgeslagen huis woonden meerdere gezinnen, de bewoners konden slechts gered worden door ze aan touwen gebonden uit de huisdeuren door het water te trekken naar het zolderraampje van het huisje links. Op deze wijze moest ook een kindje van 4 weken gered worden. Op het zoldertje van bedoeld huis waren 37 menschen gevlucht.

lot of Dutch words also found their way into English and Scottish dialects. For example, the famous herring girls (see opposite page) used a *kist* ('box') for their tools, similar to the Dutch fishermen, who had a *stoppenkist* or 'stop box' (see page 37).

Religion

Fishermen were deeply religious people, partly due to the uncertainty of their existence: would they catch lots of fish, would the ship survive, would they be able to make their way back home safely? In contrast to many other countries, the Dutch fleets respected a strict Sunday rest. There was no fishing on Sundays: it was a day of rest which started on Saturday evening, with the crew baking and eating pancakes. The pancakes would be made by an *oudste*, an eldest (see page 35). If the ship was fishing close to Lerwick, they would sail to the bay. The ships would moor at the quay or drop anchor in the bay, and the fishermen would go ashore. On Saturday afternoon, they would do their final shopping, attracting quite a bit of attention in their traditional dress, with their knickerbockers (particularly worn by fisherman from Urk and Marken) and clogs (Fig. 27). In Lerwick, there would be a special church service for Dutch fishermen in the Dutch church. *De Hoop* (see Fig. 28) would also moor in Lerwick, and the ship's minister would lead the service: this hospital-church ship would never be far off, nor would a number of naval vessels that were responsible for protecting the fleet. The Scots and English were impressed by the psalms sung during the Dutch services, which seemed to follow the movements of the sea (see box at the top of page 18). In Katwijk, this was called 'sea singing'. During weekends, the

27 FISHERMEN FROM URK AND MARKEN IN THE PORT OF LERWICK. SHETLAND MUSEUM & ARCHIVES

fishermen could also consult the physician on *De Hoop*. At the stroke of midnight on Sunday night, work on the ships would resume. In Lerwick, there is a Dutch cemetery where many Dutch fishermen are buried.

Scotland, England & Ireland

Because the Dutch fishermen dominated the herring fishing industry on the North Sea, around 1770 the Scots and English decided to build their own herring buses, which enabled them to gut herring on board. However, to their dismay, they were unable to match the quality delivered by the Dutch. They abandoned the buses, which could only be moored in larger ports. Instead, they built a larger fleet of small boats, which enabled them to bring herring ashore to smaller villages with shallower or tidal ports, and have the herring gutted there. Around 1840, this strategy proved to be a lot more successful. Herring fishing became a booming business in Scotland and England, also boosting the dissemination of the knitting patterns used in ganseys from the north to the south of Britain. How?

Herring girls

The smaller boats would land the herring in villages close to the fishing grounds. Groups of Scottish girls and women would already be waiting there to start gutting. These so-called 'herring girls' followed the fleets south by train. Some of the women travelled along the east coast, while others would go west, to the Isle of Man, Ireland and Wales. Every fishing village would have stations where these 'herring girls', 'gutting girls', 'gutter quines' or 'Scotch fisher lassies' would work in groups of three: two to gut and one to pack the herring in barrels (Fig 29, 30). Nothing was wasted: fish waste was used as fertiliser and the scales were turned into fake pearls. Gutting was always done outside, come rain or shine. The herring girls would have a kist for their tools and humble belongings. They worked long hours and were paid poorly. Their wages would depend on their speed, which increased with practice. An experienced gutter would be able to rhythmically gut and sort herring; a packer could fill a barrel, which contained a thousand herring, in an hour. The herring girls would wind bandages around their hands and fingers to protect them against the razor-sharp gutting knives and to prevent salt from entering the wounds. Despite these precautionary measures, most herring girls had raw and scratched hands – of which they were proud. Their living conditions, in shabby hostels or shacks, were far from ideal, but in all the photographs I saw they were laughing and smiling. This notion is confirmed by tape recordings made in the 1980s of a number of former herring girls: they would sing all day. If they weren't gutting herring, they would knit while waiting for the next catch to arrive. The lanolin in the wool was slightly soothing

28 THE STERN OF THE HOSPITAL-CHURCH SHIP *DE HOOP* WITH ITS CREW, DURING A VISIT TO VLAARDINGEN. THE SHIP IS IN THE OLD PORT. ALL GANSEYS READ 'HKS'. COPYRIGHT V.D. BERG'S *FOTOGRAFIE VLAARDINGEN*. CA. 1930. VLAARDINGEN CITY ARCHIVES

for their sore hands. They would often wear ganseys themselves, with short sleeves or the sleeves pulled up to keep their hands and arms free. The women in English coastal villages would always look forward to the arrival of the herring girls, as they were curious as to what knitting patterns they had been knitting. Like the Dutch knitters, the women would knit the patterns they liked and would be inspired by the work of others.

In Ireland, fishermen wore sweaters similar to the Scots and the English. In the 1930s the knitters on the Aran Islands developed the now world-famous Aran style, mainly for commercial reasons, with lots of intricate cables in bulky, natural-coloured tweed yarn.

Eventually the herring trade began to suffer from the many wars waged with England through the ages:

29 SCOTTISH HERRING GIRLS, CA. 1920, SHETLAND ISLANDS   30 SCOTTISH HERRING GIRLS, CA. 1930, SHETLAND ISLANDS

the Napoleonic Wars (which ended in 1815 and robbed the country of its European market), the First World War and the Second World War, when many fishermen lost their lives at the front. After the Second World War, many fishermen emigrated to Canada and Australia to start a new life.

Scottish & English ganseys

English ganseys are also called 'guernseys' or 'smocks'. The patterns were similar to those of the Dutch ganseys, and the motifs also had their origins in daily life. In the Netherlands, the ganseys would be named after the place the pattern came from. In England and Scotland, however, the pattern would often be named after the individual knitter or a family. For instance, Mrs Richardson's pattern looks similar to the Paessens-Moddergat 4 gansey (see the fly leaves at the back and *Dutch Traditional Ganseys* on page 131) and to the 'Betty Martin' pattern from Whitby, where no one knows who Betty Martin was. This last motif is also found in the middle part of the yoke of the Zandvoort 2 gansey (page 71).

Other ganseys that can be traced back to Scotland and England are the cabled gansey Katwijk, which closely resemble the cabled ganseys from Whitby and Flamborough in Yorkshire, and, for example, the ganseys from Scheveningen. The latter have many similarities with the ganseys that were worn on the Shetland Islands at the same time (Fig. 33, 34, 36), but their block design resembles various ganseys from the English east coast, such as the one from Scarborough. In general, the ganseys were less plain than the Dutch ones and had other combinations of motifs (Fig. 38 to 42). They also used more colours than just blue, black and natural: I have seen ganseys in red, pink, ochre, brown and various green tones. In England green was never be used, as this colour resembled the colour of the water too much. They believed that if a man went overboard, he could not be found if he was wearing green. The Scots had no problem with green, so most green ganseys are from Scotland (Fig. 42). Characteristic of the Scottish and English ganseys were the underarm gusset and shoulder strap. These gussets were diamond-shaped wedges knit between the body and the sleeve to create more arm room (Fig. 35). Something similar was done in the Netherlands, but in a different way: 3–4cm (1⅛–1½in) of stitches were picked up at the armhole, decreasing 1 stitch per row until the actual width of the sleeves was reached. The stitches would be decreased evenly towards the wrist. In very old Dutch ganseys you can still see the neck gussets

> **Ganseys in the making for a dead fisherman**
> *If the person whom the gansey was intended for died or remained at sea, the knitter would immediately stop knitting. The gansey would not be given to someone else, but was ripped out. The yarn would be kept in the cupboard for at least a year (throwing it out was not an option, as it was much too valuable), until the spirit of the fisherman had gone. Only then would the yarn be used for another gansey.*

(Fig. 37), which the knitters would bind off in the same way on the front and back so that the gansey could be worn either way. These gussets would give a bit more room to manoeuvre. Scottish and English ganseys had no tie cords. The Dutch had

31 RAYANNE AND PETER PERFORM FOR THE ENGLISH ROYAL FAMILY.
WILLIAM MOORE, SCALLOWAY, SHETLAND ISLANDS

Baffling Royalty.

Peter the Dutchman

In the summer of 1910, some boys were playing football at the gutting station in Scalloway (on the Shetland island of Mainland). They noticed an exhausted boy of about 13 or 14 years old sitting on a herring barrel, who looked at them but didn't say a word. When the game was over, the boys went home. Ten year old Jack Moore told his mother Mary about the strange boy. She sent her husband William to go look for him. The boy did not speak English, but it was clear that he was very hungry. William took him home, where he had a meal with the family. When he finished his food, he was put to bed and slept for almost 24 hours. He stayed with the family from that day on. His name was Pieter (Piet) Martens. He had signed on a Dutch herring lugger, where he had to gut herring, but because he was treated so badly he decided to run away when the ship moored in Lerwick. For some reason, Piet had decided to walk across the hills in his clogs, 18 miles northwest to Voe, where he hoped to catch a boat to Scotland or back home. But there were no boats in Voe, so he went south, towards Scalloway, walking another 17 miles – no wonder he was exhausted. Piet was 'adopted' by a family with three boys: Jack and his younger brothers Bob and Angus. Eight years before, Angus had been adopted as a baby; he had been abandoned by his mother, a herring girl (page 21) from Scotland, who had travelled to the village for the herring season. Piet, now called Peter, turned out to be a happy, strong lad who always worked hard. He started working in one of the herring factories in the village and was highly sought after. He called himself Peter Martens-Moore. He never spoke about his Dutch past, so we don't know where he was from. Maybe Brabant or Zeeland, because he joined the Belgian Army in the First World War. He got injured but survived. He left for America, where he worked in the world of illusionists and escape artists, and also appeared to have worked with the great Houdini. In the 1930s, he returned to England and married Rayanne, 'the World's Wonder Girl', a famous artiste (Fig. 31, 32). During the Second World War, they performed as illusionists and escape artists for the troops, both at home and abroad, and visited injured soldiers in hospital. They were very famous: by the end of the war, Rayanne had received 400,000 letters from soldiers and officers of all nationalities. She answered each and every letter herself. After the war, they gave two shows in sold-out theatres in the Shetland Islands. Peter died suddenly in 1957 in the English Midlands, while driving north from his home in the south of England to attend the funeral of his adoptive mother Mary in Scalloway. Bill Moore, the curator of the Scalloway Museum and son of Jack Moore, told me this story about his uncle Peter in Scalloway, Shetland Islands.

32 JACK MOORE AND PETER MARTENS-MOORE IN 1949.
WILLIAM MOORE, SCALLOWAY, SHETLAND ISLANDS

33 FISH PROCESSING BY ROBERT CHRISTIE, SCALLOWAY, CA. 1920. SCALLOWAY MUSEUM, SHETLAND ISLANDS

34 HERRING GUTTERS IN SCALLOWAY, EARLY 1900. SCALLOWAY MUSEUM, SHETLAND ISLANDS

35 UNDERARM GUSSET

36 TWO FISHERMEN FROM SCALLOWAY, LATE NINETEENTH CENTURY. SCALLOWAY MUSEUM, SHETLAND ISLANDS

37 SHOULDER STRAP

38 GANSEY FROM FOULA, SHETLAND MUSEUM, LERWICK, SHETLAND ISLANDS

39 WHITEHILLS TRIPLE ZIGZAG WITH DOUBLE CABLE. MORAY FIRTH PROJECT, SCOTLAND

40 WHITBY YORKSHIRE, CABLES AND MOSS STITCH. DEB GILLANDERS, WHITBY, ENGLAND

41 FLAGS AND LIGHTNING, SHERINGHAM, NORFOLK. THE MO SHERINGHAM MUSEUM, ENGLAND

42 BUCKIE, OPEN DIAMONDS/EYES OF GOD AND STEPS/LADDERS. MORAY FIRTH PROJECT, SCOTLAND

43 SWEDISH BOAT *ELSIE* IN SCALLOWAY. SCALLOWAY MUSEUM, SHETLAND ISLANDS

to deal with much harsher weather out at sea, while the Scots and English would stay relatively close to home.

Other countries fishing for herring

Herring fishing was not limited to the Netherlands, England, Scotland and Ireland. Germany, France and Belgium, the Nordic countries (Denmark, Norway, Sweden, Iceland and Finland) and North America (Canada and the United States) also fished for herring, some more successfully than others. Where information was found about the herring trade, I shall discuss this.

In Lerwick and Scalloway on the Shetland Islands, photographs were found showing fishermen from Sweden (Fig. 43), wearing a similar type of gansey to the Scots, English, Irish and Dutch. Marianne Horsman-Wagener found a sweater

44 THE FAROE ISLANDS, DENMARK

in Sweden with a design and motif similar to Enkhuizen 1 (*Dutch Traditional Ganseys*, page 142). Danish ganseys often had a bramble motif, as seen in the Noordwijk gansey (fly leaves at the back). This is proof that all fishermen on the North Sea and the Baltic Sea, who would also fish for herring, wore these ganseys. Photographs from the Danish Faroe Islands (Fig. 44), Brittany and Normandy show fishermen in similar ganseys. A lot of research still has to be done here.

Germany

The Germans followed the Dutch example and also started fishing for herring. Initially, they used herring buses and sailed to the Baltic Sea, but at the end of the nineteenth century there was no herring left there, forcing them to move to the North Sea. In 1872, the Vlaardingen shipowner Henri Kruthoffer set up the first lugger company in Emden: the Emder Häringsfischerei Aktien Gesellschaft. The company had six herring luggers. The company soon faced bankruptcy, but was kept afloat by Prussian state subsidies because salty herring was considered cheap food for the poor. Herring fishing never caught on in Germany, simply because the markets were too small and the railway network was too fragmented. The hinterland was hard to supply.

With the state subsidy, various lugger fleets were set up around 1900: in Bremen-Vegesack, Elsfleth, Geestemünde (now Bremerhaven) and Glückstadt. In 1911, the fleet was at its biggest, with 284 luggers. The German luggers employed a lot of Dutch fishermen from the northern coastal villages, and the shipowners from Vlaardingen had a great stake in the fleet. Photographs from that time, made in Emden, mainly show Dutch fishermen. They worked in Germany because they got paid better than at home. The Dutch system was based on the principle that each crew member would be paid a fixed percentage of the proceeds (called *besomming*, see page 37), after a deduction of 3 per cent and the load fee, a type of

45 GANSEY FROM SWEDEN, MARIANNE HORSMAN-WAGENER

25

tax charged on to the crew. The German system was based on a basic weekly wage, plus a bonus per crew member per tonne sold and travel expenses, depending on the distance. The average income of a sailor per season (which was around 20 weeks) was between 260 and 280 Dutch guilders, while a sailor on a German lugger would earn around 390 Dutch guilders in 24 weeks. However, on German luggers, sailors were expected to work on Sundays – a reason for which the very religious fishermen made the long trip to Vlaardingen, Maassluis or IJmuiden to work on Dutch luggers. During the First World War (1914–1918), many German luggers were commandeered for the war effort; German fishermen were called up to serve in the army and the herring trade collapsed. Specifically, German ganseys have not yet been found.

Belgium and France

Before 1832, the fishermen from Zeeland and the islands of Zuid-Holland would sell most of their herring in Belgium, but after the country gained independence Belgium imposed high import duties on sea fish, which had a huge impact on the fishermen's income. The Belgians managed to set up a longline fishing industry from Antwerp for a while. However, as they lacked expertise, they called in Dutch fishermen from, amongst other towns, Pernis.

Belgian fishermen, operating from English and French ports, focused on the more westerly fishing grounds (the English Channel, the Bristol Channel and St. George's) and the Spanish and Portuguese coasts. Between 1907 and 1913, various attempts were undertaken to breathe new life into herring fishing, but these were abandoned after the First World War. Horse fishing is characteristic for Belgium. The fisherman would go out to sea with his horse and nets to catch shrimps and mussels. Specifically, Belgian ganseys have not yet been found.

French fishermen also went fishing for herring quite early on – first in the Channel, and later moving ever further north. This still has to be researched, although there are some photographs of fishermen from Brittany and Normandy wearing similar plain ganseys.

Fishing for fresh fish

Along the coasts and further out on the North Sea, fishermen with *bomschuiten*, sloops and barges would sail for fresh fish. After the herring season,

46 SLOOP MIDDELHARNIS MD 4. GOEREE-OVERFLAKKEE LOCAL ARCHIVES

luggers would sometimes continue fishing for fresh fish such as mackerel, haddock and cod well into the winter. Around 1830, villages like Pernis, Zwartewaal and Middelharnis on the islands of Zuid-Holland changed to a more modern type of ship, the *chaloupe* or 'sloop' (Fig. 46). The seaworthiness and the speed of these sloops were better, and they could catch 10 to 40 per cent more fish than with a hooker. The sloops were more than 20 metres long and built for cod and haddock fishing. A new sloop would cost between 25,000 and 30,000 Dutch guilders. Because of the gutting ban (page 15), they started fishing on the Doggersbank and fishing grounds to the north. Because this fish had to be brought to the market alive, the sloops had a 'fish bun' (see box below). Live cod would yield on average 1.50 guilders per

Longliners and hooks for fishing

To fish for fresh fish, such as haddock and cod, longliners were used, with long main lines of up to 18 kilometres (11 miles) that had baited hooks on cross lines called 'snoods' (small fish or worms were used as bait). In Dutch, this was also called hoekwant *fishing.* Hoek *was the Old Dutch for hook, and* want *is the system of nets and ropes used on a ship. The fishing vessels had compartment holds called the* kaar *or* bun *that had a perforated wall which allowed sea water to flow through, keeping the catch alive.*

> **Smoking**
> *Smoking fish can be done in two ways: hot and cold. For cold smoking, the fish is smoked at a temperature of approximately 25 degrees Celsius (77 degrees Fahrenheit) for one to three days. Hot smoking only takes two to three hours, at a temperature of 80 to 100 degrees Celsius (176 to 212 degrees Fahrenheit). For cold smoking, cured fish is used, which is already cooked during the curing process. Cold-smoked fish keeps better than hot-smoked fish. Herring, eel and mackerel are the best known types of fish that are hot-smoked. The fish are brined for a short period, to give the desired salty flavour.*

fish, while a barrel of 300 salted haddock only had a commercial value of 8 guilders. Fish that was sold fresh or on ice had a value of 90 guilders. In the summer, the sloops would fish for cod, which was sold in barrels as salted fish. The vessels would make two long voyages, one from early May to early July, and one from mid-July to the end of September. They would continue fishing until the salt they had brought was all used up.

Each year, the catch decreased. In 1893, instead of two, the sloops would make only one 'salting' voyage. The voyage would last 13 to 14 weeks, with the longest voyage recorded being 15 weeks and three days. The last place where they could catch cod was De Scherpte, to the south of the mouth of the Skagerrak, 70 miles off the Danish coast. The last location where the longliners from Middelharnis, Pernis and Zwartewaal could go fishing was quickly depleted, meaning the end of the salt-fishing industry.

In 1875, the use of ice became fashionable and was an important development in the fishing industry: the fish could be kept for much longer, enabling the ships to make longer voyages. This also became a necessity, because they needed to travel ever further north to find good fishing grounds. Instead of sailing against the wind all the way back to Goeree, they would land the fish at Nieuwendiep, close to Den Helder. If the sea channels were blocked by ice drifts, they would sell the fish in Egmond aan Zee or Scheveningen. They would then drop anchor close to the shore and transfer the fish onto *bomschuiten*. In 1876 the North Sea Canal was opened, and the port of IJmuiden a short time after, which quickly became the main reception port. Every third trip, the fishermen would be able to take the train and boat home to spend four or five days with their families.

The competition from steam trawlers heralded the end of longline fishing. In 1900, the ship register in Middelharnis listed only 16 sloops. After 1912, the fishing industry had all but disappeared.

River or inland fishing

In the period after the St. Elisabeth Flood, the most important fresh-water fishing area of the Netherlands was created, the Biesbosch, which was in use until 1800. The most important types of migratory fish caught here were shad, sturgeon and salmon, with some sedentary fish also being caught. Migratory fish travel in both salt and fresh

47 VERSCHE VIS ('FRESH FISH'), JAN WILLEM 'WILLY' SLUITER (1873–1949). OIL ON CANVAS. THE CATCH IS HAULED OFF THE SHIP. FISHERMEN IN BLUE AND NASSAU BEIGE GANSEYS. KATWIJKS MUSEUM

> **Salting and drying**
> *Anchovy was salted and, like some wines, takes years to develop its characteristic flavour. It was a delicacy mainly produced for export to Germany. Of the fish caught in the Zuiderzee, it was the only type that would keep for a longer period of time (six to seven years). Another method of preservation was drying the fish in the sun. Herring, dab and flounder could be preserved in this manner.*

48 SALMON FISHERMEN WITH THEIR NETS, WOUDRICHEM 1913. STICHTING ZUIDERZEEAMBACHTEN, ENKHUIZEN

water, in contrast to sedentary fish, which spend their entire life either in salt or fresh water. Around 1900, salmon, sturgeon and shad fishing on the rivers Rhine, Waal, Lek, Maas/Meuse, Merwede, Hollands Diep, Haringvliet and Schelde, was an important source of income for the towns of Dordrecht, Zwijndrecht, Woudrichem, Klundert, Geertruidenberg, Nieuwpoort, Ammerstol, Krimpen aan de Lek, Willemstad, Moerdijk, Heerewaarden, Tiel, Lith, Charlois, Papendrecht, Capelle aan de IJssel, Hardinxveld-Giesendam, Gorinchem, Dodewaard, Ochten, Millingen, Bergen op Zoom and many others (Fig. 48). Up to around the middle of the twentieth century, the Waal was fished by a large number of *waalschokkers*. These boats would fish for salmon and eel. Salmon barges were used elsewhere as well (Fig. 49).

Salmon fishing was generally quite lucrative (Fig. 50). The large rivers were not as polluted and busy as they are now: in spring, large schools of salmon would swim upriver to spawn. Salmon was eaten regularly in that period. In the Krimpenerwaard, there are stories of maids who stipulated that they would not be served salmon for lunch more than twice a week, as it was so readily available. It seems to be just a story, as salmon was already an expensive type of fish also in those days.

Salmon was caught in three ways: with traps, seines (see box, page 29) and drift nets. Salmon traps consist of wicker fences in the water, with traps in between. Because of pollution levels, there has not been any salmon and sturgeon in the rivers since the 1950s. In the last few years, desperate attempts have been made to restore fish stock, but as of yet without much success.

Although places like Vlaardingen, Pernis and Maassluis are also on the Maas/Meuse, they are still classified as North Sea coastal towns, because they were not really involved in river fishing and instead focused more on fishing for herring and fresh fish on the North Sea. Because the fishing world was quite small and people would encounter each other regularly in different ports and at fish auctions, river fishermen also started wearing ganseys as outerwear around 1900. Beautiful ganseys were found in Charlois, Woudrichem and Willemstad, and without a doubt ganseys were also worn in other river towns such as Dordrecht, Gorinchem, Werkendam, Klundert and Geertruidenberg. However, no photographic evidence has yet been found.

DISASTERS: A HIGH PRICE TO PAY FOR FISH

By definition, fishing was a dangerous activity, as many fishermen could not swim. If you went overboard, you did not stand a chance, as your boots would fill up and your heavy, wet clothes would drag you down.

Storm was the fleet's worst enemy. The weather on the North Sea was unpredictable, and mist,

49 SALMON BOATS IN THE PORT OF WOUDRICHEM, CA. 1910. STICHTING ZUIDERZEEAMBACHTEN, ENKHUIZEN.

heavy storms and tidal waves could hit at any moment. Experienced fishermen had a good eye for the weather, but they had to rely on their own judgement and skills as they did not have radios, there were no weather forecasts, and the vessels had no lifeboats. Many ships perished in sudden storms, such as the fleet of Paesens-Moddergat in 1883. The heavily laden ships were caught by surprise when a massive storm hit within sight of the port. Only five of the 22 boats came back. The others were lost, leaving a village of orphans and 50 families in Paesens-Moddergat deprived of their breadwinner. The storm also hit the HD 19 (five dead) and HD 12 (three dead) from Den Helder, and a number of fishing vessels from Urk. In that one night, more than 200 fishermen, also from other towns in the Netherlands and England, perished on the North Sea. In reaction to the disaster, a life boat was introduced on luggers.

The ships suffered a lot of damage at sea and required constant maintenance and repair. Sometimes, however, shipowners would send out badly maintained ships for financial reasons, putting the fishermen's lives in danger.

Women often knew intuitively that a ship and their husband and/or sons had perished, even before they got the official news. There were little to no facilities for the families of dead fishermen. This meant that when their husband or father did not return, they were without income. To keep their heads above water, the destitute bereaved often had to rely on charity. Widows, for example, would knit ganseys to earn a bit of money. To not entirely abandon the fishermen's wives to their fate, societies were set up in the nineteenth century to raise money to support these families. 'A high price to pay for fish!'

Seine nets
Seine fishing is a method whereby the fish are caught using a net dragged along the sea bed, while making a circular manoeuvre.

Eel
Eel is caught with traps, pots, bobbers and eel shears, but in the past a reep would also be used. A reep is a long rope with baited cross lines, comparable to longlines.

Lamprey
Lamprey larvae live in fresh water and migrate to the sea after a few years, where they live on fish. Lampreys are caught with pots, or toten, a long line of which would be dropped in channels and gullies.

Sturgeon
Sturgeon is famous for its roe, called caviar. Sturgeons are migratory fish that swim upriver from the sea to pair and spawn. Young sturgeons will travel to the deltas where they feed on shellfish and crab. Later, they will move to the sea, where they can live to become a hundred years old. The last sturgeon caught in the Netherlands was caught in Beneden Merwede on June 26, 1952. It weighed 103 kilograms (227 pounds) and was 2.6 metres (2.84 yards) long.

Salmon seine fishing
The Domains would farm out the fishing rights on the big rivers. Mostly, seines (see above) were used to fish for salmon; sturgeon was by-catch. Hauling in the seines became a lot easier with the help of horse power on the capstan or, later, steam power. Within fifty years, salmon fishing had all but disappeared as there were no Rhine salmon left.

White fish
In addition to fishing for migratory fish, sedentary fish, whitefish (such as rock-bass), bream, white bream, ide and carp were also caught. The catch would be sold as one batch.

50 CATCHING RIVER FISH, CA. 1900. STICHTING ZUIDERZEEAMBACHTEN, ENKHUIZEN

CREW MEMBERS ON BOARD THE VL 74 JOANNA SATURNA I IN THE OUTER PORT OF VLAARDINGEN. THE SHIP WAS OWNED BY SHIPPING COMPANY J.H. WARNEKE, CA. 1905. REPRO J. SLUIMER. VLAARDINGEN MUNICIPAL ARCHIVES

2 FISHING CULTURE AROUND 1900

The fishing season was the period between May and December when the fishermen could go out to fish for herring. During voyages, the Shetland Islands would serve as a base, and vessels would often seek out a port along the English or Scottish coast to buy clean water and salt. A *bomschuit* would make around three voyages during the season, a lugger four or five. Around 1900, the season would end around mid-November to the beginning of December. This would be followed by a 'cut': fishing would stop and the luggers were made ready for winter. Everything useable on the lugger would be taken off board. It was either stored in the company attic or distributed amongst the fishermen.

Some shipowners would continue fishing during the winter by using longliners, and fish for fresh fish along the coast.

Shipping companies

Except in the Zuiderzee region, where the fishing boats were usually owned by families, most ships were owned by shipping companies. The fishermen were employed by them, working at their own risk and receiving a specific percentage of the revenue, the catch, as a reward called the *besomming*, which would differ per rank (see page 37). The shipping companies were relatively rich and not infrequently autocratic rulers within the fishing communities. They would often also own the cottages where the fishermen lived with their families, and were paid rent by those same workers. The social conditions were poor. If a fishermen signed up with one of the large fleets in Vlaardingen and Maassluis, because they could not earn enough money at home, they and their families were usually immediately evicted from their homes (Middelharnis). The fact that the first branch of the Salvation Army was set up in Yerseke indicates how bad the situation had become for many fishermen and their families. The play *Op hoop van zegen* (1900) by Herman Heijermans deals with the desperate circumstances of fishermen and their families, and the behaviour and actions of the shipowners.

A fisherman's journey would, on average, last 25 days; the income depended on the *besomming*, and the work on board was extremely difficult. A working day would usually last 13 to 14 hours. Before they could return home after a voyage, the fish had to be unloaded and the nets stowed away – extra work for which they were not paid. The reason? The fisherman had a share in the catch. After just two or three days of rest, they would prepare for another journey (Fig. 51). However, fishermen were very strong because of this hard existence, a diet of mainly fish and heavy physical work. Many of them would live to a ripe old age, unless they remained at sea. They would sit on the so-called *leugenbank*, or 'liars' bench' in the port, where they would tell each other boastful stories and fishermen's tales. In the 1910s and 1930s, the fishermen would engage in strikes for better working conditions and higher wages (Fig. 52), but they were only mildly successful.

51 CREW MEMBERS ON BOARD THE VL 147 *FLEVO IV*, MAKING THE LUGGER READY FOR A JOURNEY. OOSTHAVENKADE, CA. 1930. VLAARDINGEN MUNICIPAL ARCHIVES

52 FISHERMEN ON STRIKE. KATWIJKS MUSEUM

Vessels

Different fishing vessels were used, depending on how and where they would be fishing. Around 1900, the vessels mostly seen on the North Sea were *bomschuiten*, sloops and luggers, while *hoogaars* were most often used in Zeeland. On the Wadden Sea, *blazers*, *vletten* and *aken* were used, on the Zuiderzee *botters* and dinghies were the main vessels, and on the large rivers, fishing would take place using salmon barges and waalschokkers. The main vessels used for herring fishing and fresh fishing are described below.

Bomschuit (Fig. 53, 54, 55)

A flat-bottomed *bomschuit* without a keel was also called *bom*, but usually simply 'barge', where bom would mean *bodem* or 'bottom'. This ship

53 BOMSCHUITEN AT THE BEACH AT KATWIJK, E.A. FISCHER CÖRLIN, KATWIJK 1889, WATERCOLOUR. KATWIJKS MUSEUM

54 BOMSCHUIT BEING PULLED UP THE BEACH WITH HORSES, CA. 1900. KATWIJKS MUSEUM

55 BOMSCHUITEN IN WINTER STORAGE IN THE DUNES, KATWIJK, CA. 1900. KATWIJKS MUSEUM

pulled high up the beach to the dunes (Fig. 55). In spring, they would be pulled back down to the water line with three or four groups of harnessed horses, each group consisting of three horses.

Sloop (Fig. 56)

The sloop (derived from the French word *chaloupe*) was introduced in 1817 in the southern parts of the Netherlands and used for herring, haddock and cod fishing. When fishing for cod and haddock, the sloop was equipped with a *bun* or *kaar* (see box, page

56 SLOOP FROM MIDDELHARNIS. ORIGIN UNKNOWN

26), which had lots of small holes and would be in direct contact with the open water to keep the catch alive. Most were built in Middelharnis, but also in Vlaardingen and Pernis.

Lugger (Fig. 57)

In 1866, Adrien Eugène Maas, a shipowner from Scheveningen, brought the lugger, the French *lougre*, to the Netherlands and introduced the cotton driftnet (the *vleet*) in herring fishing. Both caused a major revolution in this industry. In 1910, the

was used by the coastal fishermen from De Zijde (the coast of North and South Holland). Coastal villages such as Scheveningen, Katwijk aan Zee, Noordwijk aan Zee, Zandvoort, Egmond aan Zee and Petten had no port. Their ships had to sail from – and land at – the beach, which was not very conducive to their lifespan. The ships had a full deck. They were used for catching and landing flatfish and roundfish, and to a lesser extent fresh herring. In the autumn, the ships would be

57 THE SAILING LUGGER VL 8 MARIA, 1914. VLAARDINGEN MUNICIPAL ARCHIVES

33

58 FISHERMAN FROM URK IN A SWEATER FROM KATWIJK.
ZUIDERZEE MUSEUM, ENKHUIZEN

herring fleet comprised 501 sailing luggers. Scheveningen had the most: 185 luggers. In 1920, there were 493 sailing luggers and 29 engine luggers; in 1930, there were only two sailing luggers left, compared with 229 engine luggers. In that year, the sailing luggers left port to fish for herring for the last time. The lay-out of the lugger was ideally suited for herring fishing with a *vleet* and to spend weeks at sea (circumstances were primitive). The cargo holds were filled with both empty barrels and barrels filled with salt for the outward journey. On the way back, the salt would be all but gone; one barrel of salt was used for every four barrels – or *kantjes* – of herring. All of the empty barrels would be filled with the gutted and salted herring and stored in the cargo holds. The drying room was intended for the storage of food and supplies.

Signing on

In the *vleet* fishing sector of around 1900, a captain of a *bomschuit* or lugger was not only responsible for the maintenance of the ship and the catches, he also had to hire crew. The crew had to sign on

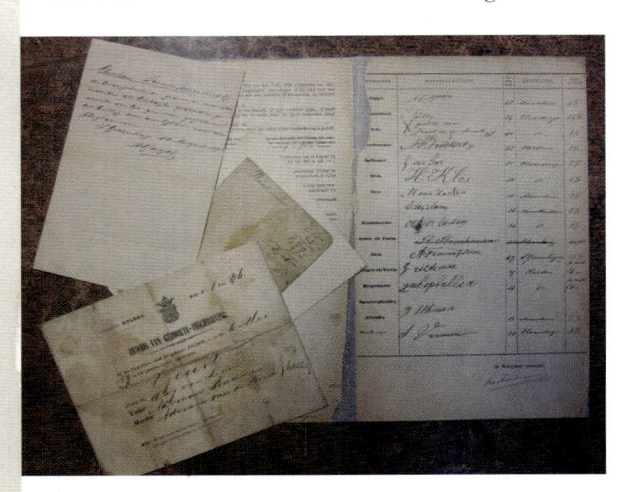

59 MUSTER LIST. VLAARDINGEN MUNICIPAL ARCHIVES

for the duration of the whole herring season. The fishermen, generally from other towns and looking for a *steetje*, a place on a ship, often could not apply directly – they had to be asked. It was not unusual for a shipowner, if he was a very successful captain, to have his son end up with the same high rank. Amongst other things, the captain was responsible for the muster list of the ship. The muster lists (Fig. 59) were the registers that indicated who had signed on, what ships they had been allocated to and at what times. They were kept at the town hall or held by the water authorities/police.

Crew

A sailing lugger had a crew of around 14 men (Fig. 60). Herring boats from Vlaardingen often had one crew member more than those from Scheveningen and Katwijk. After the arrival of the engine lugger, an engine operator or mechanic was added to the crew. The entire crew, in order of rank, comprised:
- Captain/skipper
- Chief mate/helmsman
- Engine operator or mechanic
- Sailor (usually five on board)
- Sailor-cook
- Young sailor, referred to as '7/8th'
- Eldest (usually one or two on board)
- Youngest
- Reep shooter
- Spacer.

The jobs on board had nothing to do with age, but with the number of years of working experience. All tasks were exactly prescribed by rank.

The captain and chief mate

The captain and chief mate would lead the crew, but they also did the fishing. The captains of the vessels of the coastal villages (pinks and *bomschuiten*) were called the chief mates. The second man on board was called the helmsman on a *bomschuit*, and the chief mate on other ships. Originally, the chief mate was the man at the helm, who determined the course of the ship.

Engine operator or mechanic

After the arrival of the engine lugger, the crew number expanded with the addition of an engine operator or technician; he remained below decks, at the stern, with the captain.

Sailors

The sailors were the actual herring fishermen, and so was the sailor-cook. A 7/8th could be regarded as an ordinary seamen, but had the lowest rank amongst the sailors; he earned slightly less than a full sailor, 7/8th of the crew part of the *besomming* (see pages 36 and 37).

34

Eldest

After the 7/8th came the eldest. Often, there were two eldest on board. An eldest would have four to five years of experience on a ship and would have more responsibilities. Because an eldest would be close in rank to a 7/8th, they did effectively similar work. While one eldest would help get the *vleet* out at night, the other eldest would be at the helm. In the time in between, they would switch duties. Before taking in the *vleet* early in the morning, the two eldest would set up the last on deck: a system of long planks between the crib (*krebbe*) on the port and starboard sides, into which the herring would be emptied from the nets. They would also help the sailors gut the herring, fill the barrels with the fish and then store the barrels in the hold. One of the eldest would traditionally bake pancakes on Saturday evening.

Youngest

A rank below the eldest was the youngest. A youngest would help the sailor-cook to store the nets in the *wantruimen*, which were particular net holds below deck – the word *want* is used to mean a collection of nets. There were *wantruimen* on portboard and starboard. Half a *vleet* would be stored in either room. When the nets were 'shot' (put out), the youngest was responsible for the supply of the bags or *blazen*. When the herring was gutted, he had to bring the filled basket, with three handles, to where the herring was mixed with salt in a *warrebak*, a wooden container. During mealtimes, the youngest would stay above decks on the look-out. After meals, he would clean the boiling vats, make coffee and bring it to the room below decks to the captain, chief mate and engine operator. Together with the reep shooter and spacer he would clean the crew quarters, being responsible for fetching the *puzze*, a bucket on a rope filled with sea water. The spacer and reep shooter would do most of the cleaning.

Reep shooter

A reep shooter, or *reepschieter*, was usually a young, skinny boy on his second year or season at sea. He was the second lowest in rank. He was responsible for carefully stowing the ropes, or *reep*, which the nets were attached to – from which they were disconnected when the nets were brought in, guided by the spacer – in a special place in the stern called the *reepkee*. It was important that the reep did not

60 CREW OF THE VL 192 *HENDRIKA*, CA. 1923.
VLAARDINGEN MUNICIPAL ARCHIVES

61 CREW MEMBERS OF THE WOODEN LUGGER VL 124 *PRINSES JULIANA*, CA. 1920. ARCHIVE H. V.D. BURG, VLAARDINGEN CITY ARCHIVES

get caught when the 2 to 3 kilometre (1.25 to 1.86 mile) long nets were put out again. To invoke the higher powers, the crew would call out 'Op hoop van zegen!' ('Hoping for the best!')

Spacer

All herring fishermen started their career as spacer, or *afhouder*, which was the lowest in rank. A spacer was a boy on his first year at sea. They would be young, often only 10 to 12 years, or even younger. His bunk would be in the tip of the lugger or sloop called 'the hell', because it was worst affected by the elements and went up and down like mad. As a spacer you were, by definition, sent to hell.

In longline fishing, this lowest rank was called the *speeljongen* or 'play boy'; the youngest sailor on a sloop from, for example, Middelharnis would be called the 'coffeemaker' or *kofjekokertje*, and an older crew member called *zeevader*, or 'sea father', would look out for him. If the boy had been at sea for two years he became a *ketellapper*, after another two years *inbakker*; with six years of experience he became the cook, or *kok*, and after another two years *bovenman* and then *volmatroos* – a full sailor. He could then be promoted to chief mate or even to captain or skipper. A spacer or coffeemaker would leave as a child and return from the first fishing season as a man.

Because the nets were often hauled in at night, the sailors would go back to their bunks during their day, apart from the youngest crew members. To prevent them from waking up the sailors, they had to stay above decks, whatever the weather. The younger three (the youngest, the reep shooter and the spacer) had other duties, such as frying fish, fetching coal for the sailor-cook and cleaning the quarters. The quarters were where the crew would sleep – apart from the captain, chief mate and, in later years, the engine operator, who had their own rooms at the stern – and where meals were prepared. The youngest crew members would not have to keep watch, as this was too much of a responsibility for them. Not only were the lugger and crew at stake, but the *vleet* could get caught up, crossed over or get tangled up with other *vleets*.

62 PUPILS AND TEACHERS AT THE FISHERIES SCHOOL, LOCATED IN THE TRADE BUILDING ON THE PARALLELWEG IN VLAARDINGEN, CA. 1925. FIRST PERSON FROM THE LEFT IS ZEVENHUIZEN, WHO LATER BECAME A WATERSTOKER, BOILING HOT WATER. VLAARDINGEN MUNICIPAL ARCHIVES

Education

At the end of the nineteenth century, people started to realise that it was important to offer young sailors from the age of 16 more training, so that they would have a better insight into the theoretical side of fishing (Fig. 62). For the eldest, who had a number of years of experience at sea, this training was very interesting. After a few years working as a sailor and with a diploma in hand, they could apply for a job as helmsman, chief mate or even as captain or skipper. The women who knitted or repaired the nets, would be educated at a so-called *boetschool* (Fig. 63).

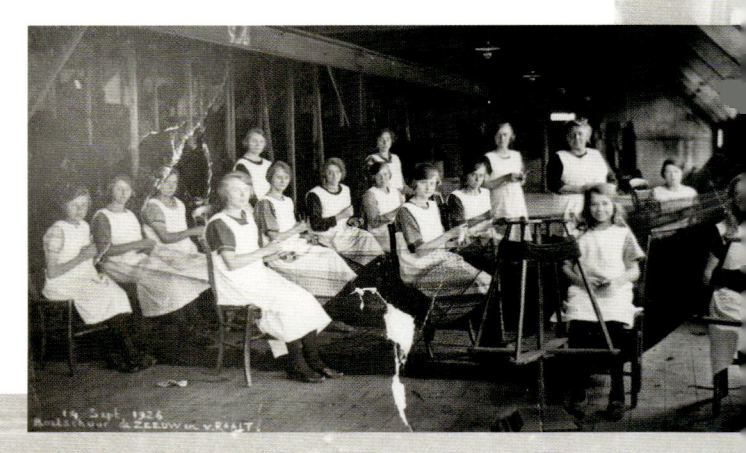

63 WOMEN MENDING NETS IN THE BARN OF SHIPPING COMPANY DE ZEEUW & VAN RAALT. SEPTEMBER 14, 1926. VLAARDINGEN MUNICIPAL ARCHIVES

Wages

Approximately 25 per cent of the *besomming* (the yield of a voyage, or of the total revenue from a fishing year or season) would be divided amongst the crew. This percentage is an estimate, because it would differ tremendously over the course of time. The amount was converted into eighths through a particular mathematical system. A captain would get 16/8th, a chief mate 12/8th, an engine operator 10/8th, a sailor 8/8th, a young sailor 7/8th, the eldest would get 6/8th, the youngest 5/8th, the reep shooter 4/8th and the spacer 3/8th. Crew members were also referred to by their percentage of the *besomming*.

Stop box & clothing

The shipping company would provide straw to sleep on and a part of the food, but a fisherman had to bring the rest himself. Straw was put in a blue and white gingham pillow, or *schuddetijk*. A fisherman's personal items, including a gutting knife, repair kit, a Bible, smoking equipment, candy, biscuits and cake, were stored in a 'stop box' or *stoppenkist*, which was often beautifully decorated with paintwork and carvings (Fig. 64). Fishermen also had to bring their own clothing. The outfit would comprise various items. The sweater was usually worn as outerwear, but also under a thick woollen coat (called a *monkje* in Katwijk, Fig. 68) or, when the weather at sea was rough, under oilskin. Fishermen would also have a sou'wester (Fig. 69), a *kas* or coat, *casjacs* (a kind of frock), long oilskin trousers and sleeves, pilo trousers (in Den Helder, a former fishing neighbourhood is called Pilobuurt after these fishing trousers) or *peukers* (Fig. 71). They would also wear *salpatters* or 'spats' around their shoes – sea boots or clogs – to protect them against the grease and dirt. In addition, they had a *voorschot* (an apron with or without a flap), jumpers, vests, jackets and long black coats, madder (red-dyed) molton undershirts with long sleeves (Fig. 70) which were supposed to protect them against rheumatism (confirmed by a study by the Academic Hospital in Leiden), English leather trousers, leather sleeves, sleeve straps, belts, socks, blue trousers, jackets, frocks and tan-coloured boiler suits and trousers. The fishermen wore large mittens to prevent injuries to the hands when hauling in the longliner nets, which had many hooks. These mittens were knit or felted and made from sheep wool (Fig. 72). Usually, the mittens had a thumb on either side, so that you could always put one on the right way and the thumb would not wear as quickly.

A fishermen's headgear would be different per town. Fishermen from Scheveningen would wear the characteristic flat cap, called *zeipnapje*; in Urk they wore a *karpoets* – a fez-type hat – or later a knitted hat; and in Volendam a cap or *ruigie*, which resembled a busby. In Noordwijk and Katwijk, the men wore a small sailor's cap; on the island of Zuid-Holland and Zeeland variants of bowler hats were worn; while in Moddergat and Zoutkamp, the men wore knitted tams. In Vlaardingen and in Den Helder, fedoras and wide-brimmed hats were popular.

When on shore, the fishermen would sometimes wear slipper-like, velvet shoes.

On board

The conditions on board were terrible. Not only looking at it with a modern eye, but also at the time. The crew's forecabins were very sparse and fulfilled none of the basic requirements that applied to the rooms where the herring barrels were stored. The quarters were always busy: it was where the entire crew lived, slept, and where meals were cooked. There would be 16 men sleeping there. On either side, there were eight small bunks, two on top of each other, with a small curtain (Fig. 66), hardly big enough to stretch out. Sometimes,

64 STOPPENKIST. KATWIJKS MUSEUM

65 CONTENTS OF A STOPPENKIST. KATWIJKS MUSEUM

men had to share a bunk. The spacer and reep shooter had the bunks in the tip of the ship, called hell. The captain and chief mate slept at the back.

In *Uitgezeild: de hoogtijdagen van de Nederlandse logger (1866–1930)* by Klaas Kornaat, Peter Zuysgeest en Henk Bubbel (Vlaardingen 2012), I read a report from 1910 by J.C. Mom, an inspector, about the conditions and the indescribable stench on board a herring lugger: 'On this fishing boat, with numerous crew, it is not only the body odour that pollutes the air, but also the evaporation of the almost always damp clothes, dirty with fish scales and other fish waste, often hung up in the same place where they would cook, smoke tobacco and sometimes dry fish, resulting in a mixture of odours difficult to describe or imagine. Consider that, in such a room, household articles such as petroleum, peat, wood, twine, tar pots, paint pots etc. are kept, and one can imagine that very little fresh sea air is to be found in such accommodation.'

In addition to condensation were frequent leaks at the bottom of the ship, meaning that there would also be stagnant water which, after a while, would turn into brown, smelly sludge that was sometimes topped with a layer of mould. The crew also suffered from mice and rats, but fleas especially could make the life of fishermen a living hell.

Provisions

Food and provisions were partly provided by the shipping company. Food like potatoes, vegetables, condensed milk, oatmeal, rice and *zeekaak* ('sea biscuit') were administered, but the fishermen had to buy certain other items, such as cheese, sugar and butter (Fig. 75). The mainstay of their food was obviously fish, which was usually fried, available in large quantities, and very healthy because of the natural fats. In addition, the diet consisted of pulses such as brown beans, grey peas and green peas, or a bean and pea soup with rice or grits, potatoes and sometimes bacon. Fishermen would eat oatmeal or rice porridge, made with cans of condensed milk. Meat, apart from smoked bacon, was too perishable and not on the menu. Fresh vegetables and fresh milk were used for as long as they could be kept fresh, but after the first week meals would primarily consist of peas and beans.

They would drink a lot of coffee, tea and beer. When an exceptionally good catch had been hauled

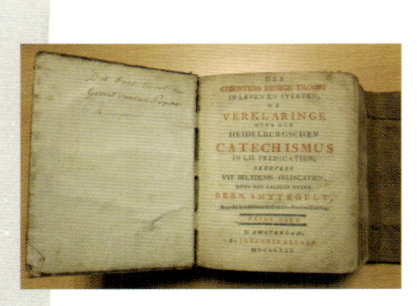

66 OFF TO BED. SEA AND PORT MUSEUM IN IJMUIDEN

CLOCKWISE FROM TOP LEFT:
67 POCKET BIBLE. KATWIJKS MUSEUM
68 MONKJE. KATWIJKS MUSEUM
69 SOU'WESTER. KATWIJKS MUSEUM
70 MADDER SHIRT. KATWIJKS MUSEUM
71 PILO TROUSERS. KATWIJKS MUSEUM
72 FELTED MITTENS WITH TWO THUMBS. SPAKENBURG MUSEUM

73 CROSS-SECTION OF A LUGGER WITH THE FORECABIN WHERE THE CREW LIVED, COOKED AND SLEPT, THE HOLDS FOR THE BARRELS OF HERRING, THE WANTRUIM, THE REEPKEE, AND THE ROOMS AT THE REAR WHERE THE CAPTAIN AND THE CHIEF MATE SLEPT. KATWIJKS MUSEUM

A fisherman's poem translated from the Vlaardingen dialect from the city archives of Vlaardingen, about the odours, the bad food, the fleas, and the miserable conditions on board:

The Lugger or the Disselvaart

Say, men who go fishing for herring
And whose lives depend on fish
Say, listen to me for a while
What I have written here

The lugger or the Disselvaart
I will not boast about it
Because I was forced to go
It was the only option I had left

I went to Vlaardingen to sign on
I said goodbye to my friends,
My parents, sister, wife and children
I hoped to see them again

That, we were blessed, did indeed happen
I was allowed to see them again
Have my wife and children around me
And still be healthy as well

My mate as well
He is back home safe and sound
Although the most recent storm
Shook many a house

And many men from our town
Were still out at sea
We were blind with worry
The wives and mothers

Luckily, after that great fear
The message arrived
That this captain and his crew
Safely withstood the storm

They are now back again
They came back safe
And unless hunger forces me
I will never go out again

Say, I have to go downstairs
To spend my time well
And see for myself
How things work on a lugger

I will not look down
On this hard life
With its rice and beer
It will never leave my thoughts

And when it is time to eat
After the prayer is said
They say the food is good
But not with enough fat

No butter on our bread
One pound for nine weeks
Who does not believe me
Has never seen it

I have to say it again
I will never forget
The worse the catch
The worse the food

No more bacon in the soup
No more butter from the cow
They call it margarine
One pound and a half

For a box of rice
One spoon full of margarine
Is also enough
Three spoons for ten people

If that is not the truth
Ask the lugger crews whether I'm lying
And if you see our quarters
They look like a pig sty

One room for fourteen men
With their knees to the fire
I would not wish it upon my enemy
This is life at sea

Two men to a bunk
You should be thankful now
Being bitten by fleas
Senseless because of the stench

I have said enough my friends
Enough for now
Go and see for yourselves
That is the best way.

Marinus (Tinus) Mellema

Marinus Mellema was born on March 1, 1885, at a time when the fishing industry in Zoutkamp and the fisheries in general were going through a hard time. A committee had even been set up to 'significantly improve the fishing fleet of Zoutkamp'. Despite the collections received, the intended Zeevischmaatschappij – 'Sea Fish Company' – never materialised. The fishing industry went further downhill. This resulted in great poverty. Many (very) young men went to Emden in Germany, where they signed on for herring luggers. They had to work hard on ships that were badly equipped and earned little money. Mellema was one of them. They left around Whitsuntide and walked together as a large group.

On 25 October 1974, Berend Zwart from Zoutkamp went to visit Tinus Mellema, then 89 years old. Below is a small part of the conversation about life on the luggers around the turn of the century and an anecdote about poverty:

'There was no money to be earned anymore around Whitsun, here or elsewhere – in Paesens-Moddergat, Wierum, etc. The idea was that, after Whitsun, there was not enough shrimp and fish to go out fishing. The ships were moored, and the men left to go fishing on luggers, mainly herring luggers, in Emden. We left [Zoutkamp] around Whitsun, with a group of around 70 men, to work on the luggers for six months. My brothers Gerrat, Kers and Jan also sailed on luggers. Some were very young, 12 or 15. I had already worked on Emden luggers for a few years when I got employed by Manus van der Schoor, a Dutch captain [from Marken]. I was 23 and the eldest on board. Together with Klaas Bakker, Ties and Sieger Bol. Later, the next journey, Jan Becker [Oostema] joined us on board; he was older. Well, we had a good time together. Siegers Hennerk (Sieger, son of Hendrik Bol) and Jan Zwart were captains from Zoutkamp. I remember that we earned 12 guilders per week, with a few per cent [of the besomming]. We were gone for 23 to 27 weeks and made three journeys in that time. In between the journeys, we spent 24 hours on shore twice. In those 24 hours we had to unload and reload the ship (with provisions) and then we would set sail again. In those days, if you had a wife, you could write home about the hard work it took to sail back to shore, because in those days all luggers had sails, not engines.

'There was one stove heater in the middle of the forecabin. We would sit around it on benches to dry up again. The bunks were behind you. A rope was attached to the ceiling, so if the ship would move about you could hold on to the rope. Regarding the food … Yes, we ate fish. Every night, fried herring, which the boys had to clean and fry, or else we'd have peas and beans. On Sunday, a few potatoes with a piece of meat, usually bacon. But not during the week; we had plenty of fish then.

'We also had plenty of fleas. One day, the fleas were so bad that as soon as we got into Emden, we all went ashore to buy powder. It came with a little blow pipe, so we could blow the powder into our bedding. But Jan [Berends] had nothing, he did not buy powder. He just went up to the deck, with his shirt in one hand and his underpants in the other hand, hitting them against the mast. "That will teach the little devils." We laughed so hard. What a strange man. When the war [First World War] broke out, the last men left the luggers. The war finished off the lugger industry.

'Poor people would get a guilder a week from the church. A poor man who has nothing, would get one guilder for himself. Sometimes you could go to the council. An old woman, Fokke Trien, went to the council once and got two quarters. She went to the mayor in Ulrum, despite having problems walking.

74 OLD TINUS MELLEMA IN HIS COTTAGE

When she arrived, she told him she had only been given two quarters. "Yes," the mayor had replied, "but isn't the air nourishment as well?" "The air is nourishment?" she said. "Dammit, you come to us and enjoy the air on the dyke, maybe you will then finally grow a pair of buttocks!" (The mayor was a lean man.) The mayor then gave her a guilder. In those days, the country was rich, but the poor people had nothing. The level of poverty was terrible here. Absolutely terrible.'

Tinus Mellema died on 8 February 1985, weeks before his hundredth birthday (Fig. 74).

COURTESY OF BEREND ZWART, DIRECTOR OF THE FISHERIES MUSEUM IN ZOUTKAMP.

75 LIST OF PROVISIONS OF THE HERRING LUGGER, *DE VIER GEZUSTERS*

The fishermen's families on shore, especially along the Zuiderzee, would eat what was caught. The fish was cooked and served on a *gatenpetiel* (a fish colander), with potatoes and melted butter and vinegar: *butter en eek*. Vegetables were hardly ever on the menu (Fig. 76).

Navigation

The sun, moon and stars were used for navigation, plus a sextant. The most accurate measurements could be obtained by measuring the sun at 12 hours local time, when the sun was at its highest point. Another measurement, the latitude, was determined by measuring the height of the Pole Star, which did not have to be done at a specific time, and which gave an idea of the latitude. A plummet with grease at the bottom was used to bring up soil samples, which were smelled and tasted in order to determine where at sea they were (Fig. 77).

in, the bottle of *jenever* might come out, but for understandable reasons the captain was not in favour of his crew drinking at sea.

They would eat *zeekaak* and *zakkoek* or *broeder* (see the box on page 42), made from a mixture of flour, beer or milk and yeast, currants and sultanas, boiled in a bag and eaten warm with some sugar or syrup. Sometimes they would bake bread, and there was margarine or butter on board. As we saw earlier, on Saturday night, one of the eldest would make pancakes.

The provisions on the luggers from Vlaardingen were much better than on those from Katwijk.

76 HAVING A MEAL IN VOLENDAM. STICHTING ZUIDERZEEAMBACHTEN, ENKHUIZEN

Broeder, Jan-in-de-zak, ketelkoek, dikke koek or poffert

Sieve the flour into a bowl and add salt. Warm up the beer until it is lukewarm. Add half of the beer and an egg to the flour. Stir in the rest of the lukewarm beer until the batter is smooth. Cover the batter with a damp cloth and leave to rise for 1 hour in a warm place. Wash the sultanas and drain well. Mix in the batter. Spoon the batter into a damp cotton bag, or broederzak, put in a pan with gently boiling water and leave to cook for 2 hours. Take a knitting needle or skewer and check to see whether the broeder is done – if there is no dough on the skewer then it is cooked. Remove from the pan. Warm up some syrup, with a knob of butter if you like. Serve the broeder warm, drizzled with syrup. Broeder can be eaten as a main course or as a dessert.

- 250g (8¾oz) of flour or self-raising flour (in the latter case, do not use yeast)
- 1 bottle of beer (can be replaced by 200ml (6¾floz) lukewarm milk + 15g (½oz) of yeast
- 1 egg
- 75g (2½oz) raisins
- 75g (2½oz) sultanas
- Pinch of salt
- Syrup or sugar
- Knob of butter (optional)

78 TWO PAIRS OF BRIDAL CLOGS FROM URK. HET OUDE RAADHUIS MUSEUM, URK

To see where the herring was, fishermen used a trained eye, distinguishing between 'thick' and 'thin' water. The colour of the water and the thickness of the plankton could show you whether there were any fish. Birds like gannets, flying above certain stretches of water, were also a good indication of herring.

77 PLUMMET. KATWIJKS MUSEUM

Lack of wind

If there was no wind and the ship could not move, the crew would do other things than fish. Smoking cigars and chewing tobacco whilst chatting was a favourite pastime. At that time, cigars and tobacco were considered to be very healthy and helped combat pests. Some hard workers hated sitting about, which is why some fishermen would use their free time for handicraft. On the luggers from Urk, fishermen used their gutting knives to cut the famous, beautifully decorated bridal clogs (Fig. 78) for their betrothed, or the charming *makelaartjes*, which decorated the tops of roofs of houses. Fishermen on the luggers from Katwijk would embroider canvas with wool (Fig. 79). Fishermen from Friesland would knit mittens. Of course, on board, there was always plenty of knitting and net repairing to do.

Signalling & fishing system

The flag signalling system was represented in the ganseys as the flag motif. In 1781, flag signals were introduced, enabling crews to signal messages to other boats in the area. The signal would correspond to actual of words in the signal book. Whole sentences could thus be communicated. The signals were all recorded in 1820 in the *Telegrafisch Sein- of Woordenboek*.
The flag system continued to be developed until the First World War when it was finally standardised.

79 EMBROIDERY, WOOL ON CANVAS, FRONT AND BACK. KATWIJKS MUSEUM

When fishing, two triangular baskets with the tips pointing in would be hoisted, to indicate their current activity to other ships.

Fishermen's wives

Women were not allowed on board. The general motto was: 'Women and cliffs are a disaster for ships.' The women would do work on land, such as repairing torn nets (*boeten*) (Fig. 80) and hawk part of the catch in the big cities. When the catch was unloaded at the beach, the women would wear the heavy baskets on a yoke and hold the remaining baskets in their arms or on top of their heads; they would then walk to the fish markets, which were often far away. The women could often be found on the dyke and the beach, looking out to see whether the ships and their husbands and sons were on their way home (Fig. 81). These were anxious times, as ships were often lost at sea.

Along the Zuiderzee, many women would work nights in the smokehouses, under bad conditions.

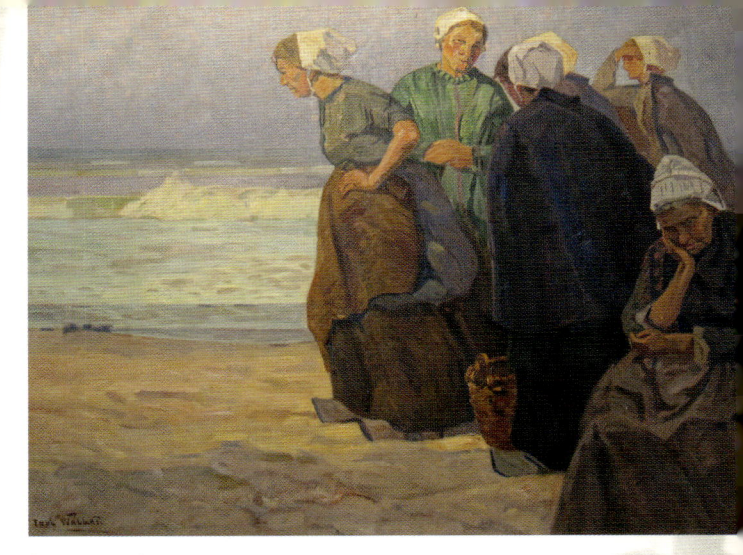

81 *FISHERMEN'S WIVES WAITING ON THE BEACH*, PAUL WALLAT (1879–1966). OIL ON CANVAS. KATWIJKS MUSEUM

The fish had to be immediately spit and skewered onto long pins when the ships came in (Fig. 82). The 1902 Spitting Act, supplementing the Labour Act, enabled women to work nights, under certain conditions. They had to earn at least 25 per cent more than during the day and could not work for more than eight hours a day. Children would also work in the smokehouses. Smokers would often have one boy and two to three helpers. The boys would strip the fish, ensuring that the spit fish would not stick together.

For women life was tough: sell and spit fish, have lots of children, accept the high infant mortality rate, make clothes for everyone, do the housework, prepare meals. Knitting was seen as relaxing, something useful to do while chatting to friends.

80 WOMAN FROM SCHEVENINGEN MENDING NETS IN THE STREET

82 SPITTING HERRING IN HARDERWIJK. STICHTING ZUIDERZEEAMBACHTEN ENKHUIZEN

Snijkoek
The fishermen would bring snijkoek from home and eat it during the trip, leaving just enough for the children when they got home again. The cake, with its high sugar content, would have started to ferment a bit, which added to the flavour and would also get the children a bit drunk.

3 KNITTING

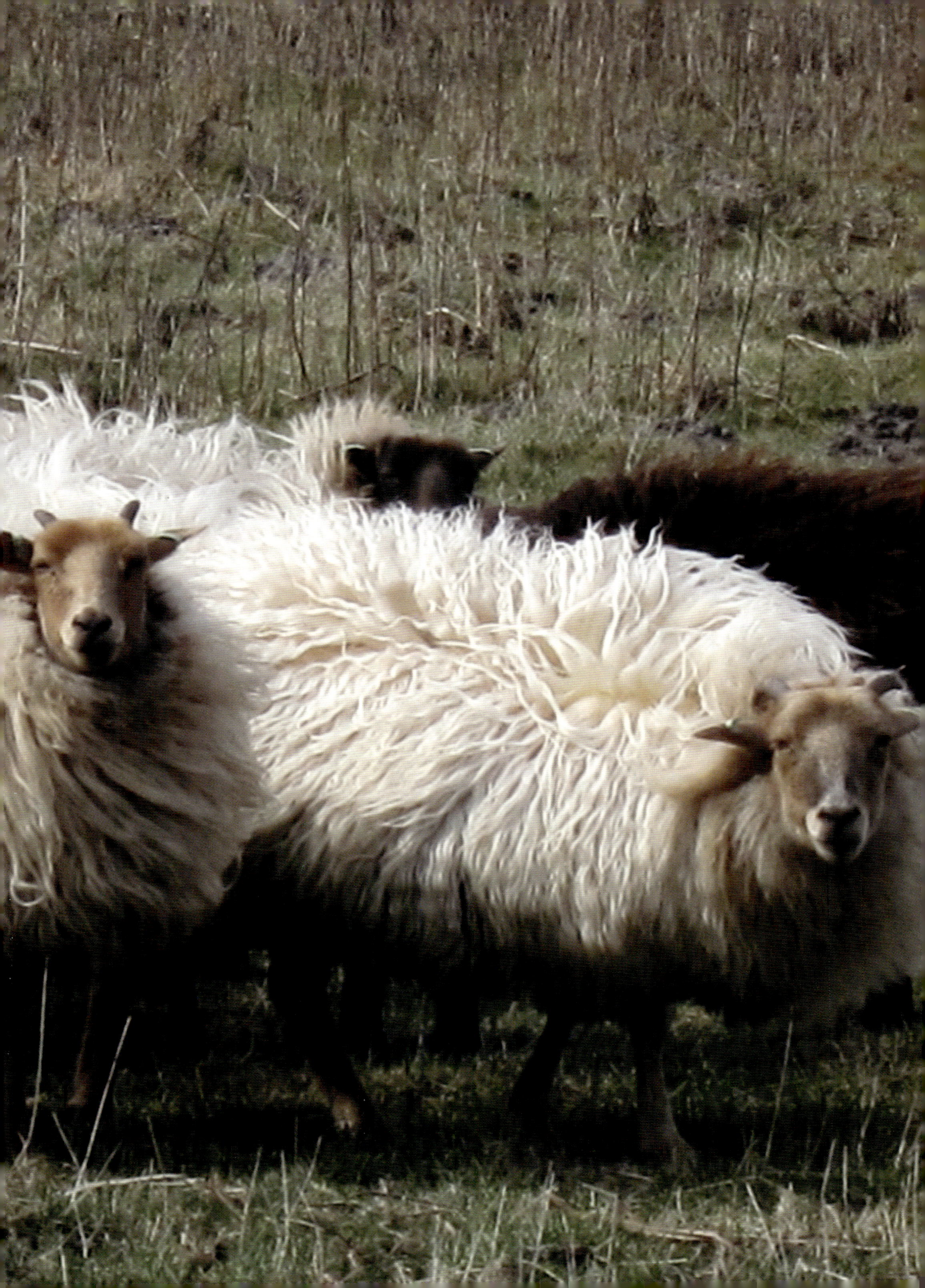

SAJET

Due to affordability and import restrictions on wool, ganseys and things like socks, stockings, undergarments, hats and mittens were knit from short belly inland Texelaar wool, called sajet or 'sagathy'. Sajet was probably named after a peddler, or derived from the word *saai* – a woollen cloth woven from a similar kind of short wool. In contrast to worsted cloth, which was woven from wool from the best part of the sheep (the back), sajet is a shiny, woollen yarn. It was used until the 1950s. Sajet cannot really be compared to any yarns that are currently available. Texelaar sheep were known for their meat and milk in addition to their wool, unlike other wool sheep such as merino sheep, which originated in Spain. Most sajet was processed in spinning mills in Veenendaal, Leiden and towns in Northern Brabant. Because of the short staple length, mills or home spinners would apply a strong twist to get a strong enough yarn. Then, two to five threads were plied together to give sajet various thicknesses (2-, 3-, 4- and 5-ply). Sajet was then dyed with colours such as indigo or woad, creating a cornflower-blue colour, and wrapped around card or wound into skeins (Fig. 83). Because of the lanolin – a natural grease in the wool which either did not fully wash out, or was added later as a spinning oil – sajet had a beautiful sheen to it. This also made the yarn warmer and more water-resistant. The pure Texelaar breed no longer exists: it has been crossed with other sheep to improve the breed's quality.

The colour system that we know now did not exist at the time, so every bulk of wool had a different colour. Ganseys were knit in colours such as Nassau blue and Nassau beige (with some red fibre spun in), marine blue, dark blue, cornflower blue, grey, black and natural wool. There weren't many other colours available. Madder, a very expensive dye, wasn't used for ganseys like it was

84 SWATCH KNITTED IN 2MM NEEDLES IN THIN SAJET, DONATED BY JEANNE DE WEERT-DOESBURG FROM WIERINGEN

in England. On the southern and eastern shores of the Zuiderzee, fishermen preferred cornflower blue. In times of mourning – which was most of the time – cornflower blue ganseys were dyed black, which resulted in a very dark blue. At a certain time, knitters decided to knit only dark blue ganseys, to avoid having to dye them a second time. Cornflower blue as a main colour slowly disappeared, but some ganseys in this colour still remain.

Sajet was a local and affordable material, but fishermen also often brought merino wool with them from England, where this good quality wool was widely available. They also brought home wool from Iceland. The Icelandic wool was sturdier, because of the colder climate, and had a great resemblance to sajet. After the Second World War, sajet was still used. In the early 1960s, however, sajet disappeared because users considered it as a poor man's yarn – it was too coarse, prickly and heavy. Knitters preferred using sock yarn or the new synthetic yarns to knit ganseys. The traditional black sajet I received from several older ladies, and with which I had the opportunity

83 BLUE AND BLACK SAJET FROM MUSEUM 'TOUDE RAADHUIS, URK

YARN FOR 2 TO 3MM (US 0 TO 2) NEEDLES

YARN FOR 2.5 TO 4MM (US 1 TO 6) NEEDLES

to knit swatches, has a beautiful sheen and cannot be compared to any yarns currently on the market. Frangipani Guernsey wool comes close, but it doesn't have the characteristic sajet sheen (Fig. 83, 84).

T-shape

The T-shape of a gansey was always knitted according to the same method: the chest size + 4–6cm (1½–2⅜in) positive ease. Cuffs were sometimes knit with a double thread for strength. Two-thirds of the total length was knitted in a round on four or five thin, double-pointed needles, much thinner than we would have now. When they reached the armholes, the work was divided into two. The armholes would be one-third of the length of the whole sweater. The front and back pieces were knitted flat on two straight needles. The back of the shoulder seam was straight, and the stitches weren't cast off but kept on the needle for later. The front was knitted up to the neckline and then the stitches divided into three parts. The shoulders were extended, and the stitches of the back and front were then knitted together and cast off at the same time, inside or outside. The remaining stitches in the middle of both sides were used for knitting the collar, in the round, wide enough to put the head through.

In the armholes stitches were picked up in the round for the sleeves. The sleeves were knitted decreasing towards the wrist. Sleeves were always knitted slightly short to keep the forearms and the hands free to work.

YARN TYPES

It is still worth the time and effort to knit your own pure wool sweater. Many store-bought, pure wool sweaters are a lot more expensive than buying the wool for a sweater you could knit yourself. If you are allergic to wool, you can also use a good-quality synthetic yarn, but sheep's wool is best. Wool stays beautiful for years and years, is elastic, warm, dirt-resistant and just a joy to wear, while synthetic yarn can be stuffy, attracts dirt and pills a lot faster, ruining your beautiful knitting in no time.

To show you the different effects you can achieve with different yarn types and thicknesses, the designs in the book are knit in various types of yarn and on different needles: from fine (2–2.5mm/US 0–1) to chunky (4.5–6mm/US 7–10). If you use even thicker yarn and needles, you will not have as many repeats, but it is still possible. To make it easier for you, a few swatches in the various yarn types and thicknesses are shown under Motifs and Patterns (page 50). Sometimes, yarn types and colours are discontinued. Your local yarn store can advise you on alternatives. When buying yarn check the total length per 50 or 100g (1¾ or 3½oz), the needle size and dye bath.

Thin or thick, sturdy or soft yarn

Whatever the needle size, you can choose between various types of worsted wool, wool mixes and synthetic yarns. We are using only pure wool and a few wool mixes, most of them plied, but also a few single-plies. Plying is the act of twisting together several threads to achieve a thicker and more robust yarn.

Some wool types feel a bit coarse at first, but will soften up during knitting. To address the coarseness, soak the sweater in cold water with a dash of Eucalan or fabric softener. Do not rinse or wring the sweater: carefully squeeze out the excess water, roll it up in a large towel and leave to dry flat, on top of another thick towel, to prevent it from sagging. The sweater will now be soft and nice to wear. Do the same with your swatch, to see and feel the effect of washing and to be able to calculate the stitch count. In some cases, yarn is held double during knitting. You can also go up half a needle size, which gives a looser-knit fabric, less gansey-like.

Amount of yarn required

How much yarn you need depends on the size of the sweater you will be knitting. The larger the sweater and

YARN FOR 3.5 TO 5MM (US 4 TO 8) NEEDLES

47

the more motifs you use, the more yarn you will need. In general, you need more balls in the case of thicker yarn. A plain men's sweater size 48 to 50 requires 1600 to 1700m (1750 to 1860yds), and a patterned sweater 1700 to 1800m (1860 to 1970yds). You can find the yarn length per ball on the ball band: sometimes you need only 500g (17⅝oz); other types you need at least 800g (28¼oz). The number of metres/yards is a better indication. Always knit a swatch first (Fig. 88, 89) to prevent disappointments.

Also check whether all the balls of yarn are from the same dye bath. The yarn will have a colour code, followed by a second number, indicating the dye bath. All these codes should be the same. It is best to buy a few extra balls of yarn; extra yarn can usually be returned or used to knit a hat or scarf.

NEEDLES & TOOLS

To be able to knit quickly, a *breischede* or 'needle holder' was used to hold the right needle (double-pointed) to keep it stable and to keep the right hand free to move the thread quickly These needle holders were made of wood or silver, nicely carved or embossed and put on a band around the waist (Fig. 85). I saw the same principle on the Shetland Isles as a puffed little leather cushion with holes in it to put the needle in. On both sides of the cushion were straps to tie it around the waist (Fig. 86). Needles didn't come in sizes, but were relatively thin.

Knitting needles are available in various materials: aluminium, steel, wood, bamboo and plastic. The lower the number, the thinner the needle: the higher the number, the thicker the needle. Use 40cm (15¾in) *straight needles* for knitting flat pieces. If you knit in the round, you can use *circular needles* by manufacturers such as KnitPro or Prym. You can also use four or five *double-pointed needles*, but this is quite complicated if you've never done it before.

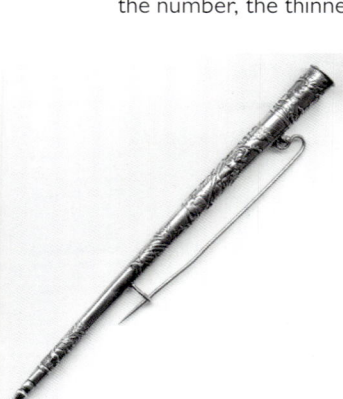

Handy tools are a *needle sizer* to check the thickness of needles, *cable needles* to make knitting cables easier, *stitch holders* to 'park' stitches which you will knit later, *stitch markers* to indicate areas such as the centre stitch or a side seam, a *lazy Kate* to keep your ball of yarn from rolling away, a *row counter* to count how many rows you've already knitted, a *(magnetic) marker* or *ruler* to keep an eye on where you are in the chart, a *knitting calculator* to re-calculate the number of rows to knit

85 NEEDLE HOLDER WITH EMBOSSED SILVER DESIGNS. COLLECTION: MRS. NEL NOORDERVLIET-JOL, SCHEVENINGEN

86 NEEDLE HOLDER USED ON THE SHETLAND ISLANDS

when you're using a different yarn, a *tape measure* and *embroidery needle* or *hook* to pick up stitches that have fallen off the needle, or to graft flat pieces of knitting.

TECHNIQUE

Ganseys were knit seamlessly, on four or five needles size 2 to 2.5mm (US 0 to 1) or less. The real needle size was never given, but people mostly used thin copper needles to knit with.

Knitting in a round

Using circular needles is a lot easier than knitting flat or using four or five needles: you can knit most stitches and have to do less purling. The charts in this book are all based on circular knitting. They show the right side of the knitting, giving you a good idea of the final result and of how the pattern is constructed (Fig. 87).

Flat knitting

Flat knitting is traditionally not a technique used for ganseys but, if you prefer, you can use this method. Keep in mind when you are calculating the number of stitches to cast on (based on your swatch) that you will need to add two extra side stitches for both the front and back. You can knit the odd rows as they are given in the chart. The even rows (the back of the work) should be knit in reverse: from left to right, all Vs as –s and all –s as Vs! (see chart key, page 53).

SIZES

Fisherwomen never followed a written pattern, but worked quite systematically: all sizes and stitches were divided into threes as mentioned before (page 10). This

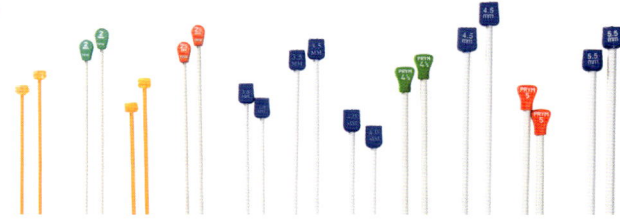

87 KNITTING ON CIRCULAR NEEDLES

is still a good guideline; however, we do now lower the front neckline and make the shoulders a bit narrower than the neck opening. Traditionally, the ganseys were worn tight across the body: chest size + 4–6cm (1½–2⅜in) of positive ease. To make the gansey more comfortable to your preference or to fashion, add 8 or 10cm (3⅛ or 4in) to the chest size. An excellent way to get the right size is by measuring a well-fitting sweater.

To keep an eye on the overall look of the sweater whilst knitting in a round, you can knit a purl stitch on both sides, suggesting a side seam. You can also hang a coloured thread in the middle of the front and the back to keep track.

STITCHES

The stitches used in ganseys are simple: knit, purl and cables. Knit stitches (i.e. stocking/stockinette) will be raised when knitting next to purled stitches, while purl stitches will be raised when knitting on top of knit stitches. Stitches are not completely square, and are wider than they are longer. That is why you will always need to knit more rows than the number of stitches you have, to create a square piece. Increasing and decreasing is done only on the sleeves. For more information about how to knit different sweater types, consult a basic knitting book. In that case, knit your chosen motifs according to the charts and follow increasing and decreasing as written in the pattern in the book. Note that your swatch has to be the same as it is written in the pattern by choosing a thinner or thicker yarn, or thinner or thicker needles.

SWATCH & STITCH COUNT

Swatches of at least 12 x 12cm (4¾ x 4¾in) – knit in both plain stocking/stockinette and pattern, in the selected yarn and with the right needle size – give you a good idea of how many stitches and rows you will get in a 10 x 10cm (4 x 4in) piece of knitting (Fig. 88, 89). As these are traditional Dutch sweaters, the method for accurately measuring their tension/gauge uses metric measurements; it is advised, therefore, that you use this system initially for these calculations, and then convert the total at the end into imperial if you wish.

Divide the desired circumference of the gansey (chest measurement + 6–8cm (equivalent to 2⅜– 3⅛in) positive ease, see also *Basic Sizes*, page 52) by 10 and multiply this by the number of stitches in 10cm (4in): this is your total number of stitches to cast on when you knit in the round. So 20 stitches in 10cm (4in) of your swatch, means in a total measurement of, for example, 104cm: 104/10 = 10.4 x 20 = 208 stitches. Or if there are 21 stitches in 10cm: 104/10 = 10.4 x 21 = 218.4. In that case, you would need to cast on 218 stitches, or a close number that matches the repeat of your chosen motif. Check the charts to see how many stitches and rows are in the motif you have selected, and adjust your stitch count as necessary. If your motif is 6 stitches wide, divide 208 stitches by 6 = 34.67 motifs. So make that 35 motifs: 6 x 35 = 210 stitches to cast on. For 218 stitches: 218/6 = 36.33. 36 x 6 = 216 stitches.

Count the same way for the number of rows you have to knit: 28 rows = 10cm. For example, if your motif is 8 rows high and the height of your gansey from the cuff is 38cm (15in) up to the armholes then 28/8 = 3.5 motifs in 10 cm. 38/10 = 3.8 x 3.5 = 13.3 motifs. You can choose then to knit 13 motifs (shorter gansey), or 14 motifs (longer gansey) before you split your work for the armholes.

Do these calculations several times, based on your swatch, to get a feel for the process. Practice makes perfect!

If you want to knit the front and back pieces separately, divide your total number of stitches in half, adding 2 side stitches to both front and back. Do the same for the sleeves. Divide

88 EXAMPLE OF A SWATCH KNITTED FOR THE VLAARDINGEN 5 GANSEY (PAGE 88) BY MARJOKE HOENDERDOS USING HJERTEGARN SUPERWASH VITAL (PURE NEW WOOL) ON 3MM (US 2) NEEDLES. 23 ST X 33 ROWS = 10 X 10CM. MOTIFS: 31 ST X 33 ROWS = 10 X 10CM. FOR THE SWATCH SHE USED 50G (1¾OZ).

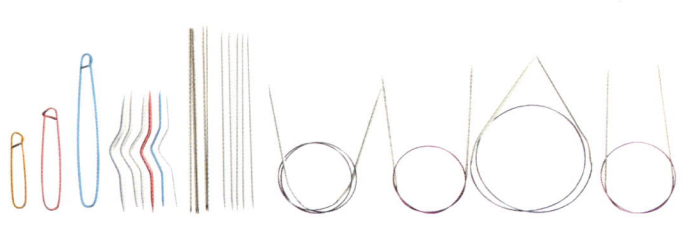

89 SWATCH, WITH THE THREAD INDICATING A HEIGHT AND LENGTH OF 10CM (4IN)

the desired length minus the cuff by 10 (cm) and multiply by the number of rows in 10cm (4in).

Make sure you always centre the middle of the motif with the middle of the front/back piece and sleeve.

You are totally free to alter a motif/pattern: instead of knitting 4 cables and 3 ladders, you can knit 5 cables and 4 ladders or 3 cables and 2 ladders, or add 2 purl stitches in between your cables instead of just 1, knit your cables over 4 instead of 6 stitches, add more repeats of the motifs or knit fewer of them, widen or narrow the motif, knit lozenges over 13 or 15 stitches instead of 11, narrow garter ridges from 3 to 2 ridges, etc. … Feel free to adjust the pattern to your liking!

MOTIFS & PATTERNS

A motif or design is the smallest stitch combination in width and height that can be repeated to form a pattern. Because of the dangers and other hardships with which fishermen had to contend at sea, they attached a lot of weight to symbolism, which can be seen in the motifs and patterns used in the ganseys. The knitters were influenced by religion, the weather, the sea, the beach, the boats, fishery, fish and daily life. All these motifs can be found in numerous variations, depending on what combinations they preferred to knit: there are no fixed rules on how to use the motifs and patterns in a gansey. The motifs and patterns charted in this book are only guidelines, indications and interpretations.

Abbreviations
Row: r
Stitch(es): st
Knit: k
Purl: p
Edge stitch(es): es
Cable crossing to the right: ccr
Cable crossing to the left: ccl

If you want to create a bigger or smaller motif or pattern, you either go up or down a needle size and use thicker or thinner yarn. Take into consideration that ganseys were knitted purposely to create a dense garment! If you want to combine motifs from various sweaters, go right ahead: it is up to you to create your own, unique gansey design. That is exactly what the fisherwomen did at the time!

Lightning bolts (weather)
If lightning strikes on land, it is scary and awe-inspiring; but nothing compares to a thunderstorm out at sea.

Squares (fishing nets, building)
Squares can represent the nets that fishermen use or the bricks of their houses. There are many types of squares.

Squares from Arnemuiden and Zandvoort

Squares from Marken, Brouwershaven, Durgerdam

Squares from Stellendam

Squares from Paesens-Moddergat

Tides (sea)
Alternating horizontal bands of stocking and motifs are called tides.

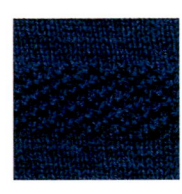

Eye of God, flower or diamond (religion)
The all-seeing eye of God is a motif that was already used in ancient times and has been found in various cultures. The motif is also called a flower (especially in Urk) or a diamond, as a symbol of prosperity. It protected fishermen and would – at least that is what their wives hoped – 'keep an eye on them' when they were in foreign ports. Machine-knit English sweaters were knit in stocking/stockinette stitch, with an eye of God on the chest consisting of one large diamond with smaller lozenges on the corners.

Eye of God

Ladders

Waves (sea)
Waves are inescapable at sea, and can be very dangerous in strong winds.

Hailstones (weather)
Hailstones were depicted in moss stitch, and in other variations on this stitch.

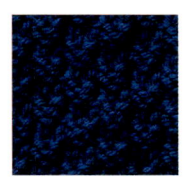

Cables (religion, boats)
Cables are used to denote stability and steadfastness. On the former isle of Urk, they stood for their bond with God. The ropes and rigging used to hoist the sails and moor the ship are symbolised through various cables.

Chains (boats)
Chains hold the anchor. In knitwork, chains can be a variation on a cable pattern, but can also be knit as alternative, horizontal bands of purl stitches.

Ladders or Jacob's ladders (religion and boats)
Out at sea, rope ladders were used to climb down into a sloop or climb on board a ship. Ladders can be knit with various-sized gaps in between. On Urk they were called Jacob's ladders, which symbolised their bond with God.

Tree of life (daily life)
The tree of life symbolises the lineage from father to son. Mothers and daughters are not part of this line; they are a separate entity. The tree of life looks a lot like herringbone, but the branches are closer together.

Arrows (fishing)
Arrows or harpoons were used at sea to kill and haul in big fish.

Garter stitch (beach)
Straight and angled garter stitch ridges represent the ridges of sand on the beach.

Lozenges (religion, fishing)
There are various types of lozenge: the eye of God and nets are also symbolised by lozenge shapes.

Herringbone (fish)
The herringbone motif is knit both horizontally and vertically.

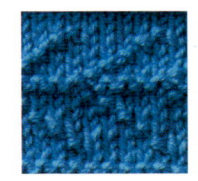

Fish nets (fishing)
All varieties of continuous and linked lozenges are inspired by fish nets.

Flags (fishing)
Flags were very important for communication at sea. The ways flags were hoisted, and the number raised, all had a specific meaning. Boats could indicate whether they had hauled in a big catch or a small one, and whether they had injured fishermen on board etc. On 'Vlaggetjesdag' or 'Flag Day', the day before the start of the herring season, and an annual feast that is still celebrated today, all the fishing boats are in port and decked with flags.

Rigging (boats)
Rigging comprises all the ropes and ties on a ship. It is used in knitting as a combination of cables and vertical motifs and used in the upper part of ganseys.

BASIC SIZES

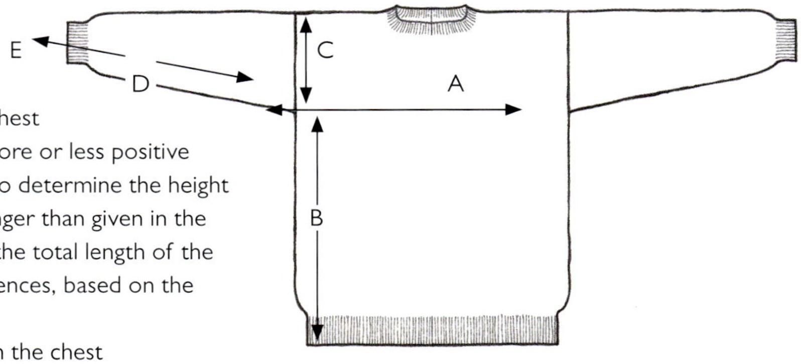

All the basic patterns in this book include 6–8cm (2⅜–3⅛in) of positive ease (3–4cm/ 1⅛–1½in) front and back, when knit flat for the chest area (A). If you like, you can adjust this to have more or less positive ease, based on your own calculations. You can also determine the height up to the armholes and make them shorter or longer than given in the patterns. The armhole height usually is a third of the total length of the sweater; but you can adjust it to your own preferences, based on the upper arm circumference.

Divide the neck and shoulder stitches based on the chest measurement plus positive ease, divided by 2. Measure the depth of the neck opening by measuring from the shoulder down to the breast bone, taking into account the height of the collar you want to knit. For the sleeve length, measure from the armpit along the arm down to the wrist. The sizes given in the patterns are standard sizes, but they are easily adjusted to fit your body type. Because all the models are T-shaped, and all ganseys are based on the chest measurements, the patterns can be easily adjusted to fit men, women, girls and boys.

Sizes	XS	S	M	L	XL	XXL
A – Chest (cm):	94	98	104	108	112	117
(in)	37	38½	41	42½	44	46
B – Height up to armhole (cm):	42	43	44	45	46	46
(in)	16½	17	17⁵⁄₁₆	17¾	18⅛	18⅛
C – Armhole height (cm):	21	21	22	23	24	24
(in)	8¼	8¼	8¾	9	9½	9½
D – Sleeve length up to forearm (incl. cuff):						
Women (cm):	45	46	47	48	49	50
(in)	17¾	18⅛	18½	18⅞	19¼	19¾
Men (cm):	48	49	50	51	52	53
(in)	18⅞	19¼	19¾	20⅛	20½	20⅞
E – Total cuff width (cm):	20	20	21	22	23	24
(in)	7⅞	7⅞	8¼	8¾	9	9½

Size	2	4	6	8	10	12	years
A – Chest (cm):	64	68	74	79	85	90	
(in)	25¼	26¾	29⅛	31⅛	33½	35⅜	
B – Height up to forearm (cm):	23	26	30	34	37	39	
(in)	9	10¼	11¾	13⅜	14⅝	15⅜	
C – Armhole height (cm):	12	13	15	16	17	18	
(in)	4¾	5⅛	5⅝	6¼	6¾	7⅛	
D – Sleeve length up to forearm (incl. cuff) (cm):	24	28	34	38	40	42	
(in)	9½	11	13⅜	15	15¾	16½	
E – Total cuff width (cm):	12	12	13	14	16	18	
(in)	4¾	4¾	5⅛	5½	6¼	7⅛	

PATTERNS & CHARTS

The motifs are easily recognisable in the chart, as they are highlighted in light blue on a dark blue background. To show you which parts of the chart form the basic motif or pattern, these stitches (below) and rows (right) are highlighted with a colour along the bottom row and right column: light blue for the first (or only) motif, green for the second repeated motif, yellow for the third, orange for the fourth, purple for the fifth motif, and so on. The centre front is indicated with a red square (see the chart key). If a motif is quite large, it sometimes has to be mirrored, starting from the centre stitch. The sweater sketch gives you a good indication of how the patterns and motifs are being knit. Cables can be knit the same way in the entire gansey, all to the right or to the left, or can sometimes be mirrored. If you want to ensure the pattern is lined up with the centre stitch, start your calculations from the middle of the pattern and count outwards – this way, you know exactly with which stitch, and where in the pattern, to start. If the multiple of the pattern doesn't – or the motif stitches don't – add up to the total number of stitches you need for your size, you can narrow or widen the motif – or place gaps in between – with 1 or more stitches, use more or fewer repeats, or knit the edge stitches (under the armhole) in plain stocking/stockinette stitch, moss stitch or another stitch that works well with the pattern. Make sure you knit a swatch if you're not quite sure of your tension/gauge or calculations. You can also copy the pattern or motif a number of times and stick these together to get a good idea of how the complete gansey pattern will look, how wide it will be, and whether you'll have to make any adjustments. This is time consuming, but will take less time than ripping out and re-knitting a gansey because the patterns don't look right.

In the knitting patterns charts are used, showing the stitches on the right side of the knitting. If you knit in the round, you can knit each row from right to left. If you knit flat, you will have to knit every second row (the even rows in the chart) from left to right and opposite to the key: all knit stitches (V) are purled and all purl stitches (–) are knit. Each motif consists of a certain number of stitches and rows, which are repeated to create a pattern (light blue in the charts). The total number of stitches in a row and the total number of rows have to be a multiple of the number of stitches and rows in a motif. The charts show the motif several times, to give an idea of what the effect is on a larger piece of knitting. This does not mean that these are the only repetitions: based on the width and length of a sweater, there are more repetitions – you can see the overall effect in the sweater sketch.

Chart key

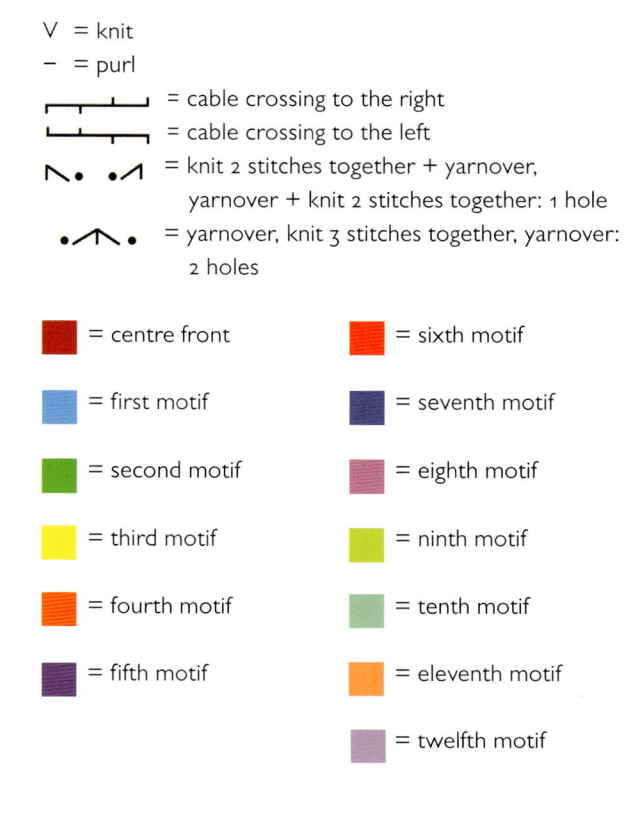

V = knit

– = purl

⌐_⌐ = cable crossing to the right

⌐‾⌐ = cable crossing to the left

↘. .↗ = knit 2 stitches together + yarnover, yarnover + knit 2 stitches together: 1 hole

•↗↖• = yarnover, knit 3 stitches together, yarnover: 2 holes

■ = centre front

■ = sixth motif

■ = first motif

■ = seventh motif

■ = second motif

■ = eighth motif

■ = third motif

■ = ninth motif

■ = fourth motif

■ = tenth motif

■ = fifth motif

■ = eleventh motif

■ = twelfth motif

HOW TO START A GANSEY

For the general knitting instruction for ganseys, the yarn and wool used are suitable for needles size 3 and 3.5mm (US 2 and 4). If you are using smaller or larger needles, or have selected a narrower or wider motif, make sure you knit a swatch to calculate your stitch count and adjust the patterns accordingly.

GENERAL KNITTING INSTRUCTIONS

What you will need:

- ∞ Enough yarn from the same dye bath, for a patterned gansey you usually need around 1700–1800m (1860–1970yds).
- ∞ Circular needles, sizes 3 and 3.5mm (US 2 and 4), 80cm (32in) long for the body and 40 and 20cm (16 and 8in) for the sleeves; or 5 double-pointed needles, sizes 3 and 3.5mm (US 2 and 4).
- ∞ Straight knitting needles size 3.5mm (US 4).
- ∞ Stitch holders.
- ∞ Thin cable needle (if necessary, see individual sweaters).
- ∞ Stitch markers or safety pins.
- ∞ Row counter.

90 LIGHTLY BLOCK THE SWEATER ON A DAMP TOWEL AND COVER IT WITH A SECOND DAMP TOWEL. LEAVE TO DRY

Knitting in a round

Measure up the person you want to knit the gansey for, or take measurements from a sweater that fits well. Check the chart and sketch of the gansey you want to knit to see how the motifs and patterns are placed, and whether the cables should be knit the same all over or mirrored on either side of the centre stitch. Make sure you knit a swatch, both in stocking/stockinette stitch and the pattern selected! Block your swatch (by pinning it on a damp towel, Fig. 90) and count the number of stitches and rows. Calculate the number of stitches in the basic motif(s) of your pattern. Measure how wide your pattern or motif is. Calculate how many stitches you should cast on for your sweater size and look at the sweater sketch to see how the motifs and patterns are knit. Determine how many repeats you should knit and what the spacing between them has to be to fit the number of stitches you are casting on.

Front and back of the sweater

Select the size you want to knit and cast on the required number of stitches (based on your swatch) on the smaller circular needles (3mm/US 2). Make sure the total number of stitches is a multiple of the number of stitches for the motif selected. Start by knitting 5–8cm (2–3⅛in) of ribbing. Switch to the larger needles (3.5mm/US 4) and continue in stocking/stockinette stitch (knit all rows) up to where you want to start with the pattern, or start knitting the motifs you selected straight away. If required, add a few stitches in the first row knitted to make sure you have a multiple of the pattern stitch count. If you are knitting cables, add 10–14 stitches, divided over the needle, as cables draw in a lot of stitches! You can decide to increase straight after the ribbing, or halfway up the body if the cables start higher up. Use a stitch marker or safety pin to indicate the start of a row, the centre stitch and the 'side seams'. Knit the body until you get to the armholes. Divide the work into a front and back. Continue knitting (on the regular needles) until the required length for the back and the front neckline. Note: knit the odd rows as they are given in the chart. Even rows (the back of the work) should be knit in reverse: from left to right, all knit stitches as purl stitches and all purl stitches as knit stitches. Once you've reached the required length for the front, divide the work in three parts (add some more stitches for the neck than for the shoulders) and put the middle stitches on a stitch holder (these are the stitches for the collar). Continue the shoulders for another 4–6cm (1½–2⅜in) – decreasing a few stitches on the inside edge for a rounded neckline – and put the remaining stitches on stitch holders. Knit the back all the way up to the nape of the neck. Knit the shoulders together as follows: knit one stitch from the front and one stitch from the back together as one stitch. Knit the next two stitches (front and back) together and pass the first stitch over. Knit and cast off the shoulder stitches. Do the same for the other shoulder. You can decide to make a visible or invisible seam; this depends on which sides you hold together. Put the stitches for the collar on a stitch holder.

Collar

Pick up all the stitches on the stitch holders on the smaller circular needles (3mm/US 2). Make sure the gap is large enough for the head (try this before you start on the sleeves) and pick up a few extra stitches to close any holes. It is best to pick up extra stitches, especially at the sides, by knitting these stitches through the front and back loop and then decreasing (some of) these stitches in the next row. Knit 4cm (1½in) or more of ribbing for the collar. Cast off loosely.

Sleeves

Divide the length of the sleeves, plus 1–2cm (⅜–¾in) extra, by the number of rows in your swatch, and calculate how often you need to knit the pattern until you get to the cuff. Calculate how many stitches you need to cast on and how many you need to achieve the right wrist circumference for the cuff. Divide the total number of rows by the difference between those two stitch counts. You now know how often and when you need to decrease. If you knit in the round, alternate your decreases on the left and the right of the centre stitch on the underside of the sleeve in order to prevent skewing. Pick up the required number of stitches for the sleeve on the large 40cm (15¾in) circular needles (size 3.5mm/US 4). In the first row, knit over every side stitch 2 stitches through the front and the back loop to avoid holes, and knit these stitches together again in the second row to end up with the number of stitches you need for the pattern. The total number of stitches should be divisible by the motif you selected. Knit the sleeve up to the required length and knit 5–6cm (2–2⅜in) ribbing for the cuff with the smaller needles (size 3mm/US 2). Cast off loosely. If you pick up the stitches from the armhole, the sweater can become quite heavy and unwieldy to hold during knitting. You can also cast on the number of stitches required and knit the sleeves separately. Sew the sleeves into the armholes using mattress stitch, which will make the seam less visible.

Finishing

Sew in the ends with a blunt-end needle. If you use a coarse wool, wash your sweater with a dash of Eucalan. Do not rinse, but block on the thick towel and leave to dry. With softer yarn, just block the sweater between two damp towels to smooth out the knitting (Fig. 90). You can also steam-iron the sweater: cover the gansey with a tea towel, set the steam iron to a fairly high setting and steam the sweater. Make sure you do not touch the knitting!

This would also press down cables and other dimensional knit stitches. By finishing off the sweaters, they will look even better.

Flat knitting

Select the right size sweater, and cast on the required number of stitches for the front and the back that is divisible by the number of stitches of your motif, based on your swatch. Add two extra side stitches (see Swatch & Stitch Count, page 49). You can knit the odd rows as they are given in the chart. The even rows (the back of the work) should be knit in reverse: from left to right, all Vs as –s and all –s as Vs!

General information

The sweaters in this book do not have detailed knitting instructions. Included are a sketch, chart(s) – based on old photographs – the sizes and a list of what you need to make the gansey. You can refer to the general knitting instructions on the opposite page. Where necessary, the introductory text for the gansey and/or the adjustments section (see pages 49–50) will give you tips and information about how the motif or pattern can be altered or adjusted. Always knit a swatch, and adjust the sizing and the stitch and row count accordingly.

Other models

Other models and knitting designs can incorporate the gansey motifs from the inspired patterns on pages 170–172. There is just a very brief instruction. Choose a model from a knitting book or magazine with a clear instruction and use the motifs from the ganseys as you would do if you were knitting the T-shape model. Make sure your swatch is equal to the number of stitches and rows in that book or magazine.

4 NORTH SEA COAST

The North Sea was traditionally the most important fishing ground for the Netherlands, with plenty of herring, cod, haddock, flatfish, roundfish, shrimp and mussels. Sometimes fishermen would venture far out at sea, but usually they fished just off the coast. The North Sea brought prosperity to the Netherlands, in particular in the seventeenth century and the end of the nineteenth and early twentieth centuries, when the catch and export figures reached record levels.

Up to the eighteenth century, the most important fishing towns for North Sea coast fishing were Callantsoog, Schoorl, Bergen and Ter Heide. Fishermen mainly used pinks, but that ended at the beginning of the nineteenth century. No ganseys were found in those places.

The North Sea fishermen were the first to come into contact with the ganseys worn as outerwear by their Scottish and English colleagues and they quickly adopted this custom. The ganseys can sometimes also be traced back to their counterparts on the other side of the North Sea.

The ganseys worn along the North Sea coast are very varied, but we can see similarities, particularly between Den Helder and Scheveningen: ganseys from Scheveningen, Zandvoort, IJmuiden and Egmond are knit in stocking/stockinette stitch up to the chest and then continue in pattern. The fishermen from these coastal towns were generally poor, and because a motif took more wool than stocking/stockinette, the motif would only be knit where it was most important: on the chest. The sleeves were also mostly knit in stocking/stockinette, or knit with a small pattern band.

91 *BOMSCHUIT* BEING PULLED UP ONTO THE BEACH AT KATWIJK BY HORSES. CA. 1900. KATWIJKS MUSEUM

NORTH HOLLAND
DEN HELDER & HUISDUINEN

Because of their location, Den Helder and Huisduinen are classified as North Sea coastal towns. However, they could also have been counted as Wadden Sea or Zuiderzee coastal villages, because the way in which the fishermen worked differed from the method applied by other North Sea coast fishermen. Some fished for fresh fish using *botters* ('smack boats'), and there were the so-called *haringbotters*, which were used to fish on the Marsdiep with open *vletten* (small, open, wooden vessels) and seines. These nets, measuring 150 to 300 metres (164 to 330 yards) long, were dragged around a school of herring. Until the Afsluitdijk was completed in 1932, this last group fished from the beach at Huisduinen, Den Helder or Texel, looking for Zuiderzee herring, a smaller type of fish. This fish would be swimming towards the Zuiderzee to spawn from the end of February until May. They would not have spawned their eggs yet and would be 'full'. The Zuiderzee herring could not be gutted but was eaten fried or smoked, as *bokking*. After May, they would fish for anchovy.

The full nets would be pulled onto the beach by ten to fifteen men, which explains the term *haringtrekkerij*, which translates as 'herring pulling'. Once the nets were full, the fishermen – wearing high water boots – would get out into the cold water, reaching up to their waists, to pull the seines onto the beach. If their boots filled up with water, they could fall over and drown.

In Den Helder, a large number of photos from around 1900 was found in the KNRM (Royal Dutch Lifeboat Society) archives. They show fishermen in various sweaters from Huisduinen and Den Helder. Two pictures show the Bakker brothers: 'De Gorrel' (Fig. 98) and 'Tabbie' (Fig. 96). There was also a third brother was nicknamed 'De Gul'. They were brave coastguards, 'knights of the sea', going out to sea in old – and sometimes leaking – *vletten* to help ships in distress, and living in their parents' and grandparents' (often uninhabitable) cottages until they were old themselves.

Some of the ganseys found here have block motifs, horizontal designs and a middle band with the eyes of God. This last motif may be inspired by or originate from Urk, as a number of people from Urk had moved to Den Helder at that time. One of the pictures shows a gansey knit sideways. The ganseys were usually blue, but a number of natural-coloured ganseys can be seen on the group pictures.

In Den Helder, the old fishing neighbourhood is called the Pilobuurt, after the pilo trousers worn by the fishermen.

THE GANSEY, DEN HELDER 1, CAN BE FOUND ON PAGE 55 OF *DUTCH TRADITIONAL GANSEYS*.

DEN HELDER 2 GANSEY

CHEST: 96CM + 6CM = 102CM (40⅛IN). TOTAL HEIGHT: 68–70CM (26¾–27½IN).

Knit a swatch first, with different sized needles if necessary. A gansey should not be knit too loosely. Follow the chart for the motif and adjust the width and/or height to your size, the yarn used and your tension/gauge. Follow the general instructions for the gansey on pages 54–55 and adjust where necessary.

Measurements

WIDTH: 2 × 51 = 102cm (40⅛in)
SHOULDERS: 16.5cm (6½in)
NECK: 17cm (6¾in)
NECKLINE DEPTH: 5–6cm (2–2⅜in)
ARMHOLE HEIGHT: 22–23cm (8¾–9in)
HEIGHT UP TO ARMHOLE, EXCL. RIBBING: 41cm (16⅛in)
SLEEVE LENGTH, EXCL. RIBBING: 43cm (17in)
WRIST CIRCUMFERENCE: approx. 23cm (9in)
RIBBING: according to preference, 5–8cm (2–3⅛in)

Materials

- 800g (28¼oz) Scheepjeswol Subtile, marine 405; or 100% merino yarn (50g (1¾oz) = approx. 125m (136¾yds))
- Circular needles, 3 and 3.5mm (US 2 and 4)
- Straight knitting needles, 3.5mm (US 4)

TENSION/GAUGE: 26 st × 34 rows on 3.5mm (US 4) needles = 10 × 10cm (4 × 4in)
RIBBING: k2, p2

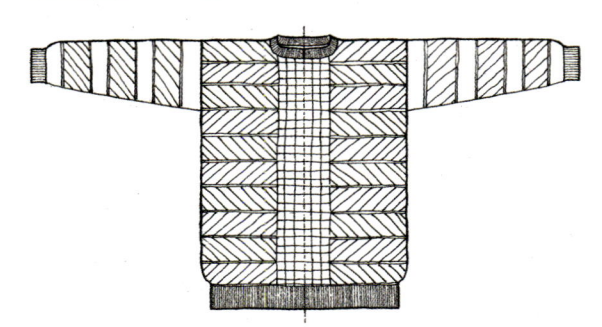

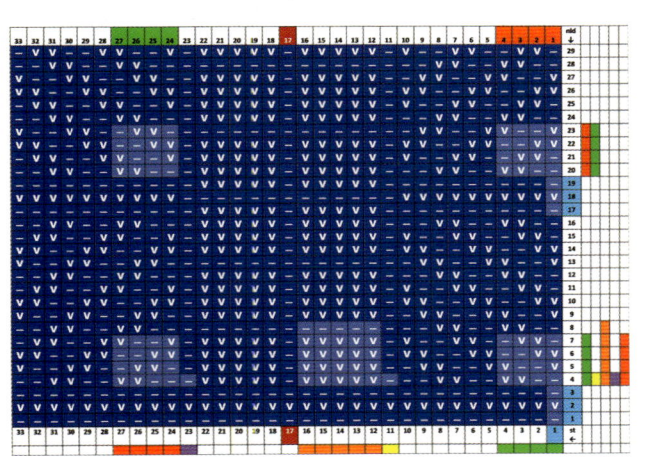

93 GRATEFUL PENSIONERS OF THE FISHERMEN SOCIETY IN DEN HELDER, CA. 1900. KNRM ARCHIVE, DEN HELDER

59

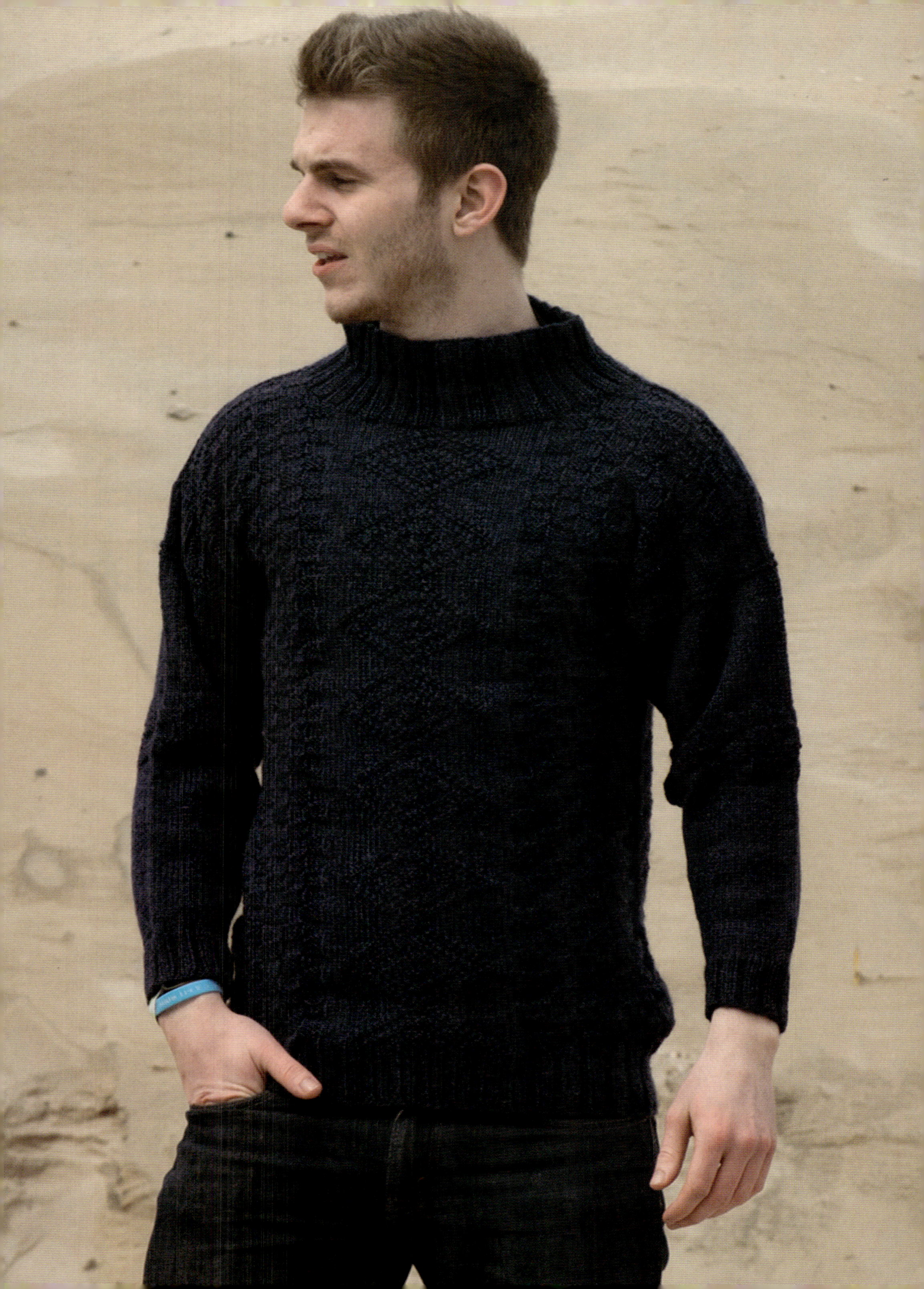

DEN HELDER 3 GANSEY

CHEST: 96CM + 6CM = 102CM (40⅛IN). TOTAL HEIGHT: 68–70CM (26¾–27½IN).

Knit a swatch first, with different sized needles if necessary. A gansey should not be knit too loosely. Follow the chart for the motif and adjust the width and/or height to your size, the yarn used and your tension/gauge. Follow the general instructions for the gansey on pages 54–55 and adjust where necessary.

Measurements

WIDTH: 2 x 51 = 102cm (40⅛in)
SHOULDERS: 16.5cm (6½in)
NECK: 18cm (7in)
NECKLINE DEPTH: 5–6cm (2–2⅜in)
ARMHOLE HEIGHT: 22–23cm (8¾–9in)
HEIGHT UP TO ARMHOLE, EXCL. RIBBING: 41cm (16⅛in)
SLEEVE LENGTH, EXCL. RIBBING: 43cm (17in)
WRIST CIRCUMFERENCE: approx. 23cm (9in)
RIBBING: according to preference, 5–8cm (2–3⅛in)

Materials

∞ Approx. 850–900g (30–31¾oz) Hjertegarn Lima, indigo marl 638; or 100% pure wool yarn (50g (1¾oz) = approx. 100m (110yds))
∞ Circular needles, 3.5 and 4mm (US 4 and 6)
∞ Straight knitting needles, 4mm (US 6)

TENSION/GAUGE: 20 st x 26 rows on 4mm (US 6) needles = 10 x 10cm (4 x 4in)

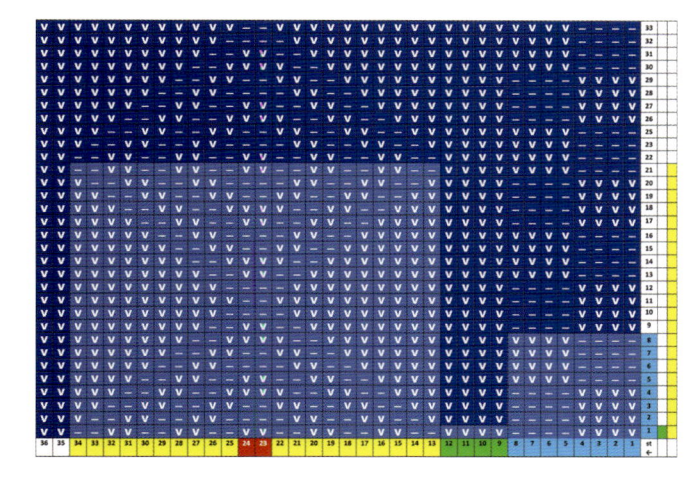

RIBBING: k2, p2

94 HAAIKE ABRAHAM JAARSMA (1881–1970) WAS A SHIP'S PILOT, BUT HE ALSO PAINTED SEASCAPES. KNRM ARCHIVES, DEN HELDER

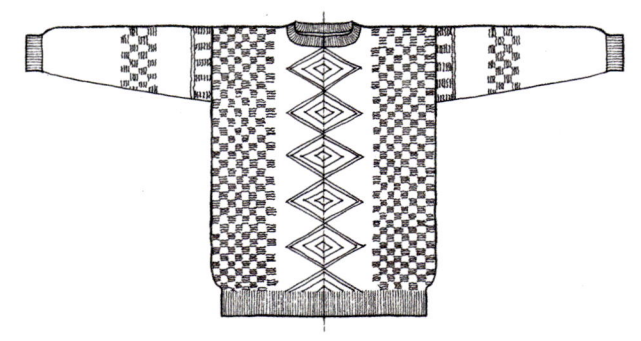

DEN HELDER 4 GANSEY

CHEST: 96CM + 6CM = 102CM (40⅛IN). TOTAL HEIGHT: 68–70CM (26¾–27½IN).

Knit a swatch first, with different sized needles if necessary. A gansey should not be too loosely knit. Follow the chart for the motif and adjust the width and/or height to your size, the yarn used and your tension/gauge. Follow the general instructions for the gansey on pages 54–55 and adjust where necessary.

Measurements
WIDTH: 2 × 51 = 102cm (40⅛in)
SHOULDERS: 16.5cm (6½in)
NECK: 18cm (7in)
NECKLINE DEPTH: 5–6cm (2–2⅜in)
ARMHOLE HEIGHT: 22–23cm (8¾–9in)
HEIGHT UP TO ARMHOLE, EXCL. RIBBING: 41cm (16⅛in)
SLEEVE LENGTH, EXCL. RIBBING: 43cm (17in)
WRIST CIRCUMFERENCE: approx. 23cm (9in)
RIBBING: according to preference, 5–8cm (2–3⅛in)

Materials
∞ Approx. 800g (28¼oz) Scheepjes Donna, blue 641; or 50% merino, 50% acrylic microfibre yarn (50g (1¾oz) = approx. 112m (122½yds))
∞ Circular needles, 3 and 3.5mm (US 2 and 4)
∞ Straight knitting needles, 3.5mm (US 4)

TENSION/GAUGE: 23 st × 32 rows on 3.5mm (US 4) needles = 10 × 10cm (4 × 4in)

RIBBING: k2, p2

95 FISHERMAN JOHAN EWALT, CA. 1900. KNRM ARCHIVES, DEN HELDER

DEN HELDER 5 GANSEY

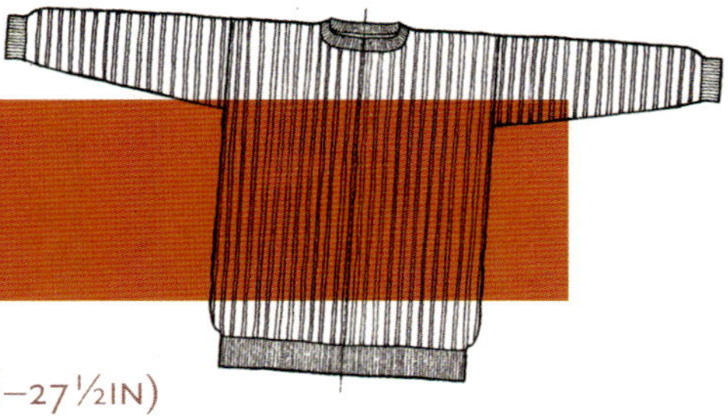

CHEST: 96CM + 6CM = 102CM (40⅛IN). TOTAL HEIGHT: 68–70CM (26¾–27½IN)

Note: This special gansey may have the T-shape, but is knit sideways, not from the bottom up. The sleeves and ribbing are worked in a round. Knit a swatch first, with different sized needles if necessary. Follow the chart for the motif and adjust the width and/or height to your size, the yarn used and your tension/gauge. Follow the general instructions for the gansey on pages 54–55 and adjust where necessary. A gansey should not be too loosely knit! Knit the motif on both the front and back pieces and the sleeves. Neckline depth: 6–7cm (2⅜–2¾in) round at the front, straight at the back of the neck. Knit back and forth according to the chart and sketch. Cast on the stitches for the entire length of the gansey – minus approx. 6cm (2⅜in) ribbing = 62–64cm (24⅜–25¼in) – and immediately start with the pattern. Pattern: *k 5 rows (back and forth), p 1 row*. Decrease for the neck after 16.5cm (6½in), knit on for another 17–18cm (6¾–7in) and gradually cast on the decreased sts again. Knit 16.5cm (6½in), cast off 22cm (approx. 8¾in) for the armhole and cast on the same number of stitches at the end of the next row. Work 51cm (20in) for the back, to the other armhole. Close the shoulder seams and one side seam. With circular needles, pick up stitches in the armholes and work the sleeves. Decrease 13 x 1 st every 4th row, then 13 x 1 st every 3rd row. In total, decrease 26x until the sleeve measures 45cm (17¾in). Make sure the pattern continues by working an extra row on one side if necessary. Pick up stitches on circular needles along the bottom hem and neck and work ribbing.

Measurements

WIDTH: 2 x 51 = 102cm (40⅛in)
SHOULDERS: 16.5cm (6½in)
NECK: 18cm (7in)
NECKLINE DEPTH: 5–6cm (2–2⅜in)
ARMHOLE HEIGHT: 22–23cm (8¾–9in)
HEIGHT UP TO ARMHOLE, EXCL. RIBBING: 41cm (16⅛in)
SLEEVE LENGTH, EXCL. RIBBING: 43cm (17in)
WRIST CIRCUMFERENCE: approx. 23cm (9in)
RIBBING: according to preference, 5–8cm (2–3⅛in)

Materials

- Approx. 700g (24⅔oz) Léttlopi, ash heather 0054; or 100% pure wool yarn (50g (1¾oz) = 100m (110yds))
- Circular needles, 3 and 3.5mm (US 2 and 4)
- Straight knitting needles, 3 and 3.5mm (US 2 and 4)

TENSION/GAUGE: 23 st x 32 rows on 3.5mm (US 4) needles = 10 x 10cm (4 x 4in)
STITCH PATTERN, FRONT/BACK: *k5 rows, p1 row*
STITCH PATTERN SLEEVES, WORKED IN A ROUND: *k3 rows, k1 row, p1 row*
RIBBING: k1, p1

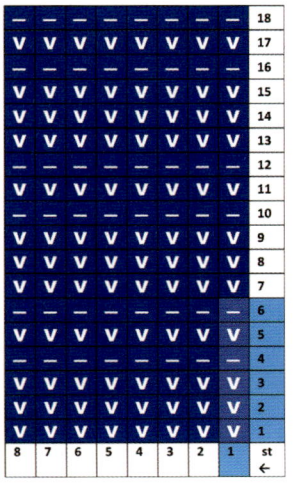

96 FISHERMAN JACOB BAKKER, 'TABBIE', CA. 1900. KNRM ARCHIVES, DEN HELDER

DEN HELDER 6 GANSEY

CHEST: 96CM + 6CM = 102CM (40⅛IN). TOTAL HEIGHT: 68–70CM (26¾–27½IN).
Knit a swatch first, with different sized needles if necessary. A gansey should not be too loosely knit. Follow the chart for the motif and adjust the width and/or height to your size, the yarn used and your tension/gauge. Follow the general instructions for the gansey on pages 54–55 and adjust where necessary.

Measurements

WIDTH: 2 × 51 = 102cm (40⅛in)
SHOULDERS: 16.5cm (6½in)
NECK: 18cm (7in)
NECKLINE DEPTH: 5–6cm (2–2⅜in)
ARMHOLE HEIGHT: 22–23cm (8¾–9in)
HEIGHT UP TO ARMHOLE, EXCL. RIBBING: 41cm (16⅛in)
SLEEVE LENGTH, EXCL. RIBBING: 43cm (17in)
WRIST CIRCUMFERENCE: approx. 23cm (9in)
RIBBING: according to preference, 5–8cm (2–3⅛in)

Material

- Approx. 750g (26½oz) Lang Merino 150, jean blue 0034; or 100% merino yarn (50g (1¾oz) = approx. 150m (164yds))
- Circular needles, 3 and 3.5mm (US 2 and 4)
- Straight needles. 3.5mm (US 4)

TENSION/GAUGE: 27 st × 37 rows on 3.5mm (US 4) needles = 10 × 10cm (4 × 4in)

RIBBING: k1, p1

97 FISHERMAN CORNELIS VERBERNE FROM DEN HELDER, CA. 1890. KNRM ARCHIVES, DEN HELDER

98 COASTGUARD WILLIAM BAKKER FROM DEN HELDER, 'DE GORREL', CA. 1900. KNRM ARCHIVES, DEN HELDER

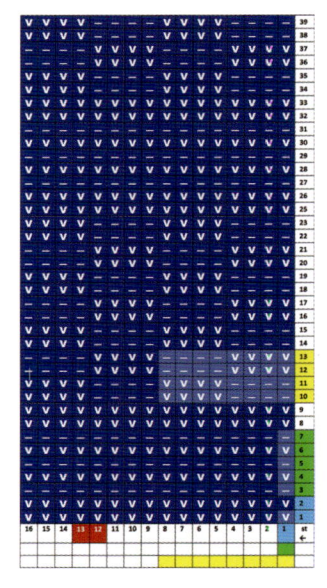

NORTH HOLLAND
PETTEN

In the eighteenth century, Petten was reasonably prosperous. The fishermen, who would pull their flat-bottomed barges onto the beach, where they would also sell the fish, also guided large ships sailing to the East and the West along the dangerous coast to Den Helder to earn some extra money. In Den Helder, a pilot would come on board the vessels to lead them to Amsterdam. However, the tide turned: the fishing trade diminished and the large ships no longer needed guides. Most fishermen moved away or went to the work on the dyke. Between 1871 and 1877, many improvements were made to the Hondsbossche and Pettemer sea defences, which meant that there were plenty of jobs. When this project was completed, poverty struck again. The mayor attempted to breathe new life into the fishing industry and set up a sea fishing company. After finding some shareholders, two complete *bomschuiten* were bought. However, the catch was disappointing. Around 1900, it was easier for fishermen to go to IJmuiden and sign up with one of the steam trawlers. On a smaller scale fishermen from Petten were relatively fruitful, using *vletten* to fish for shrimp just off the coast or from the beach. Most of them got a licence to pull their boats up to the dyke. They would often be dyke workers, who worked from five in the morning until seven at night, but had a lunch break of around three hours (because of high tide), which was perfect for a bit of fishing. They often had a bit of land to grow potatoes as well, and sometimes they had a few sheep. The money had to be earned in the summer, because the weather was too bad in the wintertime, and they would not get paid. In 1923, a last attempt was made. The Schager brothers set up the Stoomtrawlerrederij N.V. Visserij Maatschappij Petten, operating from IJmuiden.

From 1824, Petten was also a rescue boat station. The community was very close-knit. Pilots and fishermen would put some 'old man's pay' aside for those who were no longer able to fish. The dyke workers, driven by poverty, were forerunners of the socialist movement. Soon there was a very active local division of the trade union, fighting for rights that are now taken for granted. The men had to buy work shoes, boots and rain gear themselves, paying with the 1.50 to 2.50 guilders they earned a day. Long before Drees, the minister who introduced the old-age pension scheme, they organised a retirement scheme, and older workers were exempted from hard work on the dykes. To this day, there is still a socialist majority in Petten.

99 RESCUE BOAT WITH CREW ON THE BEACH OF PETTEN.
PHOTO COLLECTION FROM ZIJPER MUSEUM, SCHAGERBRUG

PETTEN GANSEY

CHEST: 84CM + 4CM = 88CM (34¾IN). TOTAL HEIGHT: 55–56CM (21¾–22IN).

Knit a swatch first, with different sized needles if necessary. A gansey should not be too loosely knit. Follow the chart for the motif and adjust the width and/or height to your size, the yarn used and your tension/gauge. Follow the general instructions for the gansey on pages 54–55 and adjust where necessary. The photo is quite vague, so the pattern is my own interpretation. Follow the motif on the chart for the front and back, and use circular needles for the sleeves. The motif has been made a bit smaller for a children's sweater: work 2 cables instead of 3. You can use the second chart for a larger sweater. The cables all lean to the left (cross front).

Measurements

WIDTH: 2 x 44 = 88cm (34¾in)
SHOULDERS: 14cm (5½in)
NECK: 16cm (6¼in)
NECKLINE DEPTH: 4–5cm (1½–2in)
ARMHOLE HEIGHT: 16–17cm (6¼–6¾in)
HEIGHT UP TO ARMHOLE, EXCL. RIBBING: 34cm (13⅜in)
SLEEVE LENGTH, EXCL. RIBBING: 34cm (13⅜in)
WRIST CIRCUMFERENCE: approx. 16cm (6¼in)
RIBBING: according to preference, 4–6cm (1½–2⅜in)

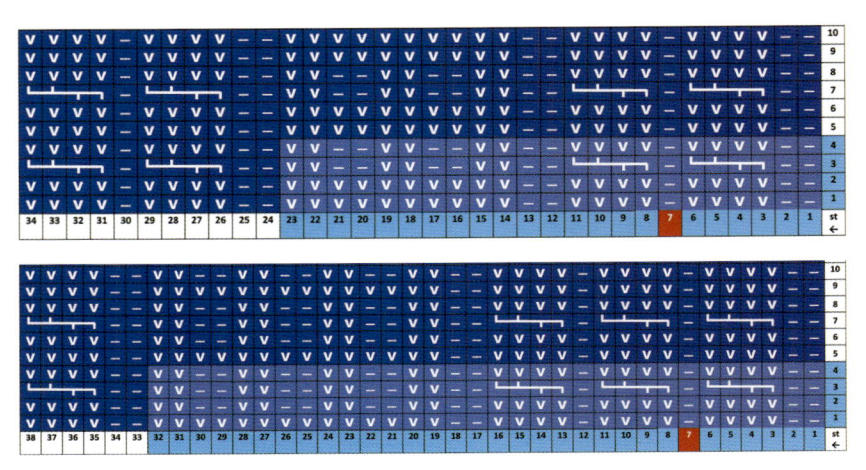

Materials

- Approx. 300g (10½oz) Lopi Einband, blue 0942; or 100% pure wool yarn (50g (1¾oz) = approx. 150m (164yds))
- Circular needles, 2.5 and 3mm (US 1 and 2)
- Straight knitting needles 3mm (US 2)
- Cable needle

TENSION/GAUGE: 27 st x 37 rows on 3mm (US 2) needles = 10 x 10cm (4 x 4in)

RIBBING: k1, p1

100 DETAIL FROM FIG. 99

NORTH HOLLAND
EGMOND AAN ZEE

Egmond aan Zee was a very poor area. People would struggle to make a living by fishing, beachcombing and poaching rabbits in the dunes, and were always afraid to get caught by *koddebaiers* or *groenpetters* (the police). Lots of people from Egmond, even young children, ended up in jail. Around 1900, it was very hard to find work. You had to walk to IJmuiden on an empty stomach, and then, if there was no work on a fishing boat, you had to walk all the way back. On the way, you could pick some blackberries and walk 10 kilometres (6.2 miles) to Alkmaar to sell these, go back and pick more berries. Blackberries were often the only fruit that grew there, but they were also seasonal. You could also go prawn fishing in the cold sea water and try to sell those.

Men, women and children would do anything to support their family. If you had some land in the dunes, this could mean the difference between life and death, because it might yield a few bags of good potatoes.

101 JACOB GLAS, CREW MEMBER OF THE RESCUE BOAT AT EGMOND AAN ZEE BETWEEN 1860 AND 1900. HISTORISCH EGMOND

THE GANSEY, EGMOND AAN ZEE 1, CAN BE FOUND ON PAGES 56–57 OF *DUTCH TRADITIONAL GANSEYS*.

EGMOND AAN ZEE 2 GANSEY

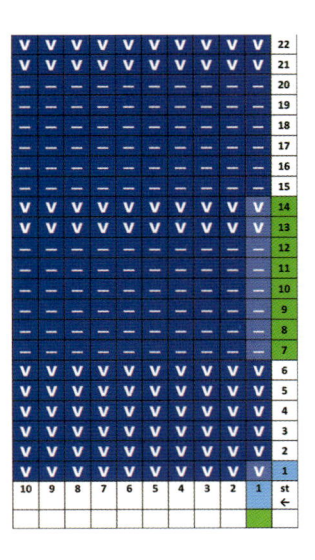

CHEST: 90CM + 6CM = 96CM (37¾IN). TOTAL HEIGHT: 68–70CM (26¾–27½IN).
Knit a swatch first, with different sized needles if necessary. A gansey should not be too loosely knit. Follow the chart for the motif and adjust the width and/or height to your size, the yarn used and your tension/gauge. Follow the general instructions for the gansey on pages 54–55 and adjust where necessary.

Measurements

WIDTH: 2 × 48 = 96cm (37¾in)
SHOULDERS: 15.5cm (6⅛in)
NECK: 17cm (6¾in)
NECKLINE DEPTH: 5–6cm (2–2⅜in)
ARMHOLE HEIGHT: 22cm (8¾in)
HEIGHT UP TO ARMHOLE, EXCL. RIBBING: 41cm (16⅛in)
SLEEVE LENGTH, EXCL. RIBBING: 43cm (17in)
WRIST CIRCUMFERENCE: approx. 22cm (8¾in)
RIBBING: according to preference, 5–8cm (2–3⅛in)

Materials

∞ Approx. 500g (17⅝oz) Lopi Einband, midnight blue 0709; or 100% pure wool yarn (50g (1¾oz) = approx. 225m (246yds))
∞ Circular needles, 2 and 2.5mm (US 0 and 1)
∞ Straight knitting needles, 2.5mm (US 1)

TENSION/GAUGE: 33 st × 54 rows on 2.5mm (US 1) needles = 10 × 10cm (4 × 4in)
RIBBING: k1, p1

67

EGMOND AAN ZEE 2 GANSEY

EGMOND AAN ZEE 3 GANSEY

CHEST: 100CM + 6CM = 106CM (41¾IN). TOTAL HEIGHT: 68–70CM (26¾–27½IN).
Knit a swatch first, with different sized needles if necessary. A gansey should not be too loosely knit. Follow the chart for the motif and adjust the width and/or height to your size, the yarn used and your tension/gauge. Follow the general instructions for the gansey on pages 54–55 and adjust where necessary.

Measurements
WIDTH: 2 × 53 = 106cm (41¾in)
SHOULDERS: 15.5cm (6⅛in)
NECK: 18cm (7in)
NECKLINE DEPTH: 5–7cm (2–2¾in)
ARMHOLE HEIGHT: 23cm (9in)
HEIGHT UP TO ARMHOLE, EXCL. RIBBING: 41cm (16⅛in)
SLEEVE LENGTH, EXCL. RIBBING: 43cm (17in)
WRIST CIRCUMFERENCE: approx. 23cm (9in)
RIBBING: according to preference, 5–8cm (2–3⅛in)

Materials
∞ Approx. 600g (21oz) Lang Donegal Merino, grey blue 034; or 100% merino yarn
  (50g (1¾oz) = approx. 190m (208yds))
∞ Circular needles, 3 and 3.5mm (US 2 and 4)
∞ Straight knitting needles, 3.5mm (US 4)

TENSION/GAUGE: 24 st × 32 rows on 3.5mm (US 4) needles
              = 10 × 10cm (4 × 4in)
RIBBING: k2, p2

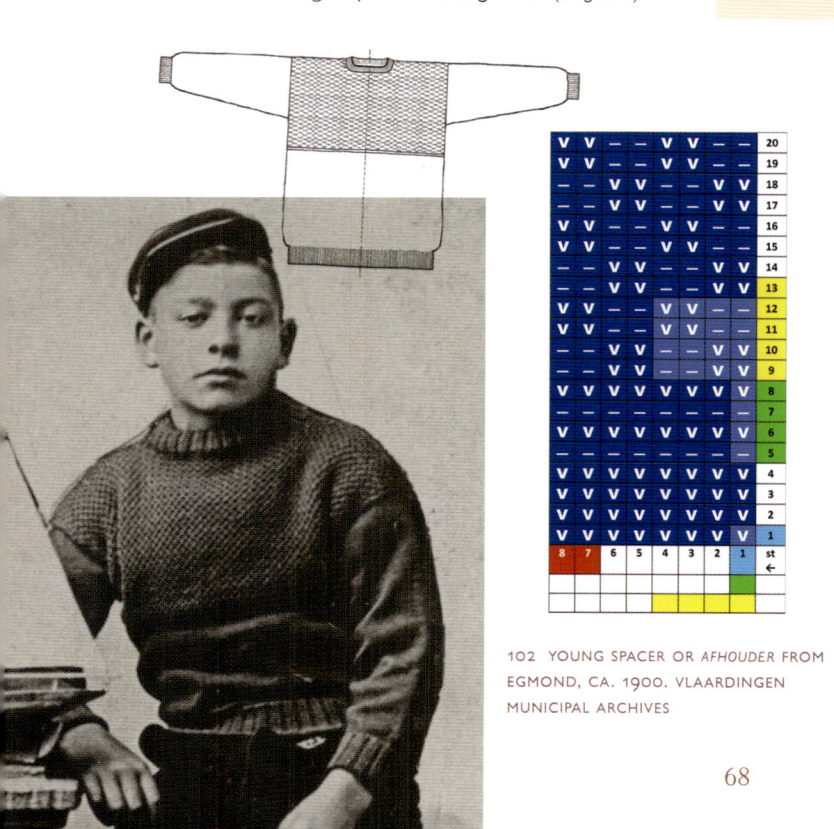

102 YOUNG SPACER OR *AFHOUDER* FROM EGMOND, CA. 1900. VLAARDINGEN MUNICIPAL ARCHIVES

68

NORTH HOLLAND
IJMUIDEN AND VELSEN

103 CREW OF A LUGGER IN THE PORT OF IJMUIDEN. SEA AND PORT MUSEUM IN IJMUIDEN

104 CREW OF THE LUGGER IJM 18, CAMELIA, FROM IJMUIDEN. SEA AND PORT MUSEUM IN IJMUIDEN

After the construction of the North Sea Canal, the new town of IJmuiden quickly outshone the old fishing village of Velsen. IJmuiden was the only port between Hoek van Holland and Den Helder, and offered a convenient mooring place in bad weather. First, ships from Zandvoort and Egmond aan Zee would use the port, which were then followed by the longliners from Middelharnis, Pernis and Zwartewaal. With the arrival of the new national fishing port in 1896 with access to the North Sea, the fish auction in 1899 and the connection to the railway network, IJmuiden soon became an important port for both herring and fresh fish. It still is the largest fishing port in the country. More and more shipowners from other fishing towns decided to settle in IJmuiden. These attracted more fishermen from all over the country, who often came to live in IJmuiden. A lot of these fishermen were from Egmond. The ganseys from IJmuiden are strongly influenced by the ones from Egmond.

IJMUIDEN GANSEY

CHEST: 96CM + 6CM = 102CM (40⅛IN). TOTAL HEIGHT: 68–70CM (26¾–27½IN).

Knit a swatch first, with different sized needles if necessary. A gansey should not be too loosely knit. Follow the chart for the motif and adjust the width and/or height to your size, the yarn used and your tension/gauge. Follow the general instructions for the gansey on pages 54–55 and adjust where necessary.

Measurements

WIDTH: 2 x 51 = 102cm (40⅛in)
SHOULDERS: 16.5cm (6½in)
NECK: 18cm (7in)
NECKLINE DEPTH: 5–6cm (2–2⅜in)
ARMHOLE HEIGHT: 22–23cm (8¾–9in)
HEIGHT UP TO ARMHOLE, EXCL. RIBBING: 41cm (16⅛in)
SLEEVE LENGTH, EXCL. RIBBING: 43cm (17in)
WRIST CIRCUMFERENCE: approx. 23cm (9in)
RIBBING: according to preference, 5–8cm (2–3⅛in)

Materials

∞ Approx. 750g (26½oz) Hjertegarn Mini Vital, dark blue 698; or 100% pure superwash wool yarn (50g (1¾oz) = approx. 150m (164yds))
∞ Circular needles, 3 and 3.5mm (US 2 and 4)
∞ Straight knitting needles, 3.5mm (US 4)
∞ Cable needle

TENSION/GAUGE: 24 st x 30 rows on 3.5mm (US 4) needles = 10 x 10cm (4 x 4in)
RIBBING: K2, p2

IJMUIDEN GANSEY

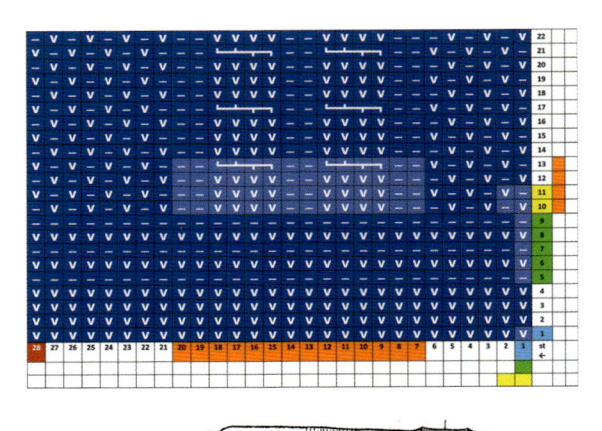

VELSEN GANSEY

CHEST: 96CM + 6CM = 102CM (40⅛IN). TOTAL HEIGHT: 68–70CM (26¾–27½IN).

This gansey looks a lot like some of the English ganseys from Staithes and Southwold/Walberswick, on the coast of Suffolk, England. Knit a swatch first, with different sized needles if necessary. A gansey should not be too loosely knit. Follow the chart for the motif and adjust the width and/or height to your size, the yarn used and your tension/gauge. Follow the general instructions for the gansey on pages 54–55 and adjust where necessary.

Measurements

WIDTH: 2 x 51 = 102cm (40⅛in)
SHOULDERS: 16.5cm (6½in)
NECK: 18cm (7in)
NECKLINE DEPTH: 5–6cm (2–2⅜in)
ARMHOLE HEIGHT: 22–23cm (8¾–9in)
HEIGHT UP TO ARMHOLE, EXCL. RIBBING: 41cm (16⅛in)
SLEEVE LENGTH, EXCL. RIBBING: 43cm (17in)
WRIST CIRCUMFERENCE: approx. 23cm (9in)
RIBBING: according to preference, 5–8cm (2–3⅛in)

Materials

∞ Approx. 800g (28¼oz) Lang Thema Nuova, navy 0025; or 100% pure wool yarn (50g (1¾oz) = approx. 118m (129yds))
∞ Circular needles, 3.5 and 4mm (US 4 and 6)
∞ Straight knitting needles, 4mm (US 6)

TENSION/GAUGE: 23 st x 32 rows on 4mm (US 6) needles = 10 x 10cm (4 x 4in)

RIBBING: k1, p1

105 FISHERMAN WEARING A GANSEY FROM SOUTHWOLD/WALBERSWICK ON THE SUFFOLK COAST, ENGLAND. DEB GILLANDERS, WHITBY, ENGLAND

106 UNKNOWN FISHERMAN FROM VELSEN. VLAARDINGEN MUNICIPAL ARCHIVES

70

NORTH HOLLAND
ZANDVOORT

107 UNKNOWN FISHERMAN FROM ZANDVOORT. ZANDVOORT VROEGER

In Zandvoort, fishermen used *bomschuiten* and fished close to the shore. While Scheveningen and Katwijk gradually moved from *bomschuiten* to luggers after the lifting of the gutting ban in 1857, Zandvoort remained faithful to these vessels for a while. In the nineteenth century, tourism became increasingly important, and by the early years of the twentieth century the fishing industry of Zandvoort was dead.

THE GANSEY, ZANDVOORT 1, CAN BE FOUND ON PAGES 58–60 OF *DUTCH TRADITIONAL GANSEYS*.

ZANDVOORT 2 GANSEY

CHEST: 96CM + 6CM = 102CM (40⅛IN). TOTAL HEIGHT: 68–70CM (26¾–27½IN).

Knit a swatch first, with different sized needles if necessary. A gansey should not be too loosely knit. Follow the chart for the motif and adjust the width and/or height to your size, the yarn used and your tension/gauge. Follow the general instructions for the gansey on pages 54–55 and adjust where necessary.

Measurements

WIDTH: 2 x 51 = 102cm (40⅛in)
SHOULDERS: 16.5cm (6½in)
NECK: 18cm (7in)
NECKLINE DEPTH: 5–6cm (2–2⅜in)
ARMHOLE HEIGHT: 22–23cm (8¾–9in)
HEIGHT UP TO ARMHOLE, EXCL. RIBBING: 41cm (16⅛in)
SLEEVE LENGTH, EXCL. RIBBING: 43cm (17in)
WRIST CIRCUMFERENCE: approx. 23cm (9in)
RIBBING: according to preference, 5–8cm (2–3⅛in)

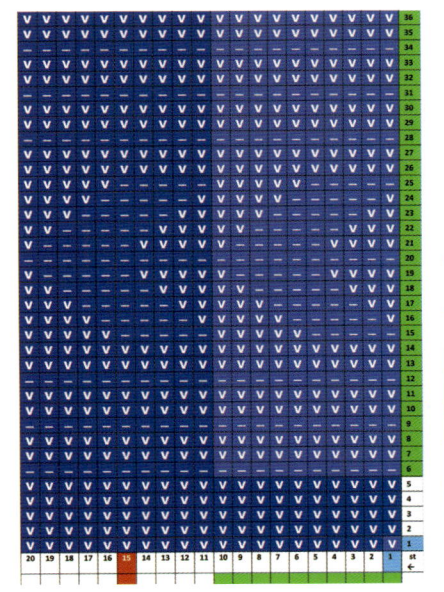

Materials

- Approx. 900–1000g (31¾–35¼oz) 5-ply Frangipani Guernsey wool, navy; or bulky 100% pure wool yarn (100g (3½oz) = approx. 195m (213yds))
- Circular needles, 2.5 and 3mm (US 1 and 2)
- Straight knitting needles, 3mm (US 2)
- Cable needle

TENSION/GAUGE: 21 st x 32 rows on 3mm (US 2) needles = 10 x 10cm (4 x 4in)
RIBBING: k2, p2

BAND UNDER CHEST

CHEST PATTERN

ZANDVOORT 3 GANSEY

CHEST: 84CM + 4CM = 88CM (34¾IN). TOTAL HEIGHT: 56–58CM (22–22¾IN).

Knit a swatch first, with different sized needles if necessary. A gansey should not be too loosely knit. Follow the chart for the motif and adjust the width and/or height to your size, the yarn used and your tension/gauge. Follow the general instructions for the gansey on pages 54–55 and adjust where necessary

Measurements

WIDTH: 2 × 44 = 88cm (34¾in)
SHOULDERS: 13.5cm (5¼in)
NECK: 14cm (5½in)
NECKLINE DEPTH: 4–5cm (1½–2in)
ARMHOLE HEIGHT: 17cm (6¾in)
HEIGHT UP TO ARMHOLE, EXCL. RIBBING: 34cm (13⅜in)
SLEEVE LENGTH, EXCL. RIBBING: 34cm (13⅜in)
WRIST CIRCUMFERENCE: approx. 16cm (6¼in)
RIBBING: according to preference, 4–6cm (1½–2⅜in)

Materials

∞ Approx. 650g (23oz) Lang Thema Nuova, marine 0035; or 100% pure wool yarn (50g (1¾oz) = approx. 118m (129yds)
∞ Circular needles, 3.5 and 4mm (US 4 and 6)
∞ Straight knitting needles, 4mm (US 6)

TENSION/GAUGE: 23 st × 32 rows on 4mm (US 6) needles = 10 × 10cm (4 × 4in)

RIBBING: k1, p1

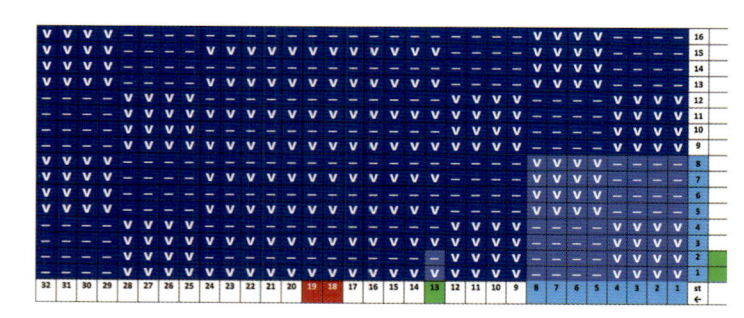

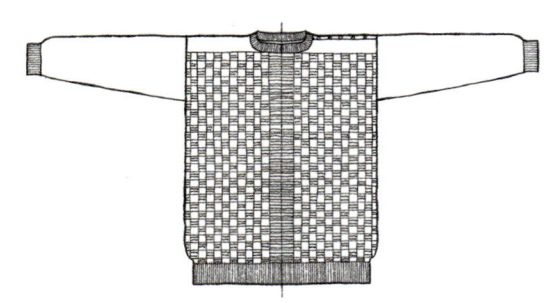

108 YOUNG FISHERMAN FROM ZANDVOORT IN THE KLEINE HOUTSTRAAT IN HAARLEM. NOORD-HOLLAND ARCHIVES

SOUTH HOLLAND
KATWIJK

At the end of the 1860s, Katwijk had the largest fishing fleet of the Netherlands, with 180 *bomschuiten*. Katwijk did not have – and still does not have – a port. Later, when modern keel ships like the lugger were introduced, the ships from Katwijk moved to the ports of Vlaardingen, IJmuiden and Scheveningen and the fleet became smaller. The period between the two wars was hard for the fisheries. Shipping companies went bankrupt because of the crisis and quite a few ships were taken out of service. The companies that survived invested in engines for the luggers in order to be less dependent on the wind. Some of the old ships were sold in the 1930s to fishermen who wanted to start for themselves: this was the start of a new generation of private ship owners. The other ships disappeared to Scandinavia, to be used as cargo ships.

Some of the people living in Katwijk still depend on fishing. The fleet has shrunk to approximately ten modern mega-ships, but the revival of the fishing school indicates that fishing is still in the blood of the Katwijk people.

109 FISHERMEN IN THE VILLAGE, CA. 1913. KATWIJKS MUSEUM

110 FISHING SCHOOL IN KATWIJK, CA 1920. KATWIJKS MUSEUM

THE GANSEYS, KATWIJK 1 AND 2, CAN BE FOUND ON PAGES 66–68 OF *DUTCH TRADITIONAL GANSEYS*.

KATWIJK 3 GANSEY

CHEST: 96CM + 6CM = 102CM (40⅛IN). TOTAL HEIGHT: 68–70CM (26¾–27½IN).

Knit a swatch first, with different sized needles if necessary. A gansey should not be too loosely knit. Follow the chart for the motif and adjust the width and/or height to your size, the yarn used and your tension/gauge. Follow the general instructions for the gansey on pages 54–55 and adjust where necessary.

Measurements

WIDTH: 2 × 51 = 102cm (40⅛in)
SHOULDERS: 16.5cm (6½in)
NECK: 18cm (7in)
NECKLINE DEPTH: 5–6cm (2–2⅜in)
ARMHOLE HEIGHT: 22–23cm (8¾–9in)
HEIGHT UP TO ARMHOLE, EXCL. RIBBING: 41–42cm (16⅛–16½in)
SLEEVE LENGTH, EXCL. RIBBING: 43cm (17in)
WRIST CIRCUMFERENCE: approx. 23cm (9in)
RIBBING: according to preference, 5–8cm (2–3⅛in)

Materials

- Approx. 850g (30oz) Lang Thema Nuova, jeans 0034; or 100% pure wool yarn (100g (3½oz) = approx. 118m (129yds))
- Circular needles, 3.5 and 4mm (US size 4 and 6)
- Straight knitting needles, 4mm (US 6)
- Cable needle

TENSION/GAUGE: 23 st × 32 rows on 4mm (US 6) needles = 10 × 10cm (4 × 4in)

RIBBING: k1, p1

111 GERRIT KUYT, CA. 1900. KATWIJKS MUSEUM

112 FISHERMAN SIMON SIP, CREW MEMBER OF THE KW
158. KATWIJKS MUSEUM

KATWIJK 4 GANSEY

This gansey is a beautiful example of different influences in one sweater: the heart from Tholen, the design from Pernis and worn by a fisherman from Katwijk.

CHEST: 96CM + 6CM = 102CM (40⅛IN). TOTAL HEIGHT: 68–70CM (26¾–27½IN).
Knit a swatch first, with different sized needles if necessary. A gansey should not be too loosely knit. Follow the chart for the motif and adjust the width and/or height to your size, the yarn used and your tension/gauge. Follow the general instructions for the gansey on pages 54–55 and adjust where necessary.

Measurements

WIDTH: 2 × 51 = 102cm (40⅛in)
SHOULDERS: 16.5cm (6½in)
NECK: 18cm (7in)
NECKLINE DEPTH: 5–6cm (2–2⅜in)
ARMHOLE HEIGHT: 22–23cm (8¾–9in)
HEIGHT UP TO ARMHOLE, EXCL. RIBBING: 41–42cm (16⅛–16½in)
SLEEVE LENGTH, EXCL. RIBBING: 43cm (17in)
WRIST CIRCUMFERENCE: approx. 23cm (9in)
RIBBING: according to preference, 5–8cm (2–3⅛in)

Materials

∞ Approx. 950g (33½oz) 5-ply Frangipani Guernsey wool, moonlight; or bulky 100% pure wool yarn (100g (3½oz) = approx. 195m (213¼yds)
∞ Circular needles, 2.5 and 3mm (US 1 and 2)
∞ Straight knitting needles, 3mm (US 2)
∞ Cable needle

TENSION/GAUGE: 21 st × 32 rows on 3mm (US 2) needles = 10 × 10cm (4 × 4in)

RIBBING: K1, p1

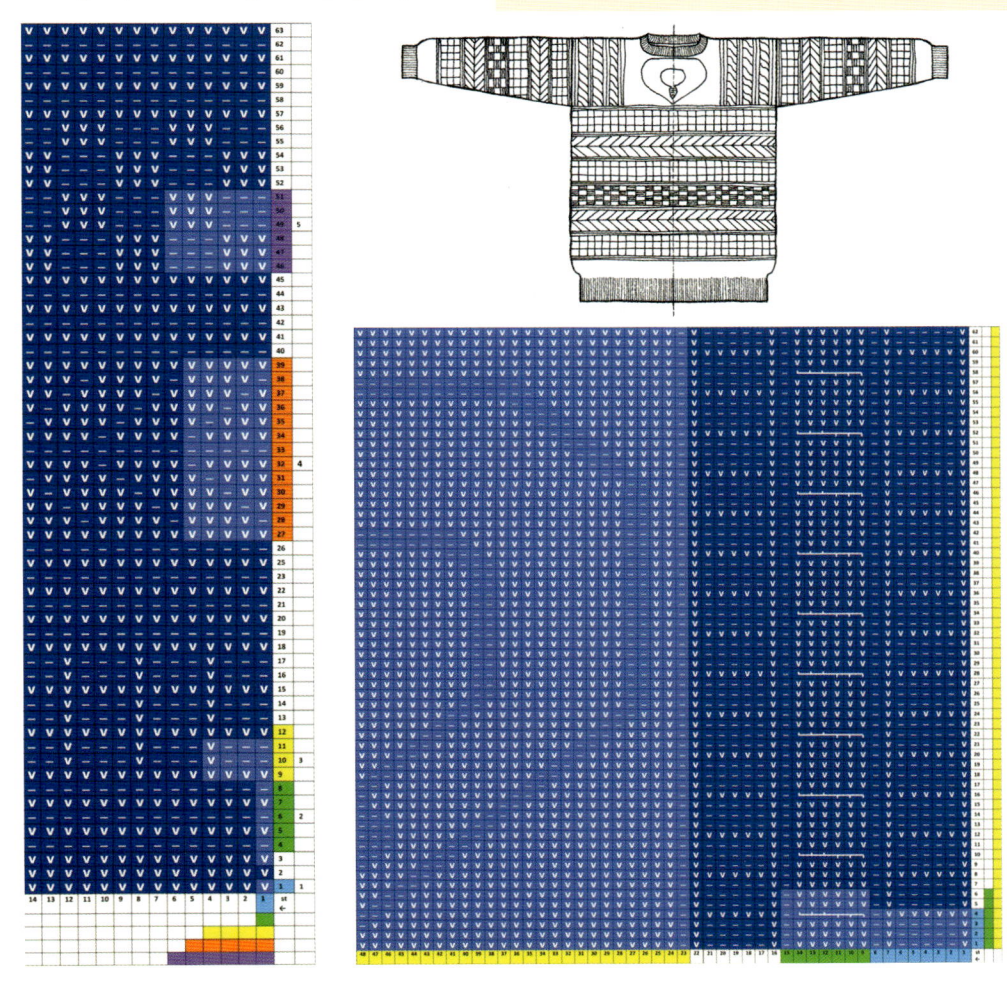

75

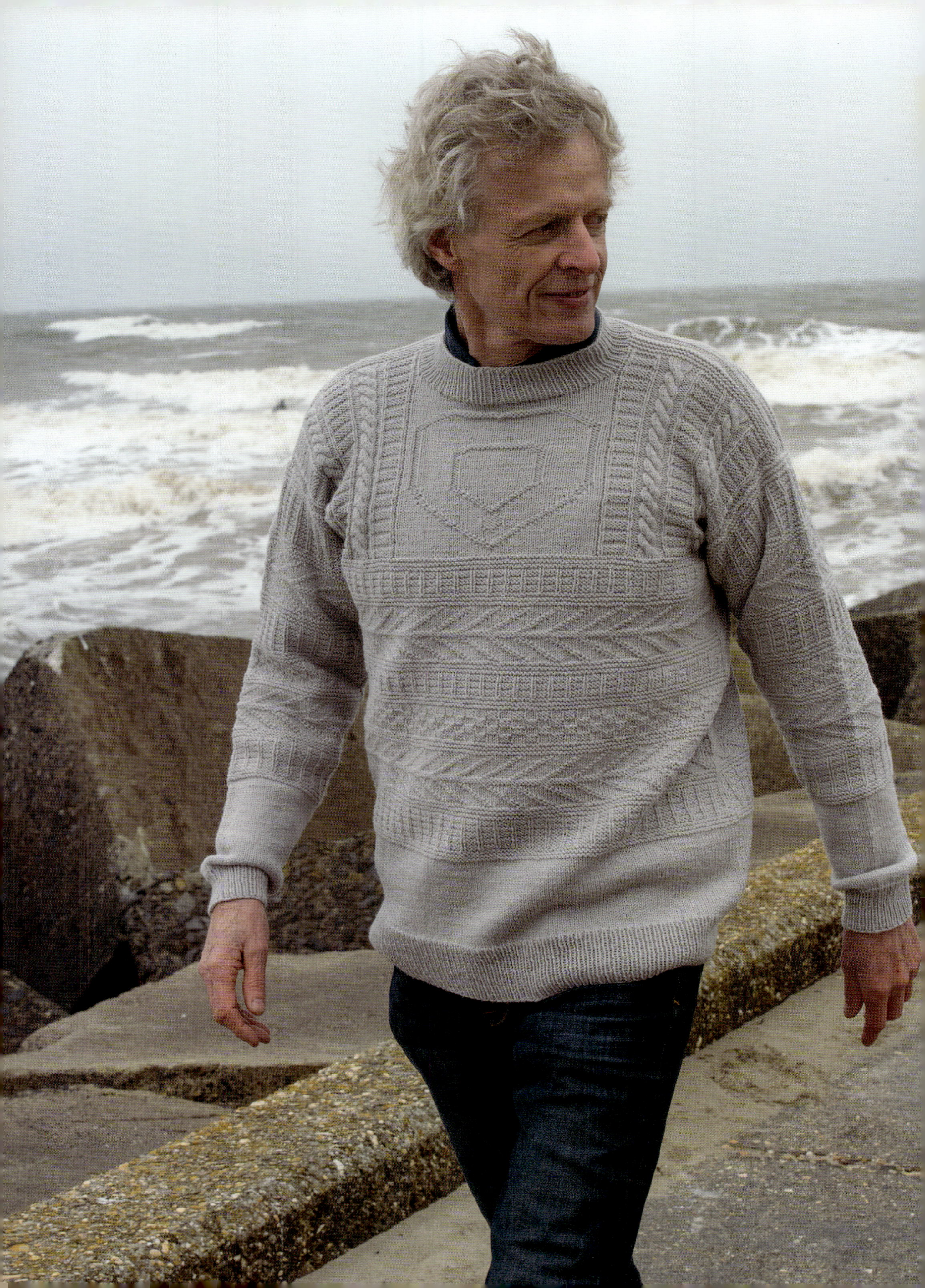

KATWIJK 5 GANSEY

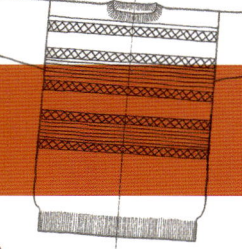

CHEST: 96CM + 6CM = 102CM (40⅛IN). TOTAL HEIGHT: 68–70CM (26¾–27½IN).

Knit a swatch first, with different sized needles if necessary. A gansey should not be too loosely knit. Follow the chart for the motif and adjust the width and/or height to your size, the yarn used and your tension/gauge. Follow the general instructions for the gansey on pages 54–55 and adjust where necessary.

Measurements

WIDTH: 2 × 51 = 102cm (40⅛in)
SHOULDERS: 16.5cm (6½in)
NECK: 18cm (7in)
NECKLINE DEPTH: 5–6cm (2–2⅜in)
ARMHOLE HEIGHT: 22–23cm (8¾–9in)
HEIGHT UP TO ARMHOLE, EXCL. RIBBING: 41–42cm (16⅛–16½in)
SLEEVE LENGTH, EXCL. RIBBING: 43cm (17in)
WRIST CIRCUMFERENCE: approx. 23cm (9in)
RIBBING: according to preference, 5–8cm (2–3⅛in)

Materials

∞ Approx. 850g (30oz) Scheepjeswol Zuiderzee, marine blue; or 100% pure wool yarn (100g (3½oz) = approx. 200m (219yds))
∞ Circular needles, 3 and 3.5mm (US 2 and 4)
∞ Straight knitting needles, 3.5mm (US 4)

TENSION/GAUGE: 21 st × 30 rows on 3.5mm (US 4) = 10 × 10cm (4 × 4in)

RIBBING: k1, p1

113 JACOB DE VREUGD, A FISHERMAN FROM KATWIJK. KATWIJKS MUSEUM

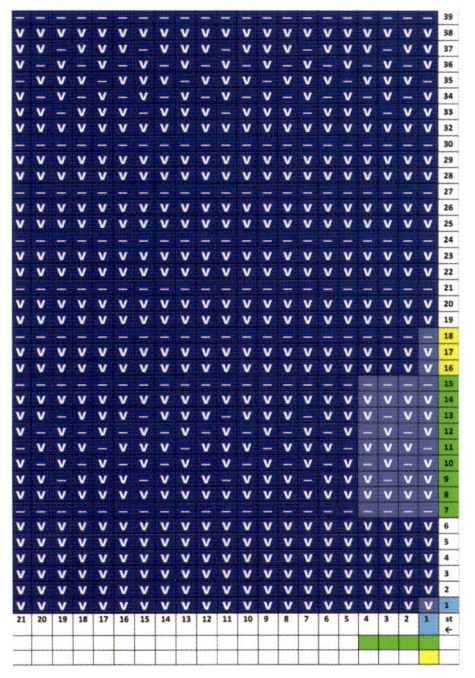

SOUTH HOLLAND
SCHEVENINGEN

Until the beginning of the twentieth century, most people in Scheveningen earned a living in the fisheries. Fishing dominated life: first, the *bomschuiten* were on the beach; later the luggers were moored in the port, with their nets hanging out to dry in the yards. And when it was storming, everyone held their breath. In comparison with places like Katwijk, Urk, Egmond aan Zee and IJmuiden, Scheveningen had always had a substantial fishing fleet. After the arrival of the lugger and the opening of the new port as a landing place for salted herring, Scheveningen quickly became an important port; the fishing fleet grew with several hundred ships and became one of the largest in the country. The First World War meant a considerable step back, and exports stagnated even more because of the crisis in the 1930s. In the Second World War the fishing industry shut down, and the Scheveningen fleet, like fleets in other villages, was largely removed by the German occupiers. After 1945 the herring fishing industry had a short revival.

The monument of a fisherman in Scheveningen, which was unveiled in 2013, contains the names of 1,350 fishermen who were lost at sea. In the First World War alone, almost 300 fishermen died at sea.

114 PIETER DE JAGER, CA. 1900.
NEL NOORDERVLIET-JOL, SCHEVENINGEN

115 A.K. GROEN WITH HIS FATHER AND W. DE GRAAF.
MUZEE SCHEVENINGEN

THE GANSEYS, SCHEVENINGEN 1, 2 AND 3, CAN BE FOUND ON PAGES 71–75 OF *DUTCH TRADITIONAL GANSEYS*.

SCHEVENINGEN 4 GANSEY

CHEST: 96cm + 6cm = 102cm (40⅛in). TOTAL HEIGHT: 68–70cm (26¾–27½in).

Knit a swatch first, with different sized needles if necessary. A gansey should not be too loosely knit. Follow the chart for the motif and adjust the width and/or height to your size, the yarn used and your tension/gauge. Follow the general instructions for the gansey on pages 54–55 and adjust where necessary.

Measurements

WIDTH: 2 x 51 = 102cm (40⅛in)
SHOULDERS: 16.5cm (6½in)
NECK: 18cm (7in)
NECKLINE DEPTH: 5–6cm (2–2⅜in)
ARMHOLE HEIGHT: 23–24cm (9–9½in)
HEIGHT UP TO ARMHOLE, EXCL. RIBBING: 41–42cm (16⅛–16½in)
SLEEVE LENGTH, EXCL. RIBBING: 43cm (17in)
WRIST CIRCUMFERENCE: approx. 23cm (9in)
RIBBING: according to preference, 5–8cm (2–3⅛in)

116 DIRK BEEKHUIZEN WITH HIS ELDEST SON, PHOTOGRAPHED IN PENZANCE, CORNWALL, ENGLAND, CA. 1895. MUZEE SCHEVENINGEN

Materials

- 800g (28¼oz) Scheepjeswol Subtile, marine 405; or 100% merino yarn (50g (1¾oz) = approx. 125m (137yds))
- Circular needles, 3 and 3.5mm (US 2 and 4)
- Straight knitting needles, 3.5mm (US 4)

TENSION/GAUGE: 26 st x 34 rows on 3.5mm (US 4) needles = 10 x 10cm (4 x 4in)

RIBBING: k2, p2

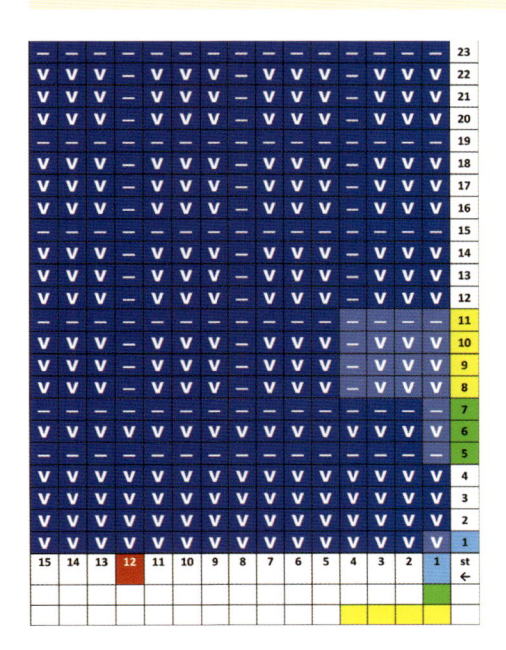

SCHEVENINGEN 5 GANSEY

CHEST: 98CM + 6CM = 104CM (41IN). TOTAL HEIGHT: 68–70CM (26¾–27½IN).

Knit a swatch first, with different sized needles if necessary. A gansey should not be too loosely knit. Follow the chart for the motif and adjust the width and/or height to your size, the yarn used and your tension/gauge. Follow the general instructions for the gansey on pages 54–55 and adjust where necessary. Increase 1–2 stitches per cable under the cables and decrease these stitches again for the shoulders (pull in the cable).

Measurements

WIDTH: 2 × 52 = 104cm (41in)
SHOULDERS: 16.5cm (6½in)
NECK: 18cm (7in)
NECKLINE DEPTH: 6–7cm (2⅜–2¾in)
ARMHOLE HEIGHT: 22–23cm (8¾–9in)
HEIGHT UP TO ARMHOLE, EXCL. RIBBING: 41cm (16⅛in)
SLEEVE LENGTH, EXCL. RIBBING: 43cm (17in)
WRIST CIRCUMFERENCE: approx. 23cm (9in)
RIBBING: according to preference, 5–8cm (2–3⅛in)

Materials

- 800g (28¼oz) SMC Baby Wool, navy 0050; or 100% merino yarn (25g (¾oz)= approx. 85m (93yds))
- Circular needles, 3 and 3.5mm (US 2 and 4)
- Straight knitting needles, 3.5mm (US 4)
- Cable needle

TENSION/GAUGE: 26 st × 36 rows on 3.5mm (US 4) needles = 10 × 10cm (4 × 4in)

RIBBING: k2, p2

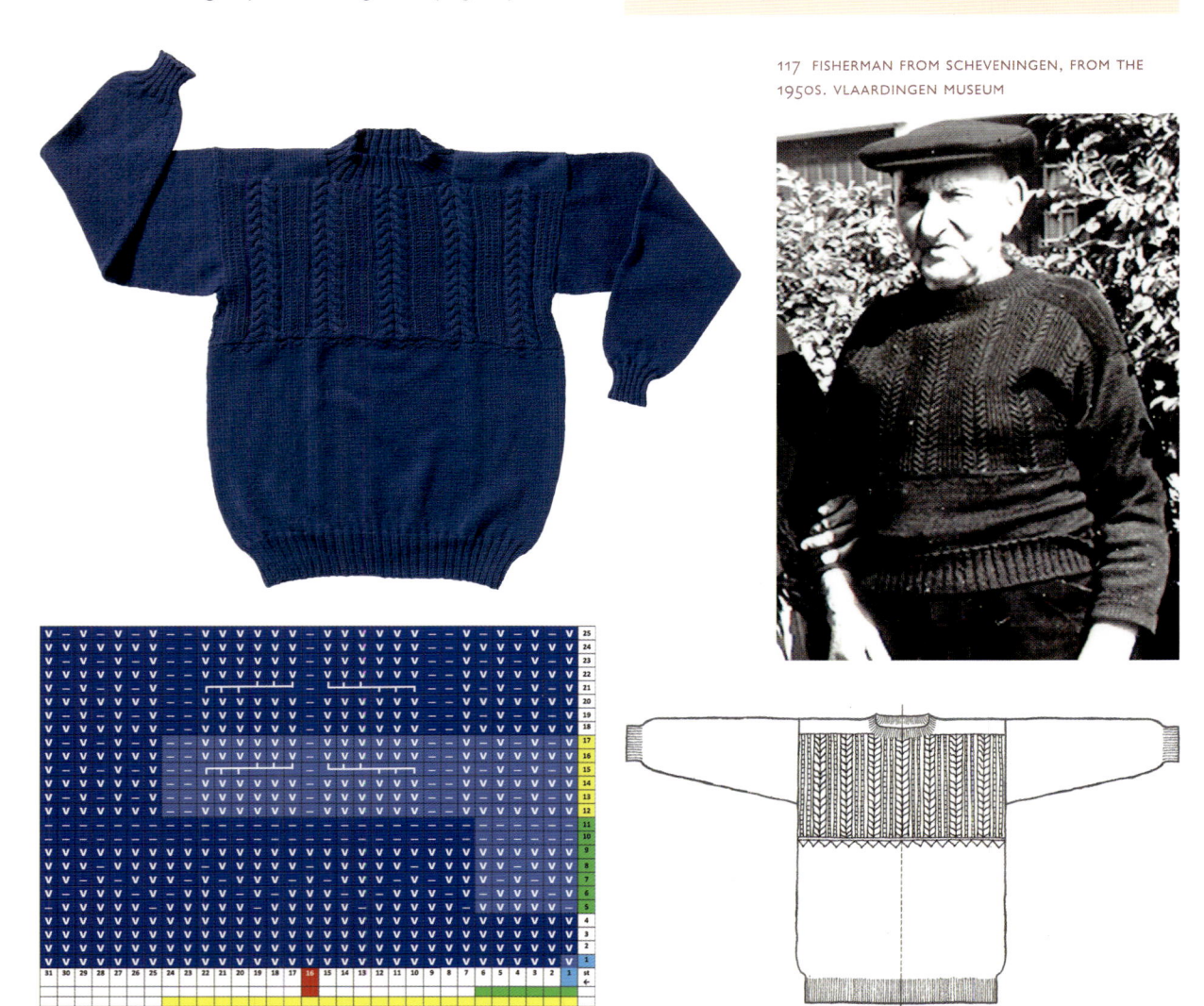

117 FISHERMAN FROM SCHEVENINGEN, FROM THE 1950S. VLAARDINGEN MUSEUM

118 TWO FISHERMEN FROM PERNIS, 1911. HISTORICAL ASSOCIATION PERNIS

SOUTH HOLLAND
PERNIS

Pernis is one of the oldest villages on the south side of the river Maas and is located in the Land van Putten. After salmon fishing on the Maas/Meuse, in the eighteenth century, sea fishing also became important. They would use longliners mainly and fish for fresh fish such as cod and haddock, travelling all the way to Iceland and Greenland. The longliner fishermen from Pernis were extremely good at their jobs and were always welcomed on the lugger fleets of Vlaardingen and Maassluis. Antwerp and Zierikzee would employ fishermen from Pernis to teach their own longliner crews. A sea lieutenant travelling on a longliner from Pernis was amazed at their professionalism:

'We, marines, are sometimes surprised at how well fishermen can make astronomical observations, find their way at sea and know exactly how to get to safe ports on foreign shores. They have a feel for the sea and know how to use the lead to find their way ... The men would explore the waters using the compass and octant, travel up to Iceland and Shetland, and felt as much at home far in the North as in their home town.'

The design of the ganseys from Pernis clearly refers to the smocked frocks as worn before the sweater became popular. These may well be the oldest ganseys in the Netherlands, because these fishermen were the first to meet Scottish and English fishermen wearing ganseys.

THE GANSEY, PERNIS 1, CAN BE FOUND ON PAGES 78–79 OF *DUTCH TRADITIONAL GANSEYS*.

PERNIS 2 GANSEY

CHEST: 102CM + 6CM = 108CM (42½IN). TOTAL HEIGHT: 68–70CM (26¾–27½IN).

Knit a swatch first, with different sized needles if necessary. A gansey should not be too loosely knit. Follow the chart for the motif and adjust the width and/or height to your size, the yarn used and your tension/gauge. Follow the general instructions for the gansey on pages 54–55 and adjust where necessary.

Measurements

WIDTH: 2 × 54 = 108cm (42½in)
SHOULDERS: 17.5cm (6⅝in)
NECK: 19cm (7½in)
NECKLINE DEPTH: 6–7cm (2⅜–2¾in)
ARMHOLE HEIGHT: 23–24cm (9–9½in)
HEIGHT UP TO ARMHOLE, EXCL. RIBBING: 41cm (16⅛in)
SLEEVE LENGTH, EXCL. RIBBING: 43cm (17in)
WRIST CIRCUMFERENCE: approx. 23cm (9in)
RIBBING: according to preference, 5–8cm (2–3⅛in)

Materials

- 700g (24⅔oz) Lang Yak, 035; or 50% merino, 50% yak yarn (50g (1¾oz) = approx. 130m (142yds))
- Circular needles, 4 and 4.5mm (US 6 and 7)
- Straight knitting needles, 4.5mm (US 7)
- Cable needle

TENSION/GAUGE: 20 st × 28 rows on 4.5mm (US 7) needles = 10 × 10cm (4 × 4in)

RIBBING: k1, p1

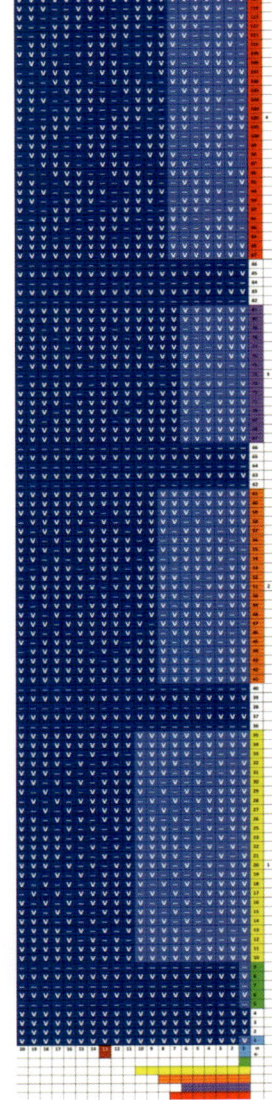

119 UNKNOWN FISHERMAN FROM PERNIS, CA. 1910. VLAARDINGEN MUNICIPAL ARCHIVE

PERNIS 3 GANSEY

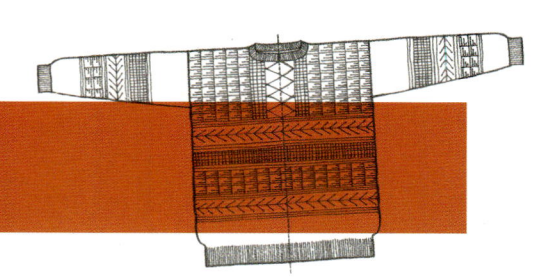

CHEST: 102CM + 6CM = 108CM (42½IN). TOTAL HEIGHT: 68–70CM (26¾–27½IN).

Knit a swatch first, with different sized needles if necessary. A gansey should not be too loosely knit. Follow the chart for the motif and adjust the width and/or height to your size, the yarn used and your tension/gauge. Follow the general instructions for the gansey on pages 54–55 and adjust where necessary.

Measurements

WIDTH: 2 x 54 = 108cm (42½in)
SHOULDERS: 17.5cm (6⅝in)
NECK: 19cm (7½in)
NECKLINE DEPTH: 6–7cm (2⅜–2¾in)
ARMHOLE HEIGHT: 23–24cm (9–9½in)
HEIGHT UP TO ARMHOLE, EXCL. RIBBING: 41cm (16⅛in)
SLEEVE LENGTH, EXCL. RIBBING: 43cm (17in)
WRIST CIRCUMFERENCE: approx. 23cm (9in)
RIBBING: according to preference, 5–8cm (2–3⅛in)

Materials

∞ 700g (24⅔oz) Léttlopi, white 0051; or 100% pure wool yarn (50g (1¾oz) = approx. 100m (110yds))
∞ Circular needles, 3.5 and 4mm (US 4 and 6)
∞ Straight knitting needles, 4mm (US 6)

TENSION/GAUGE: 19 st x 26 rows on 4mm (US 6) needles = 10 x 10cm (4 x 4in)
RIBBING: k2, p2

120 CREW MEMBER FROM PERNIS ON THE STEAM LUGGER VL 192 *HENDRIKA*, OF THE VISSCHERIJ MAATSCHAPPIJ VLAARDINGEN, CA. 1905. VLAARDINGEN MUNICIPAL ARCHIVE

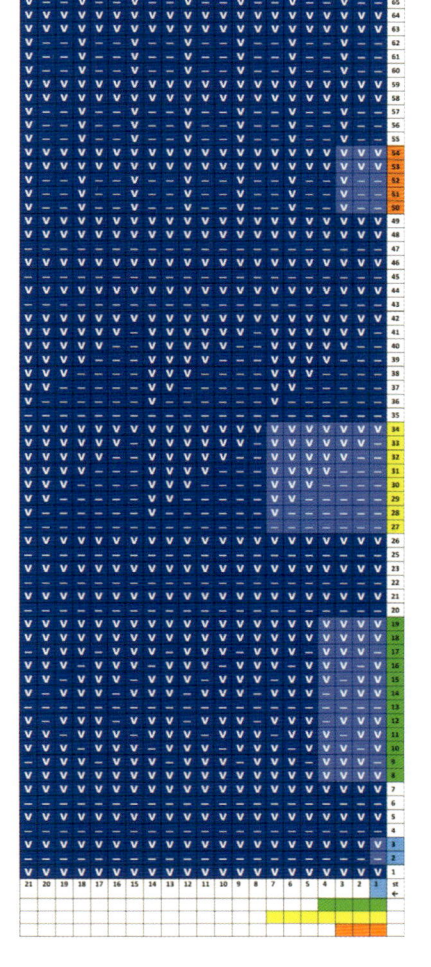

SOUTH HOLLAND
VLAARDINGEN

121 GROUP OF UNKNOWN FISHERMEN FROM VLAARDINGEN, CA. 1910.
VLAARDINGEN MUNICIPAL ARCHIVE

122 YOUNG FISHERMEN ON A BENCH AT THE *PRIKKENGAT*, ON THE CORNER OF THE *PARALLELWEG/OUDE HAVEN* ('OLD PORT'). FRONT, FROM LEFT TO RIGHT: ARIE VAN ROON, UNKNOWN, DE BIE (?) AND JAN BOERDAM. BACK, FROM LEFT TO RIGHT: SMIT AND VAN DORP, UNKNOWN. IN THE FOREGROUND, A *BENNE* ('WICKER BASKET') WITH LONGLINER. CA. 1905.
VLAARDINGEN CITY ARCHIVES

From the Middle Ages to the end of the nineteenth century, Vlaardingen was almost completely dependent on (herring) fishing. In each family, at least one person would work as a sea fisherman at a shipyard, or for one of the supply companies. The gutting monopoly which Vlaardingen, Maassluis and Enkhuizen had been granted by the County of Holland in the seventeenth century had proven to be extremely lucrative. Girls and women would do their bit by repairing nets in the large netting sheds or attics. The Anglo–Dutch sea wars (between 1652 and 1784) and the measures imposed by Napoleon at the start of the nineteenth century to boycott English trade had a dramatic impact on the fishing industry in Vlaardingen. Only after 1870 did the industry flourish again, thanks to the introduction of lighter cotton nets and the sail lugger. The expansion of the railway network helped make Germany, an important market for herring from Vlaardingen, more accessible. Vlaardingen benefited enormously from this expansion. Whilst fishing towns like IJmuiden and Scheveningen continued to invest in fishing technology, the fishermen in Vlaardingen stuck to the tried and trusted familiar methods. This caused Vlaardingen to lose its advantage. Industrialisation turned out to be the nail in the coffin. Workers could earn decent wages in the new factories, working closer to home with better career perspectives. It was no longer obvious that a young man would decide to become a fisherman. The importance of the fishing industry started to decline and by 1964, at the annual Vlaggetjesdag, the once so proud fleet had been reduced to just nine engine luggers.

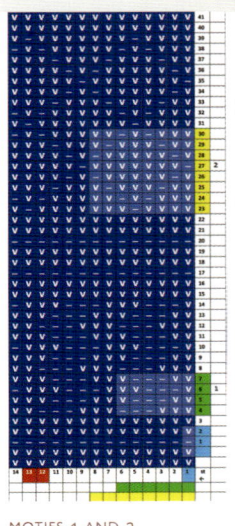

MOTIFS 1 AND 2

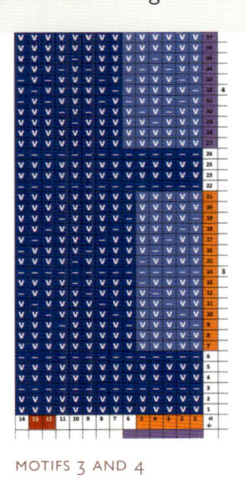

MOTIFS 3 AND 4

MOTIFS 5 AND 6

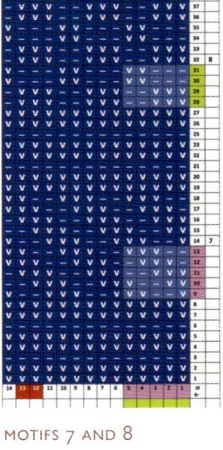

MOTIFS 7 AND 8

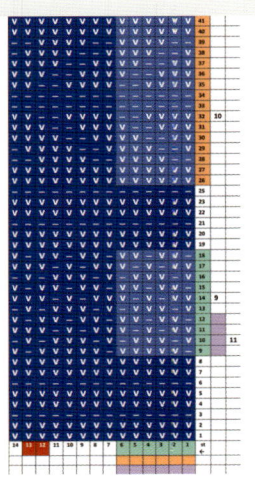

MOTIFS 9, 10 AND 11

MOTIFS 12 AND 13

MOTIFS 14 AND 15

MOTIFS 16 AND 17

MOTIFS 18 AND 19

MOTIFS 20

MOTIFS 22

MOTIF 21

MOTIFS 23 AND 24

MOTIF 25

MOTIF 26

THE GANSEYS, VLAARDINGEN 1 AND 2, CAN BE FOUND ON PAGES 81–83 OF *DUTCH TRADITIONAL GANSEYS*.

VLAARDINGEN 3 GANSEY

CHEST: 96CM + 6CM = 102CM (40⅛IN). TOTAL HEIGHT: 70CM (27½IN).

Knit a swatch first, with different sized needles if necessary. A gansey should not be too loosely knit. Follow the chart for the motif and adjust the width and/or height to your size, the yarn used and your tension/gauge. Follow the general instructions for the gansey on pages 54–55 and adjust where necessary. After the ribbing, work motifs 4, 3, 4, 22 and 9, and for the shoulders, repeat motif 4 according to the chart. Separating ridges: p1 row, k1 row, p1 row.

Measurements

WIDTH: 2 × 51 = 102cm (40⅛in)
SHOULDERS: 16.5cm (6½in)
NECK: 18cm (7in)
NECKLINE DEPTH: 5–6cm (2–2⅜in)
ARMHOLE HEIGHT: 23–24cm (9–9½in)
HEIGHT UP TO ARMHOLE, EXCL. RIBBING: 41–42cm (16⅛–16½in)
SLEEVE LENGTH, EXCL. RIBBING: 43cm (17in)
WRIST CIRCUMFERENCE: approx. 23cm (9in)
RIBBING: according to preference, 5–8cm (2–3⅛in)

Materials

- 800g (28¼oz) SMC Merino Extrafine 120, navy blue 0155; or 100% merino yarn (50g (1¾oz) = approx. 120m (131yds))
- Circular needles, 3 and 3.5mm (US 2 and 4)
- Straight knitting needles, 3.5mm (US 4)

TENSION/GAUGE: 24 st and 33 rows on 3.5mm (US 4) needles = 10 × 10cm (4 × 4in)
RIBBING: k2, p2

123 FISHERMAN C. STRUIS, CA. 1910. VLAARDINGEN MUNICIPAL ARCHIVES

VLAARDINGEN 4 GANSEY

CHEST: 96CM + 6CM = 102CM (40⅛IN). TOTAL HEIGHT: 70CM (27½IN).

Knit a swatch first, with different sized needles if necessary. A gansey should not be too loosely knit. Follow the chart for the motif and adjust the width and/or height to your size, the yarn used and your tension/gauge. Follow the general instructions for the gansey on pages 54–55 and adjust where necessary. After the ribbing, work motifs 9, 22, 9 and 21 according to the chart. Work the motif on both the front and back pieces and the sleeves (2 x motif 9). Separating ridges: p3 rows.

Measurements

WIDTH: 2 x 51 = 102cm (40⅛in)
SHOULDERS: 16.5cm (6½in)
NECK: 18cm (7in)
NECKLINE DEPTH: 5–6cm (2–2⅜in)
ARMHOLE HEIGHT: 22.75–23cm (9in)
HEIGHT UP TO ARMHOLE, EXCL. RIBBING: 41cm (16⅛in)
SLEEVE LENGTH, EXCL. RIBBING: 43cm (17in)
WRIST CIRCUMFERENCE: approx. 23cm (9in)
RIBBING: according to preference, 5–8cm (2–3⅛in)

124 CREW MEMBERS ON THE STEAM LUGGER VL192 *HENDRIKA*, OF THE VISSCHERIJ MAATSCHAPPIJ VLAARDINGEN. SECOND FROM THE LEFT (STANDING) IS ARIE VAN DIJK, CA. 1905. VLAARDINGEN MUNICIPAL ARCHIVES

Materials

- 750g (26½oz) Hjertegarn Vital, 688; or 100% pure superwash wool yarn (50g (1¾oz) = approx. 126m (138yds))
- Circular needles, 3.5 and 4mm (US 4 and 6)
- Straight knitting needles, 4mm (US 6)

TENSION/GAUGE: 22 st x 27 rows on 4mm (US 6) needles = 10 x 10cm (4 x 4in)

RIBBING: k2, p2

124 A DETAIL FROM FIG. 124

87

VLAARDINGEN 5 GANSEY

CHEST: 94CM + 6CM = 100CM (39⅜IN). TOTAL HEIGHT: 68CM (26¾IN).

Knit a swatch first, with different sized needles if necessary. A gansey should not be too loosely knit. Follow the chart for the motif and adjust the width and/or height to your size, the yarn used and your tension/gauge. Follow the general instructions for the gansey on pages 54–55 and adjust where necessary. In between the motifs, knit two rows and one ridge (p2 rows or p1 row, k1 row, p1 row – choose one). Then work motifs 23, 15, 24, 23 and 25. The pattern of the closed diamond is worked over seven rows instead of five. Shoulder motif = for staggered ridge, p1, k2 and shift the motif 1 st each row. For the sleeves, work motif 25 twice, replacing the separation ridges by k2 rows.

Measurements

WIDTH: 2 x 50 = 100cm (39⅜in)
SHOULDERS: 16.5cm (6½in)
NECK: 17cm (6¾in)
NECKLINE DEPTH: 5–6cm (2–2⅜in)
ARMHOLE HEIGHT: 21–22cm (8¼–8¾in)
HEIGHT UP TO ARMHOLE, EXCL. RIBBING: 41cm (16⅛in)
SLEEVE LENGTH, EXCL. RIBBING: 43cm (17in)
WRIST CIRCUMFERENCE: approx. 22cm (8¾in)
RIBBING: according to preference, 5–8cm (2–3⅛in)

Materials

- 900g (31¾oz) Hjertegarn Palino, dark blue 8698; or 100% merino superwash yarn (50g (1¾oz) = approx. 125m (137yds))
- Circular needles, 2.5 and 3mm (US 1 and 2)
- Straight knitting needles, 3mm (US 2)

TENSION/GAUGE: 24.8 st into 38 rows on 3mm (US 2) needles = 10 x 10cm (4 x 4in)

RIBBING: k2, p2

125 FISHERMAN FROM NOORDWIJK WEARING A GANSEY FROM VLAARDINGEN, CA. 1910. HOLLAND OPEN AIR MUSEUM, ARNHEM

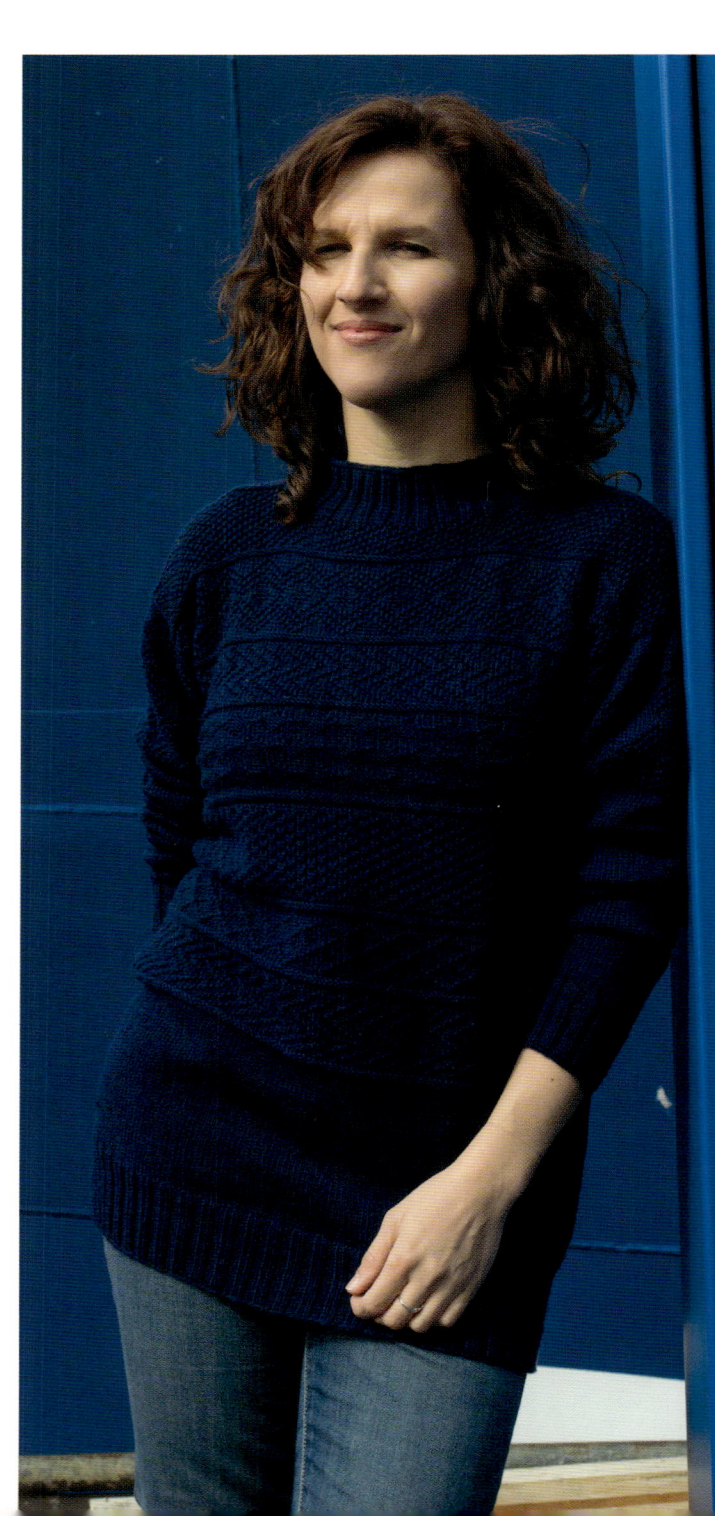

88

VLAARDINGEN 6 GANSEY

CHEST: 100CM + 6CM = 106CM (41¾IN). TOTAL HEIGHT: 68–70CM (26¾–27½IN).

Knit a swatch first, with different sized needles if necessary. A gansey should not be too loosely knit. Follow the chart for the motif and adjust the width and/or height to your size, the yarn used and your tension/gauge. Follow the general instructions for the gansey on pages 54–55 and adjust where necessary. After the ribbing, work 10cm (4in) in stockinette, and then motifs 6, 12, 2, 9, 15 and 6 according to the chart and sketch. Separating ridges: p1 row, k2 row, p1 row. For the sleeves, work motifs 5, 16 and 12.

Measurements

WIDTH: 2 × 53 = 106cm (41¾in)
SHOULDERS: 17.5cm (6⅝in)
NECK: 18cm (7in)
NECKLINE DEPTH: 6–7cm (2⅜–2¾in)
ARMHOLE HEIGHT: 23–24cm (9–9½in)
HEIGHT UP TO ARMHOLE, EXCL. RIBBING: 41cm (16⅛in)
SLEEVE LENGTH, EXCL. RIBBING: 43cm (17in)
WRIST CIRCUMFERENCE: approx. 23cm (9in)
RIBBING: according to preference, 5–8cm (2–3⅛in)

Materials

∞ 800g (28¼oz) Scheepjes Donna, light grey 666; or 50% merino, 50% acrylic microfibre yarn (50g (1¾oz) = approx. 112m (122½yds))
∞ Circular needles, 3 and 3.5mm (US 2 and 4)
∞ Straight knitting needles, 3.5mm (US 4)

TENSION/GAUGE: 26 st × 32 rows on 3.5mm (US 4) needles = 10 × 10 cm (4 × 4in)

RIBBING: k2, p2

126 BOELE, A FISHERMAN FROM VLAARDINGEN, CA. 1910. VLAARDINGEN MUNICIPAL ARCHIVES

VLAARDINGEN 7 GANSEY

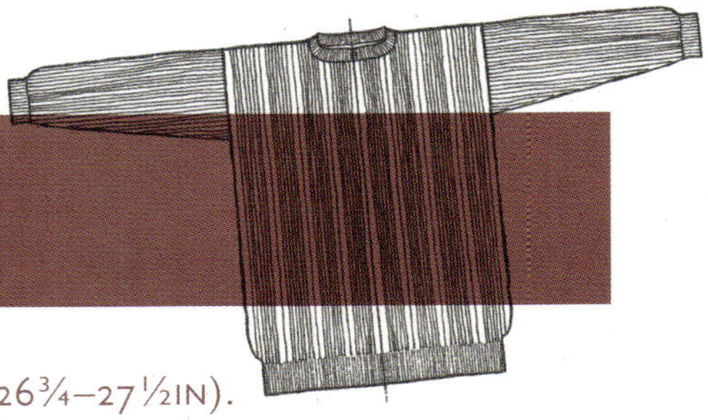

CHEST: 96CM + 6CM = 102CM (40⅛IN). TOTAL HEIGHT: 68–70CM (26¾–27½IN).

Note: This special gansey may have the T-shape, but is knit sideways, not from the bottom up. Cast on the stitches for the entire length of the gansey (minus approx. 6cm (2⅜in) ribbing = 64cm (25¼in)) and immediately start with the pattern. Knit a swatch first, with different sized needles if necessary. Follow the chart for the motif and adjust the width and/or height to your size, the yarn used and your tension/gauge. A gansey should not be too loosely knit. Work the motif on both the front and back pieces and the sleeves. Neckline depth; 5–6cm (2–2⅜in) round at the front, straight at the back of the neck. Work according to the chart and sketch. Pattern: *k 14 rows (back and forth), p1 row, k3 rows, p1 row.* Decrease for the neck after 16.5cm (6½in), knit on for another 18cm (7in) and gradually cast on the decreased sts again. Knit 16.5cm (6½in), cast off 22cm (8¾in) for the armhole and cast on the same number of stitches at the end of the next row. Work 51cm (20in) for the back, to the other armhole. Close the shoulder seams and side seams. With circular needles, pick up stitches in the armholes and work the sleeves. Pick up stitches on circular needles along the bottom hem and neck and work ribbing.

Measurements

WIDTH: 2 × 51 = 102cm (40⅛in)
SHOULDERS: 16.5cm (6½in)
NECK: 18cm (7in)
NECKLINE DEPTH: 5–6cm (2–2⅜in)
ARMHOLE HEIGHT: 22–23cm (8¾–9in)
HEIGHT UP TO ARMHOLE, EXCL. RIBBING: 41cm (16⅛in)
SLEEVE LENGTH, EXCL. RIBBING: 43cm (17in)
WRIST CIRCUMFERENCE: approx. 23cm (9in)
RIBBING: according to preference, 5–8cm (2–3⅛in)

Materials

∞ Approx. 750g (26½oz) Léttlopi, ocean blue 9419; or 100% pure wool yarn (50g (1¾oz) = 110m (120¼yds))
∞ Circular knitting needles. 3.5 and 4mm (US 4 and 6)
∞ Straight knitting needles, 3.5 and 4mm (US 4 and 6)

TENSION/GAUGE: 20 st × 28 rows on 4mm (US 6) needles = 10 × 10cm (4 × 4in)
STITCH PATTERN FRONT/BACK: *k5 rows, p1 row*
STITCH PATTERN SLEEVES, WORKED IN THE ROUND: *k3 rows, p1 row, k1 row, p1 row*
RIBBING: k1, p1

127 UNKNOWN FISHERMAN, CA. 1910. VLAARDINGEN MUNICIPAL ARCHIVES

SOUTH HOLLAND VOORNE-PUTTEN
ZWARTEWAAL

128 FISHERMEN FROM ZWARTEWAAL WITH THEIR CATCH, CA. 1920. ORIGIN UNKNOWN

Zwartewaal is a small village on the Brielse Maas in South Holland, located between Spijkenisse and Brielle, in the region of Voorne-Putten. It is part of the municipality of Brielle and now has around 1900 inhabitants. In the past, fishermen from this village were the first to take their longliners all the way to Iceland to go fishing. At one point, up to 95 per cent of the population lived off fishing: they would sail on hookers or sloops, or work in a cooperage, basket weaving shop, supply store or workshop. The ganseys from Zwartewaal have some beautiful patterns and, together with those from Pernis, are probably the oldest found in the country.

THE GANSEYS, ZWARTEWAAL 1 AND 2, CAN BE FOUND ON PAGES 87–89 OF *DUTCH TRADITIONAL GANSEYS*.

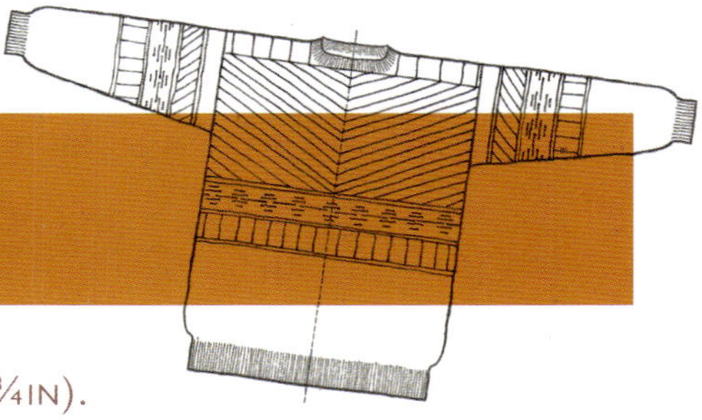

ZWARTEWAAL 3 GANSEY

CHEST: 94CM + 6CM = 100CM (39 3/8IN). TOTAL HEIGHT: 68CM (26 3/4IN).

Knit a swatch first, with different sized needles if necessary. A gansey should not be too loosely knit. Follow the chart for the motif and adjust the width and/or height to your size, the yarn used and your tension/gauge. Follow the general instructions for the gansey on pages 54–55 and adjust where necessary.

Measurements

WIDTH: 2 × 50 = 100cm (39 3/8in)
SHOULDERS: 16.5cm (6 1/2in)
NECK: 17cm (6 3/4in)
NECKLINE DEPTH: 5–6cm (2–2 3/8in)
ARMHOLE HEIGHT: 21–22cm (8 1/4–8 3/4in)
HEIGHT UP TO ARMHOLE, EXCL. RIBBING: 41cm (16 1/8in)
SLEEVE LENGTH, EXCL. RIBBING: 43cm (17in)
WRIST CIRCUMFERENCE: approx. 22cm (8 3/4in)
RIBBING: according to preference, 5–8cm (2–3 1/8in)

Materials

∞ Approx. 750g (26 1/2oz) Léttlopi, lapis blue heather 1403; or 100% pure wool yarn (50g (1 3/4oz) = 100m (110yds))
∞ Circular needles, 3.5 and 4mm (US 4 and 6)
∞ Straight knitting needles, 3.5 and 4mm (US 4 and 6)

TENSION/GAUGE: 17 st × 25 rows in on 4mm (US 6) needles = 10 × 10cm (4 × 4in)

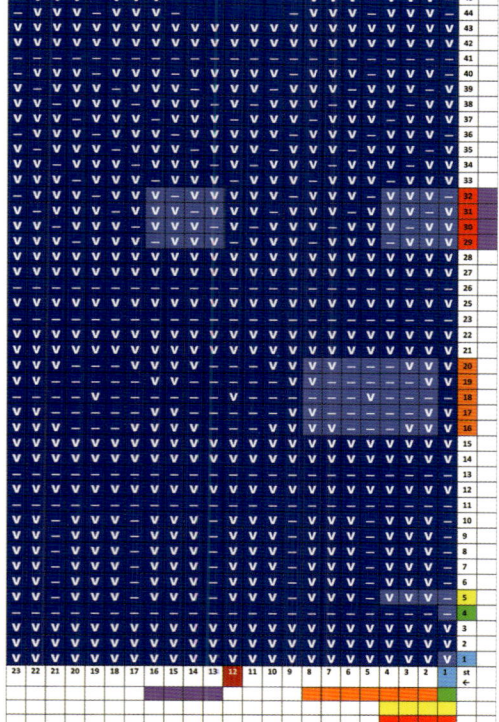

RIBBING: k1, p1

129 THE FISHERMAN FROM ZWARTEWAAL, CA. 1895. VLAARDINGEN MUSEUM

92

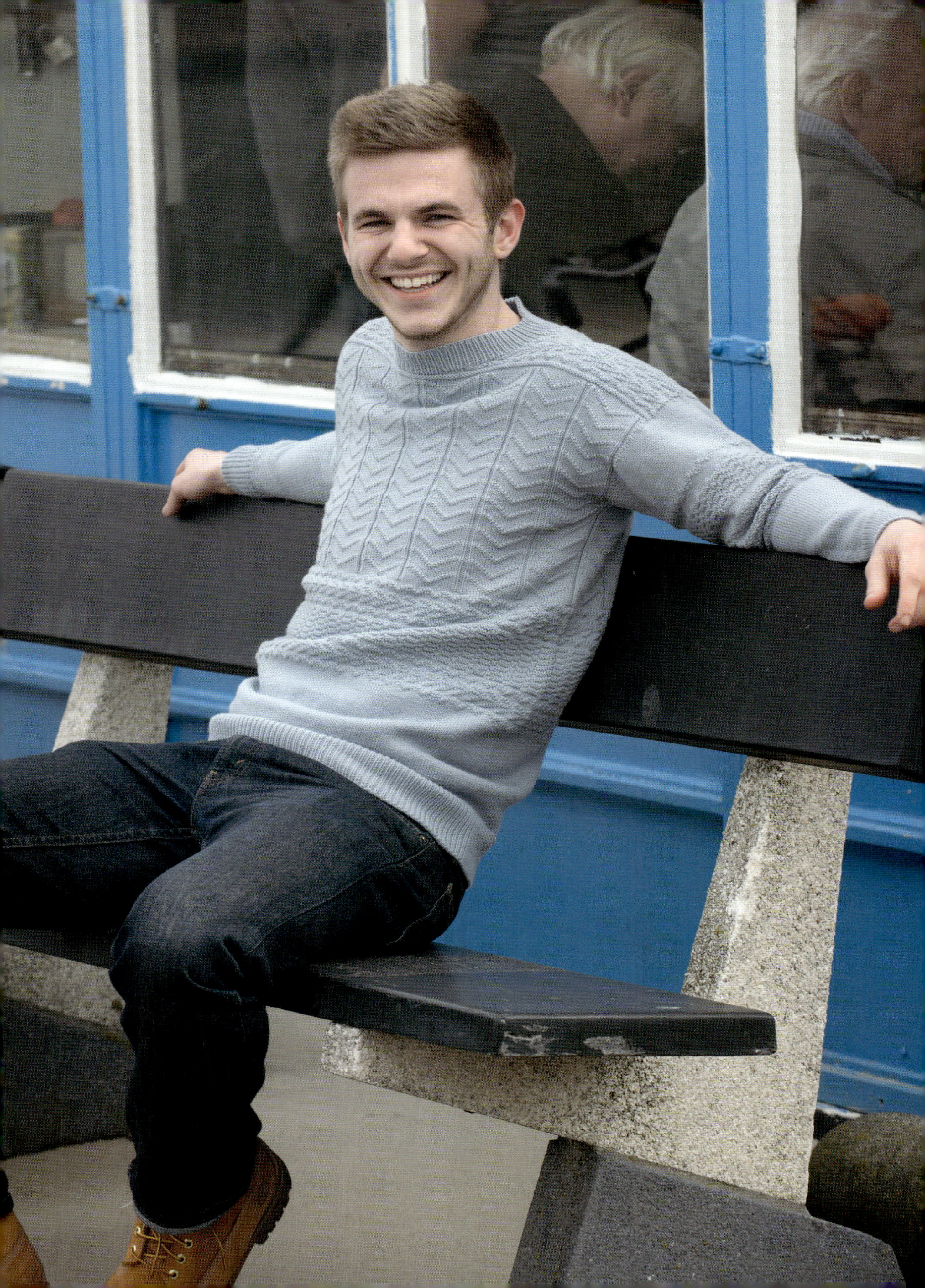

ZWARTEWAAL 4 GANSEY

CHEST: 94CM + 6CM = 100CM (39⅜IN). TOTAL HEIGHT: 68CM (26¾IN).

Knit a swatch first, with different sized needles if necessary. A gansey should not be too loosely knit. Follow the chart for the motif and adjust the width and/or height to your size, the yarn used and your tension/gauge. Follow the general instructions for the gansey on pages 54–55 and adjust where necessary.

Measurements

WIDTH: 2 × 50 = 100cm (39⅜in)
SHOULDERS: 16.5cm (6½in)
NECK: 17cm (6¾in)
NECKLINE DEPTH: 5–6cm (2–2⅜in)
ARMHOLE HEIGHT: 21–22cm (8¼–8¾in)
HEIGHT UP TO ARMHOLE, EXCL. RIBBING: 41cm (16⅛in)
SLEEVE LENGTH, EXCL. RIBBING: 43cm (17in)
WRIST CIRCUMFERENCE: approx. 22cm (8¾in)
RIBBING: according to preference, 5–8cm (2–3⅛in)

Materials

∞ Approx. 750g (26½oz) Lang Merino 150, light grey 0123; or 100% merino yarn (50g (1¾oz) = 150m (164yds))
∞ Circular knitting needles, 3 and 3.5mm (US 2 and 4)
∞ Straight knitting needles, 3 and 3.5mm (US 2 and 4)

TENSION/GAUGE: 27 st × 37 rows on 3.5mm (US 4) needles = 10 × 10cm

RIBBING: K1, p1

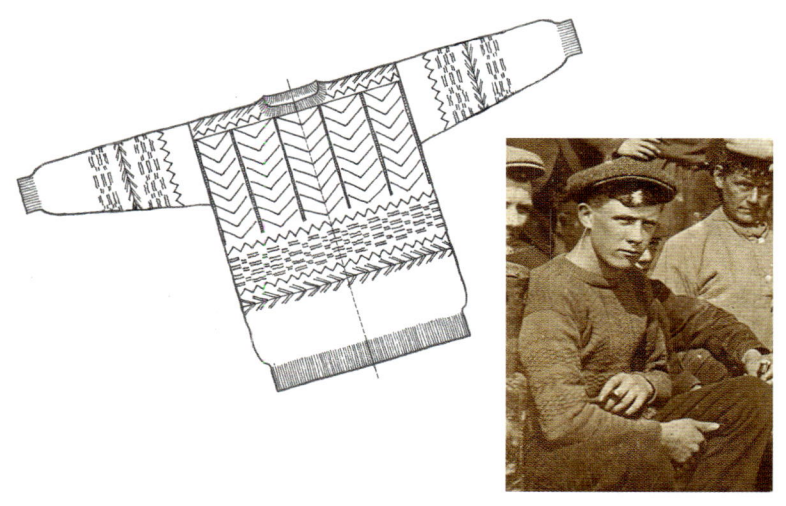

130 SHIP'S CREW. THE REAR SIDE OF THE PHOTOGRAPH READS: SHIPPING COMPANY DE EENDRACHT, DIR. H. DE KORVER, CA. 1912. VLAARDINGEN MUNICIPAL ARCHIVES

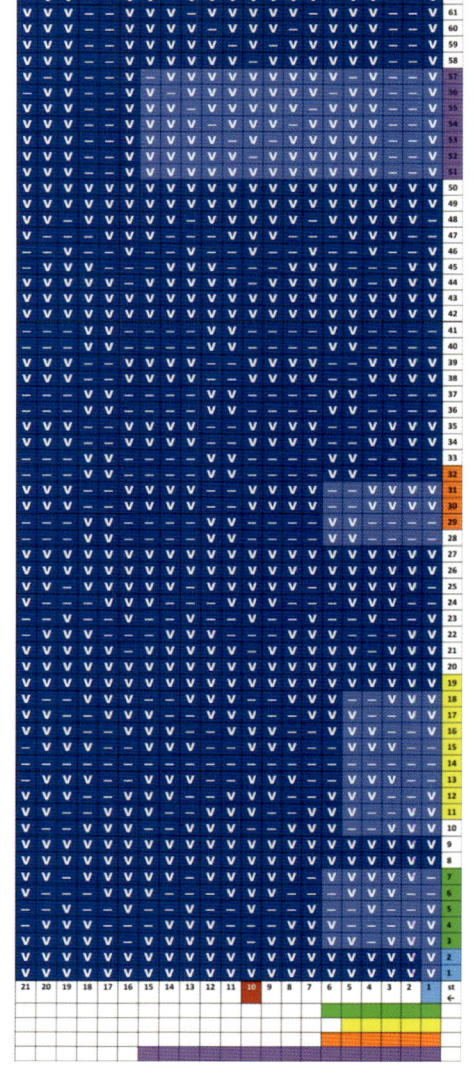

131 FISHERMAN MATTHEUS FROM MIDDELHARNIS.
GOEREE-OVERFLAKKEE LOCAL ARCHIVES

SOUTH HOLLAND GOEREE-OVERFLAKKEE
MIDDELHARNIS

For Middelharnis, the nineteenth century was an extremely difficult period with wars, failed harvests, poor catches and the port silting up. The fishermen here got paid significantly less than elsewhere and lived in great poverty. The relationship with the shipowners was not great, causing dozens of fishermen to go to 'the other side': Vlaardingen and Maassluis. The ones who stayed behind often travelled to Vlaardingen and even to IJmuiden, where the fleet would be moored after the port of Middelharnis had silted up.

When the First World War struck – making many victims among the fishermen, and with the remaining sloops being sold at a good price after the war – fishing completely disappeared from Middelharnis.

THE GANSEYS, MIDDELHARNIS 1 AND 2 (CALLED OUDDORP 1) CAN BE FOUND ON PAGES 91 AND 97 OF *DUTCH TRADITIONAL GANSEYS*.

MIDDELHARNIS 3 GANSEY

CHEST: 94CM + 6CM = 100CM (39 3/8 IN). TOTAL HEIGHT: 69CM (27 1/8 IN).

Knit a swatch first, with different sized needles if necessary. A gansey should not be too loosely knit. Follow the chart for the motif and adjust the width and/or height to your size, the yarn used and your tension/gauge. Follow the general instructions for the gansey on pages 54–55 and adjust where necessary.

Measurements
WIDTH: 2 x 50 = 100cm (39 3/8 in)
SHOULDERS: 16.5cm (6 1/2 in)
NECK: 17cm (6 3/4 in)
NECKLINE DEPTH: 5–6cm (2–2 3/8 in)
ARMHOLE HEIGHT: 21–22cm (8 1/4–8 3/4 in)
HEIGHT UP TO ARMHOLE, EXCL. RIBBING: 41cm (16 1/8 in)
SLEEVE LENGTH, EXCL. RIBBING: 43cm (17in)
WRIST CIRCUMFERENCE: approx. 22cm (8 3/4 in)
RIBBING: according to preference, 5–8cm (2–3 1/8 in)

Materials
∞ Approx. 750g (26 1/2 oz) Hjertegarn Mini Vital, dark blue 698; or 100% pure superwash wool yarn (50g (1 3/4 oz) = 150m (164yds))
∞ Circular needles, 3 and 3.5mm (US 2 and 4)
∞ Straight knitting needles, 3 and 3.5mm (US 2 and 4)

TENSION/GAUGE: 24 st x 30 rows on 3.5mm (US 4) needles = 10 x 10cm (4 x 4in)
RIBBING: k1, p1

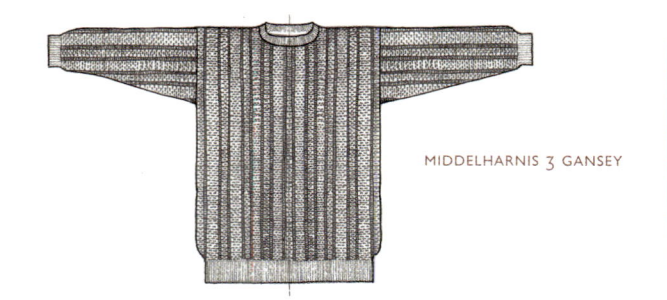

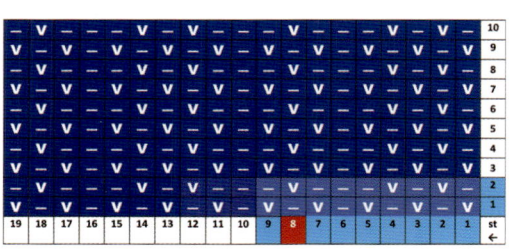

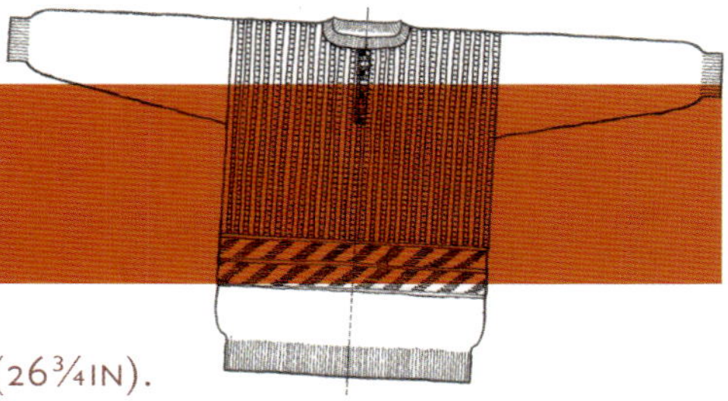

MIDDELHARNIS 4 GANSEY

CHEST: 94CM + 6CM = 100CM (39⅜IN). TOTAL HEIGHT: 68CM (26¾IN).
Knit a swatch first, with different sized needles if necessary. A gansey should not be too loosely knit. Follow the chart for the motif and adjust the width and/or height to your size, the yarn used and your tension/gauge. Follow the general instructions for the gansey on pages 54–55 and adjust where necessary.

Measurements
WIDTH: 2 x 50 = 100cm (39⅜in)
SHOULDERS: 16.5cm (6½in)
NECK: 17cm (6¾in)
NECKLINE DEPTH: 5–6cm (2–2⅜in)
ARMHOLE HEIGHT: 21–22cm (8¼–8¾in)
HEIGHT UP TO ARMHOLE, EXCL. RIBBING: 41cm (16⅛in)
SLEEVE LENGTH, EXCL. RIBBING: 43cm (17in)
WRIST CIRCUMFERENCE: approx. 22cm (8¾in)
RIBBING: according to preference, 5–8cm (2–3⅛in)

Materials
- Approx. 450g (15¾oz) Lopi Einband, navy 0118; or 100% pure wool yarn (50g (1¾oz) = 150m (164yds))
- Circular needles 2 and 2.5mm (US 0 and 1) or 3 and 3.5mm (US 2 and 4) (yarn held double)
- Straight knitting needles, 2 and 2.5mm (US 0 and 1) or 3 and 3.5mm (US 2 and 4) (yarn held double)

TENSION/GAUGE: 33 st x 54 rows on 2.5mm (US 1) needles = 10 x 10cm (4 x 4in)
RIBBING: k2, p2

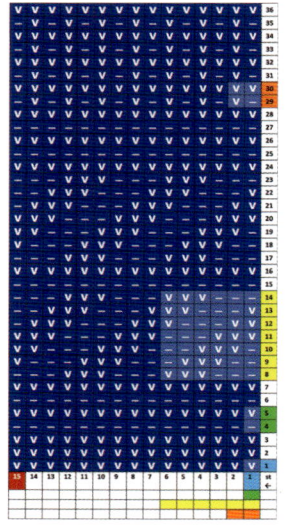

SPLIT: *After dividing the work into a front and back piece, work 24 more rows in pattern (take care to work the even row as a mirror of the chart), and then divide the work for the split as follows: work 55 sts, bind off 5 sts, work 55 sts. For the fold, cast on 8 extra sts on the right-hand side. After 12.5cm (5in), from the inside edge put 18 st (+8 st for the right side) on a stitch holder and work the remaining stitches until the armhole measures 23cm (9in). Bind off the sts for the front and back shoulders using a knit bind-off. Front split: Pick up 41 sts and work 6 ridges. After 3 ridges, make 3 buttonholes: bind off a few sts, enough to fit a button through, and cast on the same number of sts in the next row. Sew on three wooden or bone buttons.*

132 FISHERMAN MATTHIJS VISSER, CA. 1895. GOEREE-OVERFLAKKEE LOCAL ARCHIVE

SOUTH HOLLAND GOEREE-OVERFLAKKEE
STELLENDAM

Until the middle of the eighteenth century, Goeree and Overflakkee were two separate islands. In 1751, the province of Holland ordered a dam to be built between the two islands, the so-called Statendam. A few decades later, land alongside the dam was reclaimed. In one of these *polders* – these low tracts of land enclosed by the dyke – the village of Stellendam was founded. It is the youngest village on Goeree-Overflakkee. Fishing is an important source of income, and shrimp from Stellendam is still very popular. The Stellendam fleet, like the one from Ouddorp, is moored in the new Deltahaven.

134 FISHERMEN FROM GOEDEREEDE-HAVENHOOFD (TOP LEFT TO RIGHT: JAN TANIS & WOUT GROENENDIJK), OUDDORP (BOTTOM LEFT) AND STELLENDAM (BOTTOM RIGHT), CA. 1900. PUBLISHED WITH THE PERMISSION OF MRS LEENTJE TANIS-REDERT FROM GOEDEREEDE-HAVENHOOFD AND MRS GIELTJE GROENENDIJK-MOERKERKE FROM GOEDEREEDE. COURTESY OF MRS ADRIANA DEN HERTOG, GOEDEREEDE

THE GANSEY, STELLENDAM 1, CAN BE FOUND ON PAGE 93 OF *DUTCH TRADITIONAL GANSEYS*.

STELLENDAM 2 GANSEY

CHEST: 96CM + 6CM = 102CM (40 1/8IN). TOTAL HEIGHT: 68CM (26 3/4IN).

Knit a swatch first, with different sized needles if necessary. A gansey should not be too loosely knit. Follow the chart for the motif and adjust the width and/or height to your size, the yarn used and your tension/gauge. Follow the general instructions for the gansey on pages 54–55 and adjust where necessary.

Measurements

WIDTH: 2 × 51 = 102cm (40 1/8in)
SHOULDERS: 16.5cm (6 1/2in)
NECK: 18cm (7in)
NECKLINE DEPTH: 5–6cm (2–2 3/8in)
ARMHOLE HEIGHT: 21–22cm (8 1/4–8 3/4in)
HEIGHT UP TO ARMHOLE, EXCL. RIBBING: 41cm (16 1/8in)
SLEEVE LENGTH, EXCL. RIBBING: 43cm (17in)
WRIST CIRCUMFERENCE: approx. 23cm (9in)
RIBBING: according to preference, 5–8cm (2–3 1/8in)

Materials

- Approx. 750g (26 1/2oz) SMC Merino Extrafine 120, jeans 0154; or 100% merino yarn (50g (1 3/4oz) = approx. 120m (131 1/4yds))
- Circular needles, 3 and 3.5mm (US 2 and 4)
- Straight knitting needles, 3.5mm (US 4)

TENSION/GAUGE: 24 st × 33 rows on 3.5mm (US 4) needles = 10 × 10cm (4 × 4in)

RIBBING: k2, p1

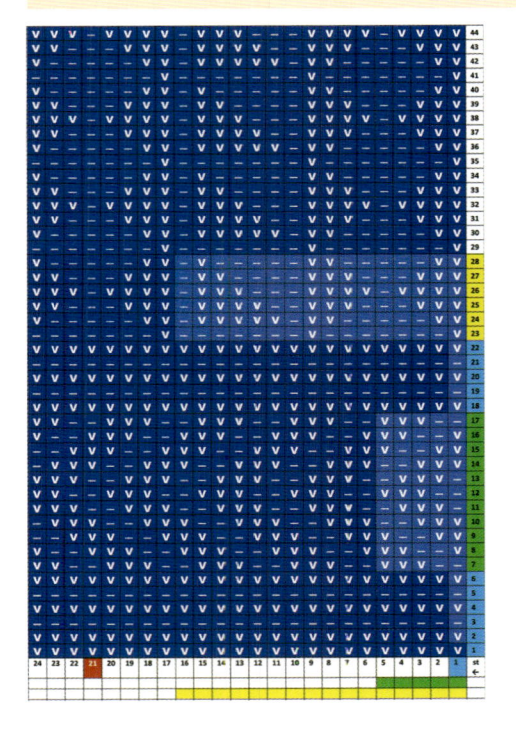

133 FISHERMAN FROM STELLENDAM, CA. 1900. DETAIL FROM FIG. 134

SOUTH HOLLAND GOEREE-OVERFLAKKEE
GOEDEREEDE-HAVENHOOFD

In the villages on Goeree, Ouddorp, Goedereede and Stellendam, fishing became more and more important in the second half of the nineteenth century. They even built a new fishing village: Goedereede-Havenhoofd. The only Dutch pope, Adrianus, was a priest in Goedereede. In 1918, fishermen from Goedereede brought 900 barrels of port ashore, which they had fished out of the sea. The port was salvaged from a ship that had hit a mine. The population of Goedereede had a great party and were drunk for days. Since 2013, this event is celebrated every year, in the form of the Goereese Port Days.

THE SKETCH AND CHART FOR THE GANSEY GOEDEREEDE-HAVENHOOFD 1 CAN BE FOUND ON PAGE 95 OF *DUTCH TRADITIONAL GANSEYS*.

GOEDEREEDE-HAVENHOOFD 2 GANSEY

CHEST: 102CM + 6CM = 108CM (42½IN). TOTAL HEIGHT: 68–70CM (26¾–27½IN).

Knit a swatch first, with different sized needles if necessary. A gansey should not be too loosely knit. Follow the chart for the motif and adjust the width and/or height to your size, the yarn used and your tension/gauge. Follow the general instructions for the gansey on pages 54–55 and adjust where necessary.

Measurements
WIDTH: 2 × 54 = 108cm (42½in)
SHOULDERS: 17.5cm (6⅝in)
NECK: 19cm (7½in)
NECKLINE DEPTH: 6–7cm (2⅜–2¾in)
ARMHOLE HEIGHT: 23–24cm (9–9½in)
HEIGHT UP TO ARMHOLE, EXCL. RIBBING: 41cm (16⅛in)
SLEEVE LENGTH, EXCL. RIBBING: 43cm (17in)
WRIST CIRCUMFERENCE: approx. 23cm (9in)
RIBBING: according to preference, 5–8cm (2–3⅛in)

Materials
- Approx. 700g (24⅔oz) Loret Karman RAW Superwash, night blue; or 100% pure superwash wool yarn (100g (3½oz) = approx. 250m (273½yds))
- Circular needles, 3 and 3.5mm (US 2 and 4)
- Straight knitting needles, 3mm (US 2)
- Cable needle

TENSION/GAUGE: 21 st × 26 rows on 3.5mm (US 4) needle = 10 × 10cm (4 × 4in)
RIBBING: k1, p1

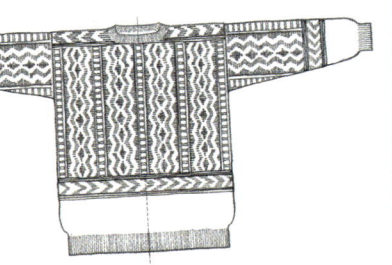

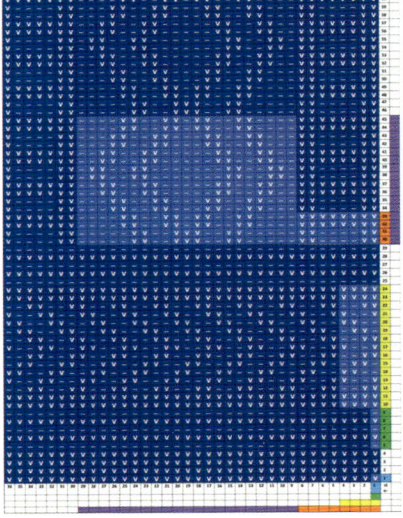

135 FISHERMAN JAN TANIS FROM GOEDEREEDE-HAVENHOOFD (STANDING), CA. 1900. PUBLISHED WITH THE PERMISSION OF MRS LEENTJE TANIS-REDERT FROM GOEDEREEDE-HAVENHOOFD AND MRS GIELTJE GROENENDIJK-MOERKERKE FROM GOEDEREEDE

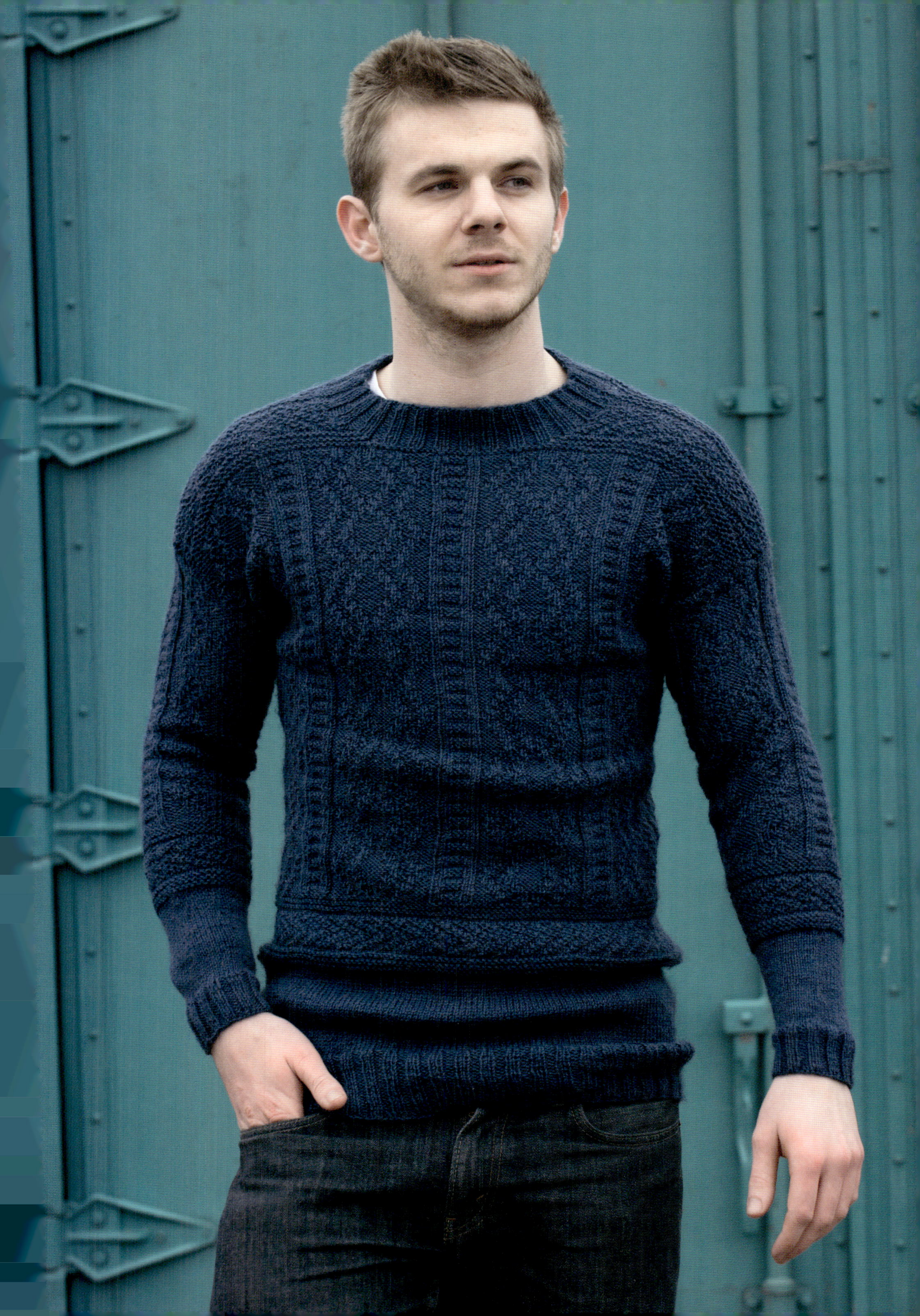

GOEDEREEDE-HAVENHOOFD 3 GANSEY

CHEST: 96CM + 6CM = 102CM (40⅛IN). TOTAL HEIGHT: 68–70CM (26¾–27½IN).

Knit a swatch first, with different sized needles if necessary. A gansey should not be too loosely knit. Follow the chart for the motif and adjust the width and/or height to your size, the yarn used and your tension/gauge. Follow the general instructions for the gansey on pages 54–55 and adjust where necessary.

Measurements

WIDTH: 2 × 51 = 102cm (40⅛in)
SHOULDERS: 16.5cm (6½in)
NECK: 17cm (6¾in)
NECKLINE DEPTH: 5–6cm (2–2⅜in)
ARMHOLE HEIGHT: 22–23cm (8¾–9in)
HEIGHT UP TO ARMHOLE, EXCL. RIBBING: 41cm (16⅛in)
SLEEVE LENGTH, EXCL. RIBBING: 43cm (17in)
WRIST CIRCUMFERENCE: approx. 23cm (9in)
RIBBING: according to preference, 5–8cm (2–3⅛in)

Materials

∞ 800g (28¼oz) Rauma Strikkegarn, dark sky blue 143; or 100% pure wool yarn (50g (1¾oz) = approx. 105m (115yds))
∞ Circular needles, 3 and 3.5mm (US 2 and 4)
∞ Straight knitting needles, 3.5mm (US 4)

TENSION/GAUGE: 22 st × 27 rows on 3.5mm (US 4) needles = 10 × 10cm (4 × 4in)

RIBBING: k2, p2

136 FISHERMAN WOUT GROENENDIJK FROM GOEDEREEDE-HAVENHOOFD (STANDING), CA. 1900. PUBLISHED WITH THE PERMISSION OF MRS LEENTJE TANIS-REDERT FROM GOEDEREEDE-HAVENHOOFD AND MRS GIELTJE GROENENDIJK-MOERKERKE FROM GOEDEREEDE

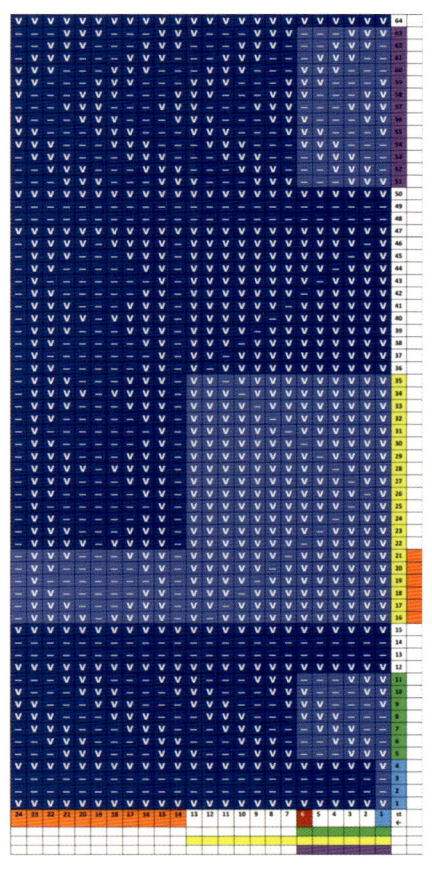

137 PHOTOGRAPH FROM 1918: FISHERMEN FROM OUDDORP, FROM LEFT TO RIGHT: HANS KASTELEIN, KEES V.D. KLOOSTER AND AREN V.D. KLOOSTER. COURTESY OF A.J. KASTELEIN, GOEDEREEDE

SOUTH HOLLAND GOEREE-OVERFLAKKEE
OUDDORP

Mrs Gieltje Groenendijk-Moerkerke from Goedereede told the following story:
Before, during and after the Second World War, there was great poverty in the fishing sector, especially in Ouddorp. One visiting family member kept his jacket on the entire time. It was very hot in their little cottage, so he was asked why he didn't take it off. He replied: 'I'm only wearing half a sweater, a sweater without sleeves.' There was no money to buy the wool that was needed for the sleeves. He did have one other sweater, but he wore that only when we went out to sea.

The port of Ouddorp was built in 1860–1861 and expanded through the years. It is now used as a marina. Even older than this port is the Kil port, close to De Val. The people living here already fished for herring at De Val around 1415. The port is now silted up and the fleet uses the new Deltahaven at Stellendam.

The fleet of Ouddorp made the news in April 2005, when three crew members of the cutter Ouddorp 1 (OD-1) were killed when their vessel hit a bomb from the Second World War. The bomb had gotten into their nets and exploded when they were hauling in the net.

THE GANSEY, OUDDORP 1, CAN BE FOUND ON PAGES 96–97 OF *DUTCH TRADITIONAL GANSEYS*, AND IS FROM MIDDELHARNIS (SEE ALSO PAGE 7 OF THE SAME BOOK)

OUDDORP 1 GANSEY

CHEST: 94CM + 6CM = 100CM (39⅜IN). TOTAL HEIGHT: 68–70CM (26¾–27½IN).

Knit a swatch first, with different sized needles if necessary. A gansey should not be too loosely knit. Follow the chart for the motif and adjust the width and/or height to your size, the yarn used and your tension/gauge. Follow the general instructions for the gansey on pages 54–55 and adjust where necessary.

Measurements

WIDTH: 2 x 50 = 100cm (39⅜in)
SHOULDERS: 16.5cm (6½in)
NECK: 17cm (6¾in)
NECKLINE DEPTH: 5–6cm (2–2⅜in)
ARMHOLE HEIGHT: 21–22cm (8¼–8¾in)
HEIGHT UP TO ARMHOLE, EXCL. RIBBING: 41cm (16⅛in)
SLEEVE LENGTH, EXCL. RIBBING: 43cm (17in)
WRIST CIRCUMFERENCE: approx. 22cm (8¾in)
RIBBING: according to preference, 5–8cm (2–3⅛in)

Materials

- 550g (19½oz) Lopi Einband, blue 0942; or 100% pure wool yarn (50g (1¾oz) = approx. 225m (246yds))
- Circular needles, 2.5 and 3mm (US 1 and 2)
- Straight knitting needles, 3mm (US 2)

TENSION/GAUGE: 25 st x 32 rows on 3mm (US 2) needles = 10 x 10cm (4 x 4in)

RIBBING: K2, p2

138 HANS KASTELEIN FROM OUDDORP. COURTESY OF A.J. KASTELEIN, GOEDEREEDE. DETAIL FROM FIG. 137

OUDDORP 2 GANSEY

CHEST: 98CM + 6CM = 104CM (41IN). TOTAL HEIGHT: 68–70CM (26¾–27½IN).

Knit a swatch first, with different sized needles if necessary. A gansey should not be too loosely knit. Follow the chart for the motif and adjust the width and/or height to your size, the yarn used and your tension/gauge. Follow the general instructions for the gansey on pages 54–55 and adjust where necessary.

Measurements

WIDTH: 2 x 52 = 104cm (41in)
SHOULDERS: 16.5cm (6½in)
NECK: 18cm (7in)
NECKLINE DEPTH: 6–7cm (2⅜–2¾in)
ARMHOLE HEIGHT: 22–23cm (8¾–9in)
HEIGHT UP TO ARMHOLE, EXCL. RIBBING: 41cm (16⅛in)
SLEEVE LENGTH, EXCL. RIBBING: 43cm (17in)
WRIST CIRCUMFERENCE: approx. 23cm (9in)
RIBBING: according to preference, 5–8cm (2–3⅛in)

Materials

- 850g (30oz) Scheepjeswol Zuiderzee, off white; or 100% pure wool yarn (100g (3½oz) = approx. 85m (93yds))
- Circular needles, 3 and 3.5mm (US 2 and 4)
- Straight knitting needles, 3.5mm (US 4)

TENSION/GAUGE: 21 st x 30 rows on 3.5mm (US 4) needles = 10 x 10cm (4 x 4in)

RIBBING: k1, p1

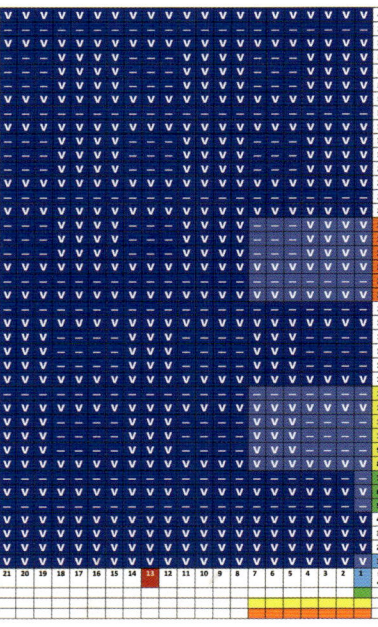

139 FISHERMAN FROM OUDDORP, CA. 1900. PUBLISHED WITH THE PERMISSION OF MRS LEENTJE TANIS-REDERT FROM GOEDEREEDE-HAVENHOOFD AND MRS GIELTJE GROENENDIJK-MOERKERKE FROM GOEDEREEDE. (RIGHT)

ZEELAND NOORD-BEVELAND
COLIJNSPLAAT

Colijnsplaat was founded in 1598, after the reclamation of the Oud-Noord-Bevelandpolder. The name comes from the salt marsh called 'Colinsplate', which was first mentioned in 1489 and was partly reclaimed.

During the 1953 floods, the miracle of Colijnsplaat took place: a number of men tried to hold up the flashboards and supports for the dyke, which threatened to collapse because of the high water. A cargo ship that had cut adrift in the storm was thrown against the crack in the dyke, and acted as a breakwater, thus saving Colijnsplaat from being flooded. A monument from 1993, with the name 'Houen Jongens', by the sculptor Jan Haas, is a reminder of that fateful day.

The Veerse Gatdam, which was completed in 1961, blocked Veere off from the sea for good. The fishing fleets of Veere and Arnemuiden moved to Colijnsplaat. The port also has a fish auction.

140 IN THE PORT OF COLIJNSPLAAT, CA. 1950. MARITIME MUSEUM ROTTERDAM

COLIJNSPLAAT GANSEY

CHEST: 80cm + 2cm = 82cm (32¼in). TOTAL HEIGHT: 54–56cm (21¼–22in).

Knit a swatch first, with different sized needles if necessary. A gansey should not be too loosely knit. Follow the chart for the motif and adjust the width and/or height to your size, the yarn used and your tension/gauge. Follow the general instructions for the gansey on pages 54–55 and adjust where necessary.

141 DETAIL FROM FIG. 140

Measurements
WIDTH: 2 x 41 = 82cm (32¼in)
SHOULDERS: 13.5cm (5¼in)
NECK: 14cm (5½in)
NECKLINE DEPTH: 4–5cm (1½–2in)
ARMHOLE HEIGHT: 16cm (6¼in)
HEIGHT UP TO ARMHOLE, EXCL. RIBBING: 33cm (13in)
SLEEVE LENGTH, EXCL. RIBBING: 34cm (13⅜in)
WRIST CIRCUMFERENCE: approx. 16cm (6¼in)
RIBBING: according to preference, 4–6cm (1½–2⅜in)

Materials
- 400g (14oz) 5-ply Frangipani Guernsey Wool, navy; or bulky 100% pure wool yarn (100g (3½oz) = approx. 195m (104yds))
- Circular needles, 2.5 and 3mm (US 1 and 2)
- Straight knitting needles, 3mm (US 2)

TENSION/GAUGE: 21 st x 32 rows on 3mm (US 2) needles = 10 x 10 cm (4 x 4in)
RIBBING: k1, p1

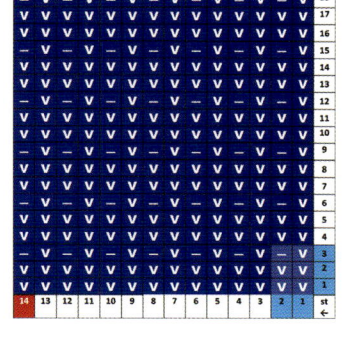

ZEELAND ZEEUWS-VLAANDEREN
BRESKENS

Visschersklub-Breskens.

142 VISSCHERSCLUB BRESKENS WITH, IN THE FOREGROUND, A SMALL BOY WHO IS – AT MOST – FOUR YEARS OLD AND SMOKING A PIPE. ZEEUWS ARCHIVE

The first fishing boat in Bresken was only registered in 1890 (the BR 1). In 1891, Breskens had nine *hoogaarzen* – clinker-built, flat-bottomed vessels which were mainly used for fishing on flatfish and shrimp. After the First World War, the fishing boats were gradually equipped with more and more powerful engines. Immediately after Second World War, the fishermen from Breskens were allowed to salvage food and other items from ships that had been sunk by the Germans, of which they could keep half. After the war, fishermen from Urk and Texel came to Breskens to join them on herring fishing trips on the southern North Sea fishing grounds. They built new, larger and more modern ships, complete with detection equipment. As a result, this part of the North Sea was virtually depleted. The catches became smaller and the fishing vessels from Urk and Texel disappeared from Breskens. The fishermen from Breskens went back to the old fishing methods, fishing restrictions were imposed and the allowable engine power was reduced.

As a result, the herring stocks in the southern North Sea improved and fishing for herring is now possible again. However, the herring has to be frozen immediately on landing. This cannot be done in Breskens, but only in Oostende and Scheveningen.

BRESKENS 1 GANSEY

CHEST: 96CM + 6CM = 102CM (40⅛IN). TOTAL HEIGHT: 68CM (26¾IN).

Knit a swatch first, with different sized needles if necessary. A gansey should not be too loosely knit. Follow the chart for the motif and adjust the width and/or height to your size, the yarn used and your tension/gauge. Follow the general instructions for the gansey on pages 54–55 and adjust where necessary.

Measurements

WIDTH: 2 x 51 = 102cm (40⅛in)
SHOULDERS: 16.5cm (6½in)
NECK: 17cm (6¾in)
NECKLINE DEPTH: 5–6cm (2–2⅜in)
ARMHOLE HEIGHT: 22–23cm (8¾–9in)
HEIGHT UP TO ARMHOLE, EXCL. RIBBING: 41cm (16⅛in)
SLEEVE LENGTH, EXCL. RIBBING: 43cm (17in)
WRIST CIRCUMFERENCE: approx. 23cm (9in)
RIBBING: according to preference, 5–8cm (2–3⅛in)

Materials

- 850g (30oz) Hjertegarn Lima, saxe blue 2176; or 100% pure wool yarn (50g (1¾oz) = approx. 100m (110yds))
- Circular needles, 3.5 and 4mm (US 4 and 6)
- Straight knitting needles, 4mm (US 6)

TENSION/GAUGE: 20 st x 26 rows on 4mm (US 6) needles: = 10 x 10cm (4 x 4in)

RIBBING: K2, p2

143 GANSEY BRESKENS 1, DETAIL FROM FIG. 142

107

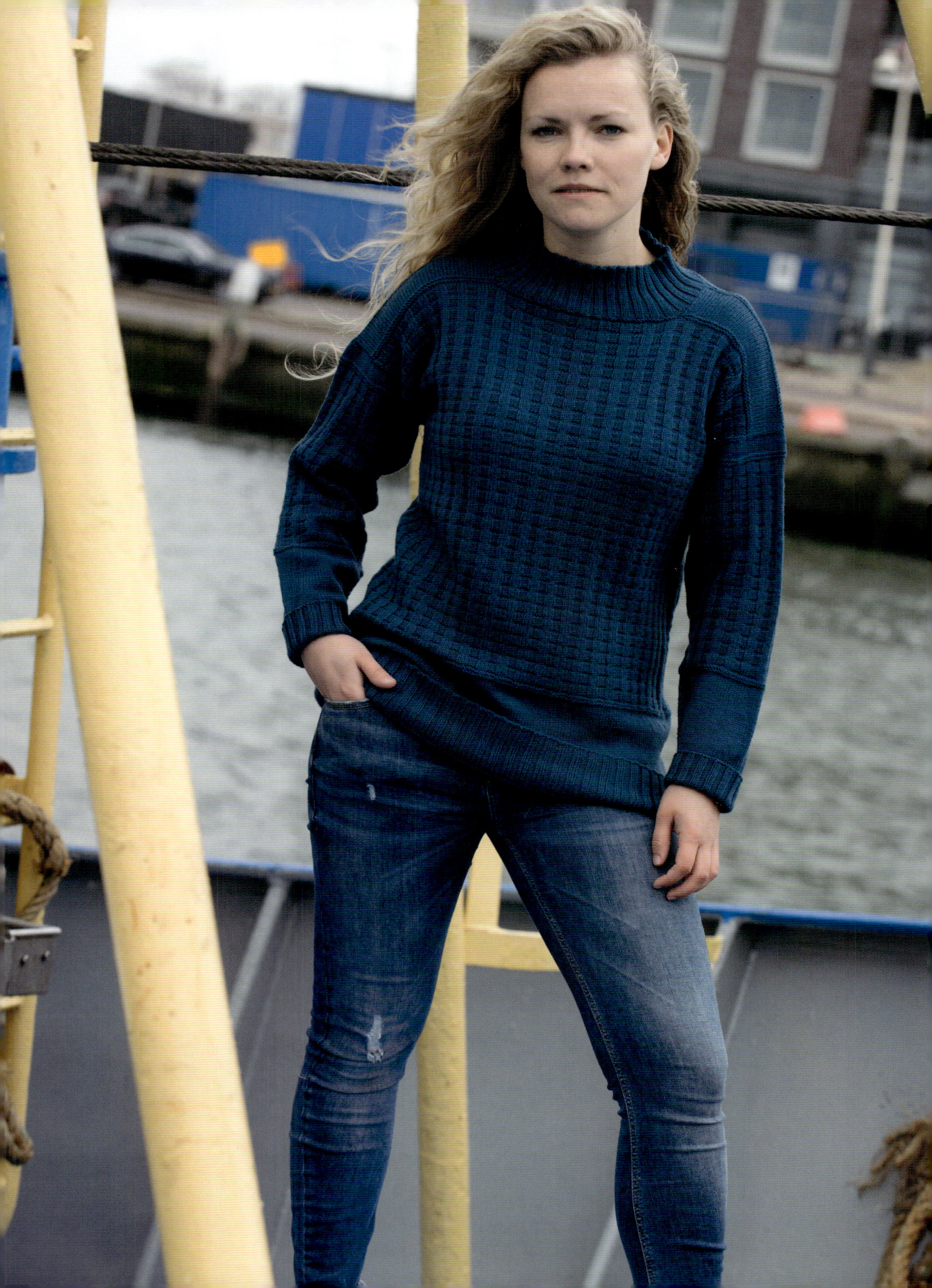

BRESKENS 2 GANSEY

CHEST: 96CM + 6CM = 102CM (40⅛IN). TOTAL HEIGHT: 68CM (26¾IN).

Knit a swatch first, with different sized needles if necessary. A gansey should not be too loosely knit. Follow the chart for the motif and adjust the width and/or height to your size, the yarn used and your tension/gauge. Follow the general instructions for the gansey on pages 54–55 and adjust where necessary.

Measurements

WIDTH: 2 × 51 = 102cm (40⅛in)
SHOULDERS: 16.5cm (6½in)
NECK: 17cm (6¾in)
NECKLINE DEPTH: 5–6cm (2–2⅜in)
ARMHOLE HEIGHT: 22–23cm (8¾–9in)
HEIGHT UP TO ARMHOLE, EXCL. RIBBING: 41cm (16⅛in)
SLEEVE LENGTH, EXCL. RIBBING: 43cm (17in)
WRIST CIRCUMFERENCE: approx. 23cm (9in)
RIBBING: according to preference, 5–8cm (2–3⅛in)

Materials

- 700g (24⅔oz) Lang Merino 150, petrol 0133; or 100% merino yarn (50g (1¾oz) = approx. 150m (164yds))
- Circular needles, 3 and 3.5mm (US 2 and 4)
- Straight knitting needles, 3.5mm (US 4)

TENSION/GAUGE: 27 st × 37 rows on 3.5mm (US 4) needles = 10 × 10cm (4 × 4in)
RIBBING: k2, p2

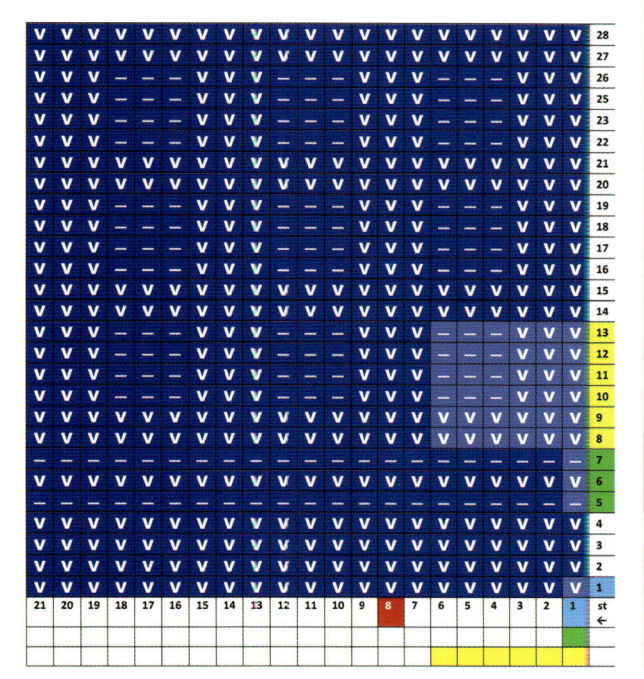

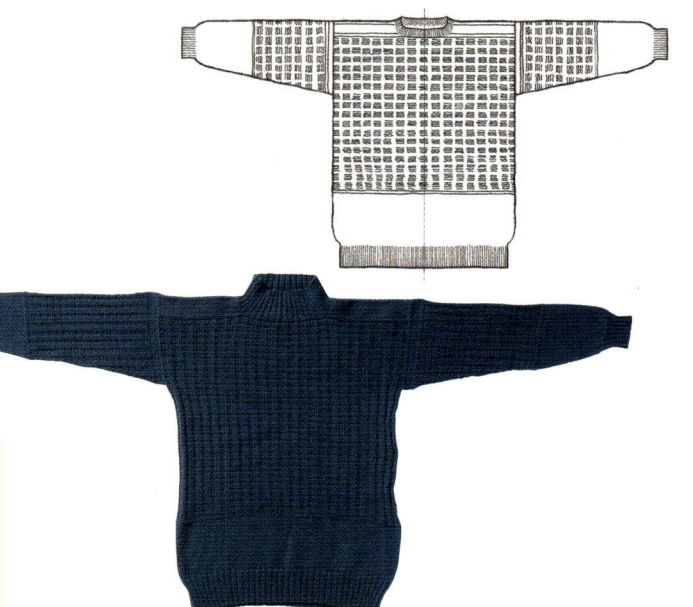

144 BRESKENS 2 GANSEY, DETAIL FROM FIG. 142

SALMON BOATS IN THE PORT OF WOUDRICHEM, CA. 1900.
FISHERIES MUSEUM HET ARSENAAL, WOUDRICHEM

5 MAJOR RIVERS

Around 1900, the rivers – still clear and not yet polluted by industry – were busy with fishermen, fishing for salmon, sturgeon, shad, whitefish and eel. *Zalmschouwen*, small barge-like fishing boats, were pulled up the river by other, more powerful boats, often all the way to Germany, in order to fish downriver from there. The fish caught were then distributed by train and cart, and even exported to Germany. Via the same routes, North Sea fish were transported the other way, to the big cities in the hinterland and to Germany, Belgium, and France.

Countless towns and cities practised this type of river fishing. Still, there are hardly any photos of fishermen with sweaters from those towns. From three towns, Charlois (Rotterdam), Woudrichem and Willemstad, we did find old photographs of sweater-wearing fishermen, a number of which are described here. There have to be a lot more, but this requires further research.

SOUTH HOLLAND
CHARLOIS

145 LOTS OF SHIPS IN THE HARBOUR, CA. 1900.
HISTORICAL SOCIETY OF CHARLOIS

146 BOATS OWNED BY CAPTAIN BLOM.
HISTORICAL SOCIETY OF CHARLOIS

Charlois (pronounced as 'Sharloos') is located in the De Reijerwaard area, gifted by Philip of Burgundy to his son Charles the Bold in 1458. He gave permission to build dykes. He also determined that the dyked area should 'from now on be referred to as the Land of Charollais'. Possibly, the name comes from the county of Charolais in France, which also belonged to Charles the Bold.

In 1873, the municipality of Katendrecht was added to Charlois, and in 1895 it was itself annexed by Rotterdam, where the construction of a huge port was started. There was only a little bit of fishing going on here, mainly small-scale river fishing. The shipyards, however, were of great economic value.

A sneaky trick
Captain Blom from Charlois had been mooring his two fishing boats in an old part of the port, the Rietdijk, for years. It was a real eyesore for the municipality – also because they had big plans for this area. They agreed he was allowed to keep his boats there until they had to come out of the water for the winter. But, long before the season was at an end, he had to tar his boats and decided to pull them ashore for a day and a night. When he came back the next day to go fishing, he saw to his disgust that the municipality had filled up the small port with sand as soon as he had lifted his boats out of the water! (Fig. 146)

147 YARD CREW. HISTORICAL SOCIETY OF CHARLOIS

CHARLOIS GANSEY

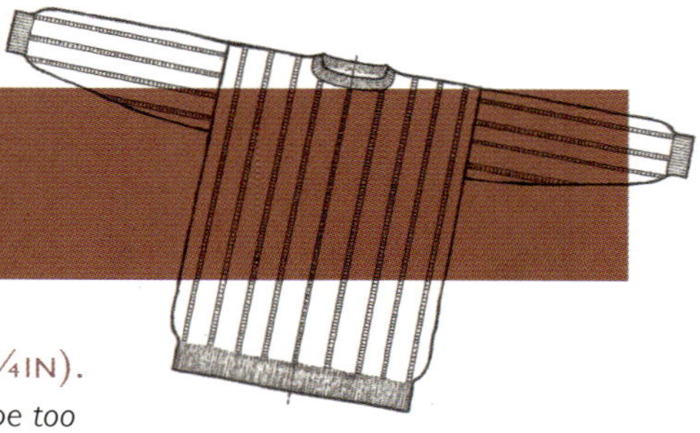

CHEST: 96CM + 6CM = 102CM (40⅛IN). TOTAL HEIGHT: 68CM (26¾IN).
Knit a swatch first, with different sized needles if necessary. A gansey should not be too loosely knit. Follow the chart for the motif and adjust the width and/or height to your size, the yarn used and your tension/gauge. Follow the general instructions for the gansey on pages 54–55 and adjust where necessary.

Measurements
WIDTH: 2 × 51 = 102cm (40⅛in)
SHOULDERS: 16.5cm (6½in)
NECK: 18cm (7in)
NECKLINE DEPTH: 5–6cm (2–2⅜in)
ARMHOLE HEIGHT: 22–23cm (8¾–9in)
HEIGHT UP TO ARMHOLE, EXCL. RIBBING: 41cm (16⅛in)
SLEEVE LENGTH, EXCL. RIBBING: 43cm (17in)
WRIST CIRCUMFERENCE: approx. 23cm (9in)
RIBBING: according to preference, 5–8cm (2–3⅛in)

Materials
- 700g (24⅔oz) Lang Donegal Merino, blue 035; or 100% merino yarn (50g (1¾oz) = approx. 150m (164yds))
- Circular needles, 2.5 and 3mm (US 1 and 2)
- Straight knitting needles, 3mm (US 2)

TENSION/GAUGE: 26 st × 41 rows on 3mm (US 2) needles = 10 × 10cm (4 × 4in)
RIBBING: k1, p1

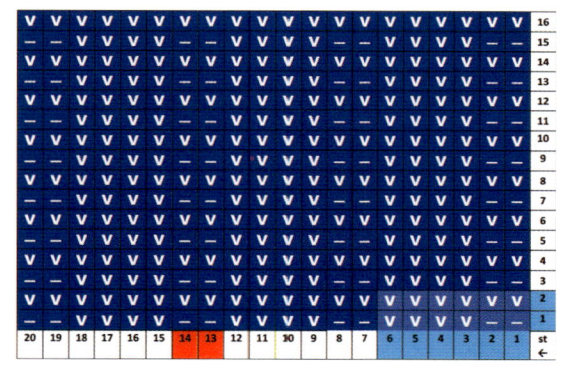

NORTH BRABANT
WOUDRICHEM

The Brabant town of Woudrichem (known in the local dialect as Woerkum) is a unique place where the rivers Maas/Meuse and Waal join up, and the provinces of Gelderland, Brabant and South Holland meet. In 1362, the fortress town was granted fishing rights by count Dirk Loeff van Horne, Lord of Altena. Across from Woudrichem, on the other side of the river Maas, he had Castle Loevestein built in 1361. Woudrichem still has these fishing rights, which apply to an area that is visible from the tower, 'as far as the eye can see'. These rights were also given to the burghers and their children – i.e. to the people living in the fortress. The Cooperative Association De Hoop now owns the fishing rights.

Its favourable location enabled fishing on the rivers Maas and Waal, and the Waal's connection to the sea, the Boven Merwede. People would fish for pike and perch, salmon, eel, sturgeon, twaite, shad, houting (whitefish) and eel. Because of the pollution of the rivers, fish stocks have deteriorated dramatically since the 1950s.

148 SALMON FISHING IN WOUDRICHEM, PACKING THE SALMON, CA. 1910. STICHTING ZUIDERZEEAMBACHTEN, ENKHUIZEN

WOUDRICHEM 1 GANSEY

CHEST: 98CM + 6CM = 102CM (40 1/8 IN). TOTAL HEIGHT: 68–70CM (26 3/4–27 1/2 IN).
Knit a swatch first, with different sized needles if necessary. A gansey should not be too loosely knit. Follow the chart for the motif and adjust the width and/or height to your size, the yarn used and your tension/gauge. Follow the general instructions for the gansey on pages 54–55 and adjust where necessary.

Measurements

WIDTH: 2 × 51 = 102CM (40 1/8 IN)
SHOULDERS: 16.5CM (6 1/2 IN)
NECK: 18CM (7IN)
NECKLINE DEPTH: 6–7CM (2 3/8–2 3/4 IN)
ARMHOLE HEIGHT: 22–23CM (8 3/4–9IN)
HEIGHT UP TO ARMHOLE, EXCL. RIBBING: 41CM (16 1/8 IN)
SLEEVE LENGTH, EXCL. RIBBING: 43CM (17IN)
WRIST CIRCUMFERENCE: approx. 23CM (9IN)
RIBBING: according to preference, 5–8CM (2–3 1/8 IN)

Materials

- 800g (28¼oz) Lang Thema Nuova, royal blue 0054; or 100% pure wool yarn (50g (1¾oz) = approx. 118m (129yds))
- Circular needles, 3.5 and 4mm (US 4 and 6)
- Straight knitting needles, 4mm (US 6)
- Cable needle

TENSION/GAUGE: 23 st x 32 rows on 4mm (US 6) needles = 10 x 10cm (4 x 4in)

RIBBING: k2, p2

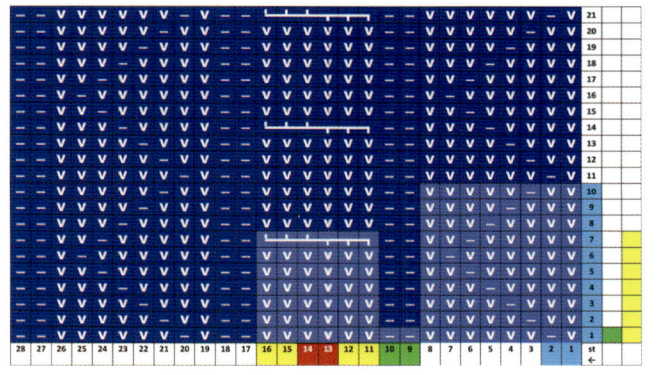

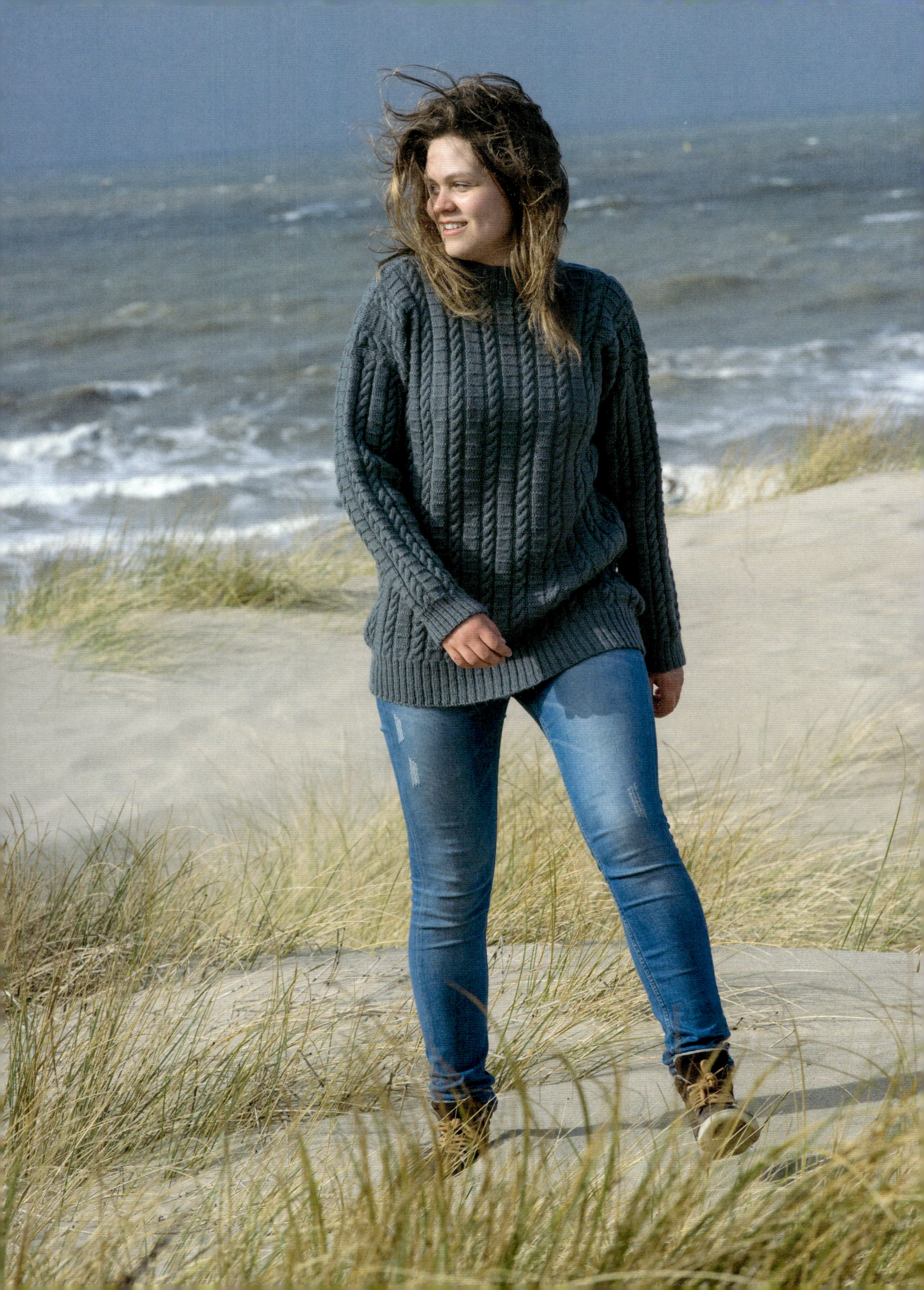

WOUDRICHEM 2 GANSEY

CHEST: 100CM + 6CM = 106CM (41¾IN). TOTAL HEIGHT: 68–70CM (26¾–27½IN).

Knit a swatch first, with different sized needles if necessary. A gansey should not be too loosely knit. Follow the chart for the motif and adjust the width and/or height to your size, the yarn used and your tension/gauge. Follow the general instructions for the gansey on pages 54–55 and adjust where necessary.

Measurements

WIDTH: 2 x 53 = 106cm (41¾in)
SHOULDERS: 17.5cm (6⅝in)
NECK: 18cm (7in)
NECKLINE DEPTH: 5–7cm (2–2¾in)
ARMHOLE HEIGHT: 23cm (9in)
HEIGHT UP TO ARMHOLE, EXCL. RIBBING: 41cm (16⅛in)
SLEEVE LENGTH, EXCL. RIBBING: 43cm (approx. 17in)
WRIST CIRCUMFERENCE: approx. 23cm (9in)
RIBBING: according to preference, 5–8cm (2–3⅛in)

Materials

∞ Approx. 700g (24⅔oz) Loret Karman RAW Superwash, grey; or 100% pure superwash wool yarn (100g (3½oz) = approx. 250m (273½yds))
∞ Circular needles, 3 and 3.5mm (US 2 and 4)
∞ Straight knitting needles, 3.5mm (US 4)
∞ Cable needle

TENSION/GAUGE: 21 st x 26 rows on 3.5mm (US 4) needles = 10 x 10cm (4 x 4in)

RIBBING: k2, p2

149 SALMON FISHERMEN IN WOUDRICHEM, 1913. STICHTING ZUIDERZEEAMBACHTEN, ENKHUIZEN

150 FISHERMEN KNITTING FYKES IN WILLEMSTAD. THE MAURITSHUIS MUSEUM, WILLEMSTAD

NORTH BRABANT
WILLEMSTAD

Willemstad is a fortress town in the municipality of Moerdijk in North Brabant, where the Volkerak and the Hollands Diep meet. In the past, there was a salting close to Willemstad. John IV of Glymes, Marquis of Bergen op Zoom, decided to reclaim it, as a result of which the town of Ruigenhil was founded in 1565. In 1583, the Spaniards occupied the area of Steenbergen, and William of Orange decided to fortify Ruigenhil and make it into a fortress. His son, Prince Maurits, granted the town city rights in 1585, and the city (*stad*) of Willem was given its new official name: Willemstad. In 1607, Coenraat Norenburch built the first church for Protestant worship in the Netherlands in this town. Prince Maurits offered financial support, on the condition that the church would have a round or octagonal shape. In 1623, Maurits had the Princehof built in Willemstad (now called the Mauritshuis).

The building was the town hall of the municipality of Willemstad in 1973, until it was annexed by the municipality of Moerdijk in 1997. One of the titles of the current King Willem-Alexander is Lord of Willemstad.

In 1874, Willemstad was the centre of the Stellingen of the Hollands Diep and the Volkerak. These were built to protect Holland against armed forces from North Brabant who wanted to cross the Hollands Diep and close off ship access to it.

The fishermen of Willemstad mainly fished for salmon, sturgeon, shad, eel, etc., like other river fishermen.

WILLEMSTAD GANSEY

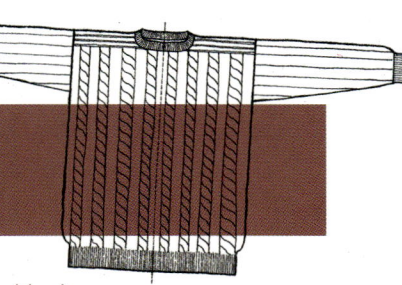

CHEST: 102CM + 6CM = 108CM (42½IN). TOTAL HEIGHT: 68–70CM (26¾–27½IN).

Knit a swatch first, with different sized needles if necessary. A gansey should not be too loosely knit. Follow the chart for the motif and adjust the width and/or height to your size, the yarn used and your tension/gauge. Follow the general instructions for the gansey on pages 54–55 and adjust where necessary.

Measurements
WIDTH: 2 × 54 = 108cm (42½in)
SHOULDERS: 17.5cm (6⅝in)
NECK: 19cm (7½in)
NECKLINE DEPTH: 6–7cm (2⅜–2¾in)
ARMHOLE HEIGHT: 23–24cm (9–9½in)
HEIGHT UP TO ARMHOLE, EXCL. RIBBING: 41cm (16⅛in)
SLEEVE LENGTH, EXCL. RIBBING: 43cm (17in)
WRIST CIRCUMFERENCE: approx. 23cm (9in)
RIBBING: according to preference, 5–8cm (2–3⅛in)

151 FISHERMAN FROM WILLEMSTAD, CA 1930. HISTORICAL ASSOCIATION, WILLEMSTAD

Materials
- 750g (26½oz) Hjertegarn Vital, 698; or 100% pure superwash wool yarn (50g (1¾oz) = approx. 130m (142⅙yds))
- Circular needles, 3 and 3.5mm (US 2 and 4)
- Straight knitting needles, 3.5mm (US 4)
- Cable needle

TENSION/GAUGE: 23 st × 33 on 3.5mm (US 4) needles = 10 × 10cm (4 × 4in)

RIBBING: k1, p1

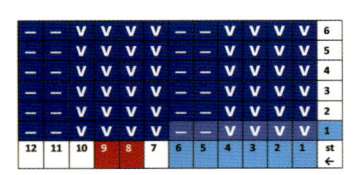

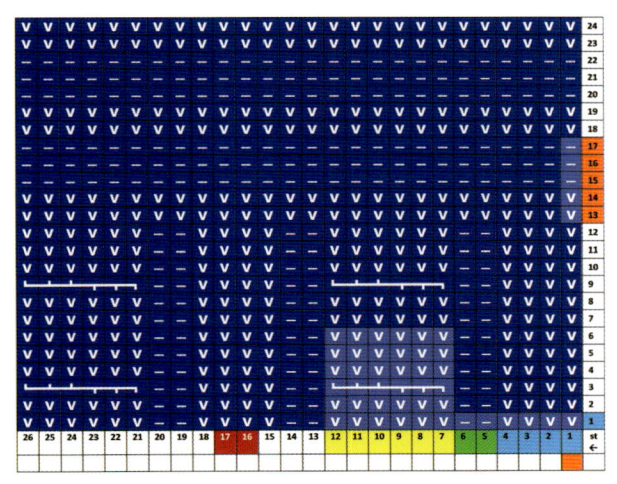

A HERRING BARGE AND BARGE FROM WIERUM, 1895.
STICHTING ZUIDERZEEAMBACHTEN ENKHUIZEN

6 WADDEN SEA COAST

Of all the Wadden Sea Islands, only Texel had its own fleet. The other islands focused more on whaling, but around 1900 fishing became problematic because the fish stocks were depleted. Many fishermen from the islands, and in particular from Terschelling, moved to German fishing towns like Emden in order to sign on to the herring luggers. In the municipality of Dongeradeel, fishermen mainly fished at sea for haddock, cod and flatfish. Because there was no port, the ships dropped anchor on the flats of the Wadden Sea. The close-knit communities in Wierum, Ternaard and Moddergat have long had a fishing culture and there is evidence of a connection with the fishermen in Hollum, on the island of Ameland. Unfortunately no sweaters have been found there. Engwierum, Ee and Dokkumer Nieuwezijlen also belonged to this fishing area. In addition to trawler fishing, the fishermen of Dongeradeel and Ameland specialised in the fishing with longliners (see page 26). After 1900, the importance of the fisheries declined because of the low fish stocks, the competition from trawlers and the larger fishing ports which had better international marketing channels.

Many fishermen from this area signed up with the herring luggers along the Holland coast and in Germany, and later started fishing for shrimp on the Wadden Sea. The fishermen also greatly benefited from the emergence of Zoutkamp as a centre of trade for shrimp, and later from the fishing port with auction at Lauwersoog.

NORTH HOLLAND TEXEL
OOSTEREND

Texel is the only Dutch Wadden island with its own fishing fleet. It is one of the most modern in the country. The fleet consists of approximately 11 North Sea cutters and eight shrimp cutters. These last ships fish only on the Wadden Sea. The main species they fish for are sole and plaice. In the seventeenth century, Oudeschild was a town of international importance, because of the Texel Roadstead. Many VOC (*Vereenigde Oost-Indische Compagnie* – Dutch East India Company) ships started their long voyage to the East from here. This was the village's own 'golden age', as the ships would also buy supplies at Texel. All the streets in the town are named after former naval heroes and pirates who travelled to the Far East from Oudeschild. The drinking water for the ships came from water wells that were owned by an orphanage in Den Burg, and which were therefore called 'orphan wells'. Oudeschild used to have its own fish auction, but now the catch is sold at Den Helder. There used to be a port in Oosterend as well, but this silted up in the nineteenth century.

Oosterend was home to most of the Texel North Sea fishermen of Texel, but Oudeschild is the port of Texel, where the ships from Oosterend are also moored.

152 CREW OF A SHIP FROM OOSTEREND, TEXEL, CA. 1910. MUSEUM KAAP SKIL, OUDESCHILD

OOSTEREND 1 GANSEY

CHEST: 102CM + 6CM = 108CM (42½IN). TOTAL HEIGHT: 68–70CM (26¾–27½IN).

Knit a swatch first, with different sized needles if necessary. A gansey should not be too loosely knit. Follow the chart for the motif and adjust the width and/or height to your size, the yarn used and your tension/gauge. Follow the general instructions for the gansey on pages 54–55 and adjust where necessary.

Measurements
WIDTH: 2 x 54 = 108cm (42½in)
SHOULDERS: 17.5cm (6⅝in)
NECK: 19cm (7½in)
NECKLINE DEPTH: 6–7cm (2⅜–2¾in)
ARMHOLE HEIGHT: 23–24cm (9–9½in)
HEIGHT UP TO ARMHOLE, EXCL. RIBBING: 41cm (16⅛in)
SLEEVE LENGTH, EXCL. RIBBING: 43cm (17in)
WRIST CIRCUMFERENCE: approx. 23cm (9in)
RIBBING: according to preference, 5–8cm (2–3⅛in)

Materials
∞ 850–900g (30–31¾oz) Hjertegarn Lima, dark blue 1660; or 100% pure wool yarn (50g (1¾oz) = approx. 100m (110yds))
∞ Circular needles, 4 and 4.5mm (US 6 and 7)
∞ Straight knitting needles 4.5mm (US 7)
∞ Cable needle

TENSION/GAUGE: 20 st x 28 rows on 4.5mm (US 7) needles = 10 x 10cm (4 x 4in)

RIBBING: k2, p2

DETAIL FROM FIG. 152

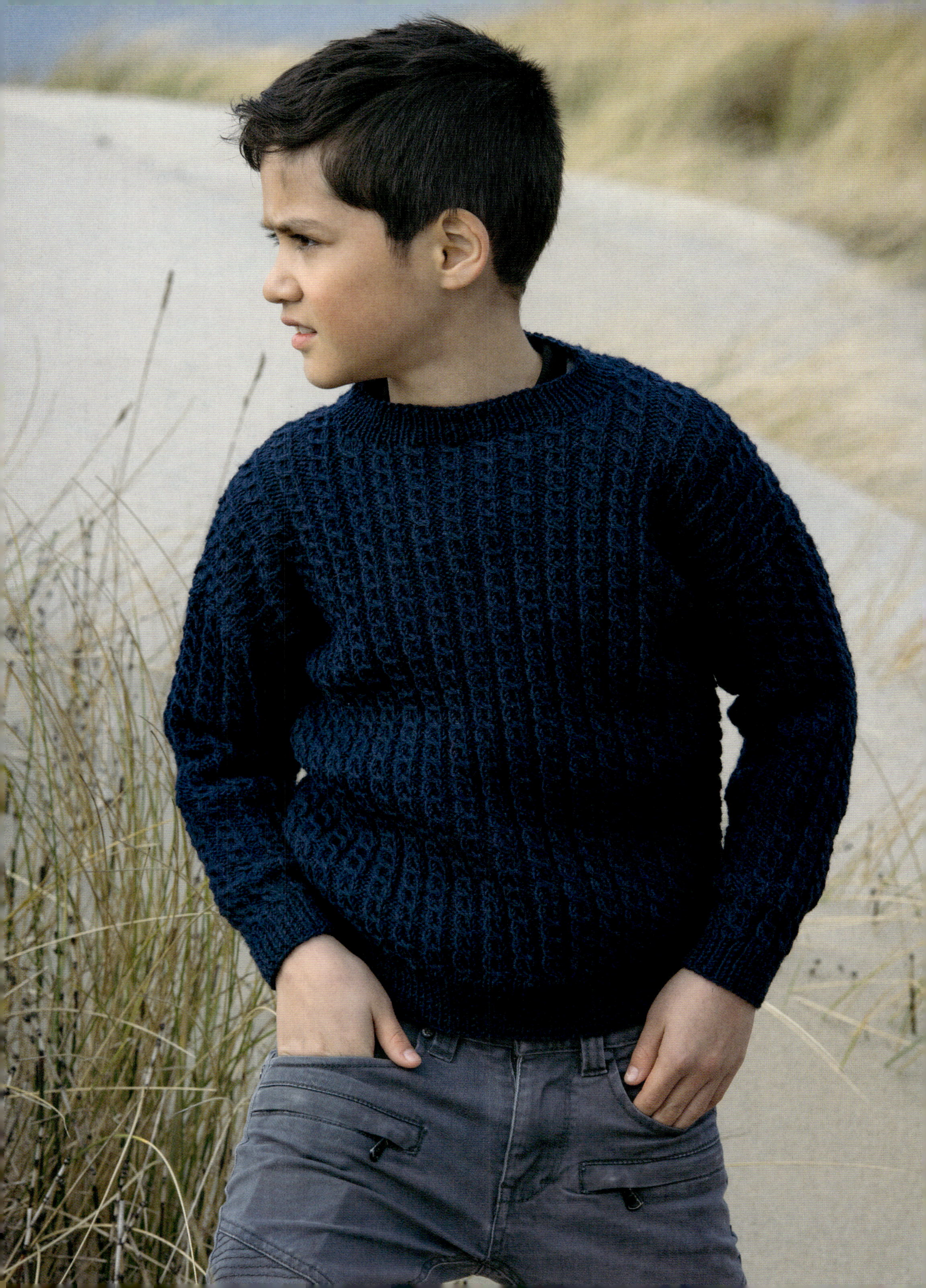

OOSTEREND 2 GANSEY

CHEST: 74CM + 4CM = 78CM (30¼IN). TOTAL HEIGHT: 44–45CM (17⁵⁄₁₆–17¾IN) (CHILD'S GANSEY)

Note: The cable is made by slipping 1 st on the cable needle and crossing it over 3 sts to the left. Knit a swatch first, with different sized needles if necessary. A gansey should not be too loosely knit. Follow the chart for the motif and adjust the width and/or height to your size, the yarn used and your tension/gauge. Follow the general instructions for the gansey on pages 54–55 and adjust where necessary.

DETAIL FROM FIG. 152

Measurements

WIDTH: 2 × 39 = 78cm (30¼in)
SHOULDERS: 12.5cm (5in)
NECK: 13cm (5⅛in)
NECKLINE DEPTH: 4–5cm (1½–2in)
ARMHOLE HEIGHT: 15cm (6in)
HEIGHT UP TO ARMHOLE, EXCL. RIBBING: 25cm (9¾in)
SLEEVE LENGTH, EXCL. RIBBING: 28cm (11in)
WRIST CIRCUMFERENCE: approx. 14cm (5½in)
RIBBING: according to preference, 3–4cm (1⅛–1½in)

Materials

- 400g (14oz) 5-ply Frangipani Guernsey Wool, navy; or bulky 100% pure wool yarn (100g (3½oz) = approx. 195m (213¼yds))
- Circular needles, 2.5 and 3mm (US 1 and 2)
- Straight knitting needles, 3mm (US 2)
- Cable needle

TENSION/GAUGE: 21 st × 32 rows on 3mm (US 2) needles = 10 × 10cm (4 × 4in)

RIBBING: k1, p1

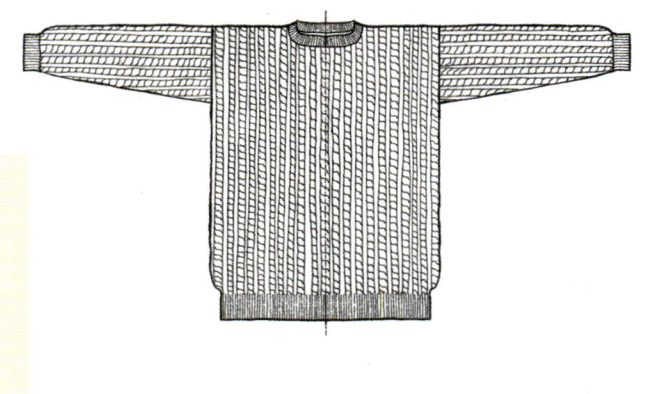

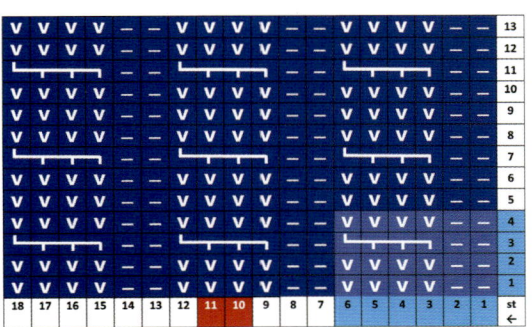

OOSTEREND 3 GANSEY

This sweater has not been completely knit, but the chart, the sketch and the swatch should give you enough information to get started. Knit a swatch first, with different sized needles if necessary. A gansey should not be too loosely knit. Follow the chart for the motif and adjust the width and/or height to your size, the yarn used and your tension/gauge. Follow the general instructions for the gansey on pages 54–55 and adjust where necessary.

Materials

- ∞ Approx. 750g (26½oz) SMC Merino Extrafine 120, cloud blue 0156; or 100% merino yarn (50g (1¾oz) = approx. 120m (131¼yds))
- ∞ Circular needles, 3 and 3.5mm (US 2 and 4)
- ∞ Straight knitting needles, 3.5mm (US 4)
- ∞ Cable needle

TENSION/GAUGE: 26 st x 34 rows on 3.5mm (US 4) needles = 10 x 10cm (4 x 4in)

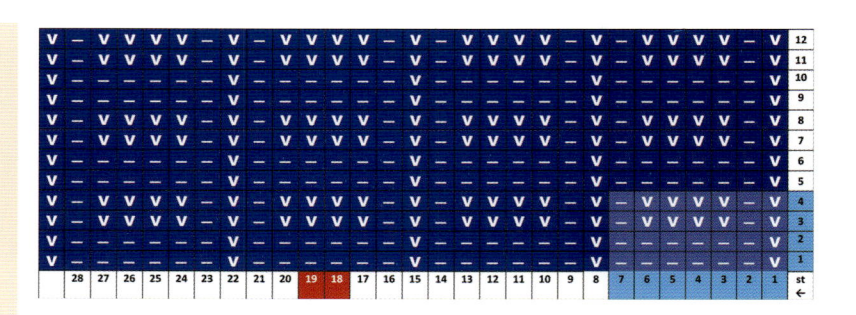

FRONT

BACK

153 FISHERMAN KLAAS VLAS OF THE TX 15, OOSTEREND, TEXEL, CA. 1930. MUSEUM KAAP SKIL, OUDESCHILD

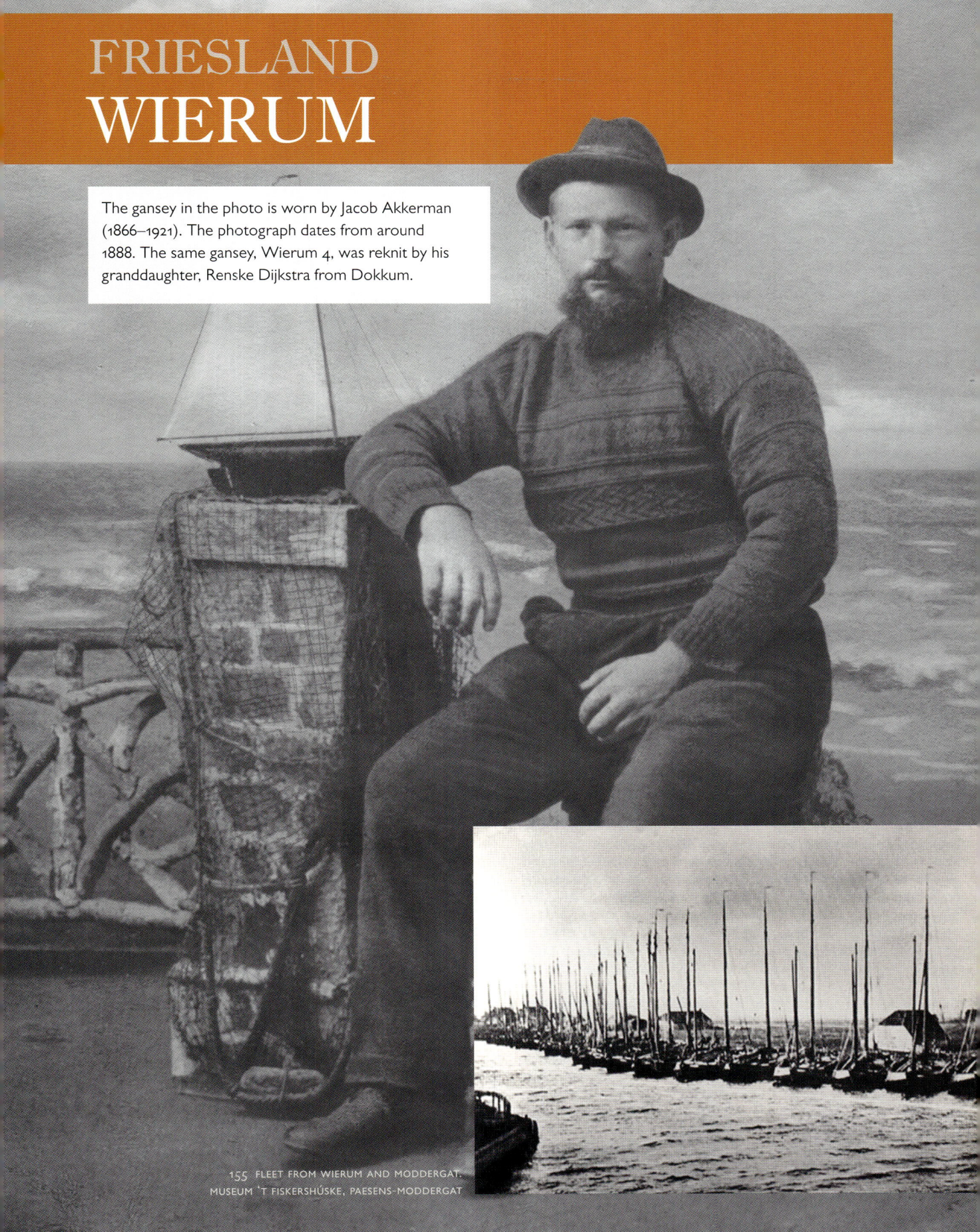

154 JACOB AKKERMAN. COURTESY OF MRS RENSKE DIJKSTRA, DOKKUM THROUGH MUSEUM 'T FISKERSHÚSKE, PAESENS-MODDERGAT

FRIESLAND
WIERUM

The gansey in the photo is worn by Jacob Akkerman (1866–1921). The photograph dates from around 1888. The same gansey, Wierum 4, was reknit by his granddaughter, Renske Dijkstra from Dokkum.

155 FLEET FROM WIERUM AND MODDERGAT. MUSEUM 'T FISKERSHÚSKE, PAESENS-MODDERGAT

THE GANSEYS, WIERUM 1, 2 AND 3, CAN BE FOUND ON PAGES 121–124 OF *DUTCH TRADITIONAL GANSEYS*.

WIERUM 4 GANSEY

CHEST: 102CM + 6CM = 108CM (42½IN). TOTAL HEIGHT: 68CM (26¾IN)

Knit a swatch first, with different sized needles if necessary. A gansey should not be too loosely knit. Follow the chart for the motif and adjust the width and/or height to your size, the yarn used and your tension/gauge. Follow the general instructions for the gansey on pages 54–55 and adjust where necessary.

Measurements

WIDTH: 2 x 54 = 108cm (42½in)
SHOULDERS: 17.5cm (6⅝in)
NECK: 19cm (7½in)
NECKLINE DEPTH: 6–7cm (2⅜–2¾in)
ARMHOLE HEIGHT: 23–24cm (9–9½in)
HEIGHT UP TO ARMHOLE, EXCL. RIBBING: 41cm (16⅛in)
SLEEVE LENGTH, EXCL. RIBBING: 43cm (17in)
WRIST CIRCUMFERENCE: approx. 23cm (9in)
RIBBING: according to preference, 6–8cm (2⅜–3⅛in)

Materials

∞ Approx. 850g (30oz) Scheepjeswol Zuiderzee, cornflower blue; or 100% pure wool yarn (100g (3½oz) = approx. 200m (219yds))
∞ Circular needles, 3 and 3.5mm (US 2 and 4)
∞ Straight knitting needles, 3.5mm (US 4)

TENSION/GAUGE: 21 st x 30 rows on 3.5mm (US 4) needles = 10 x 10cm (4 x 4in)
RIBBING: k2, p2

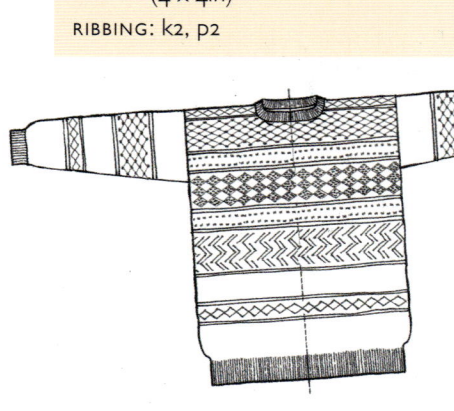

156 CHURCH OF WIERUM

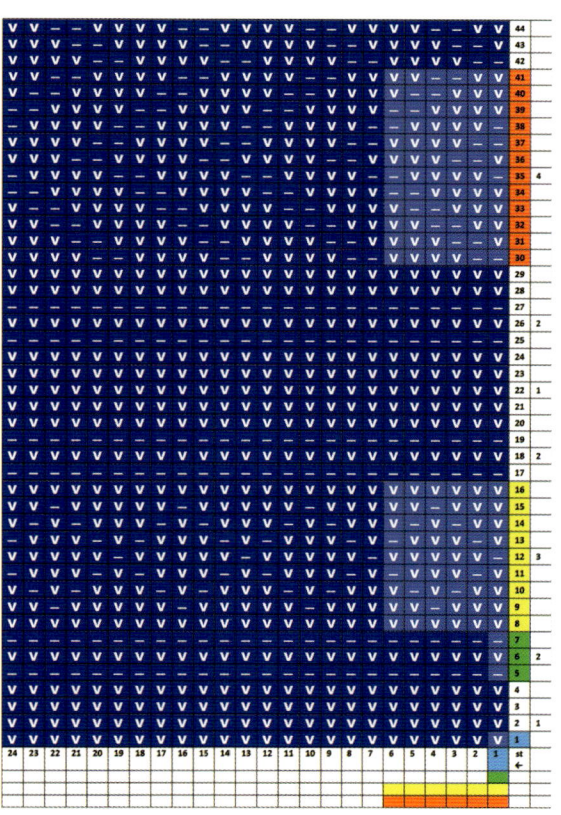

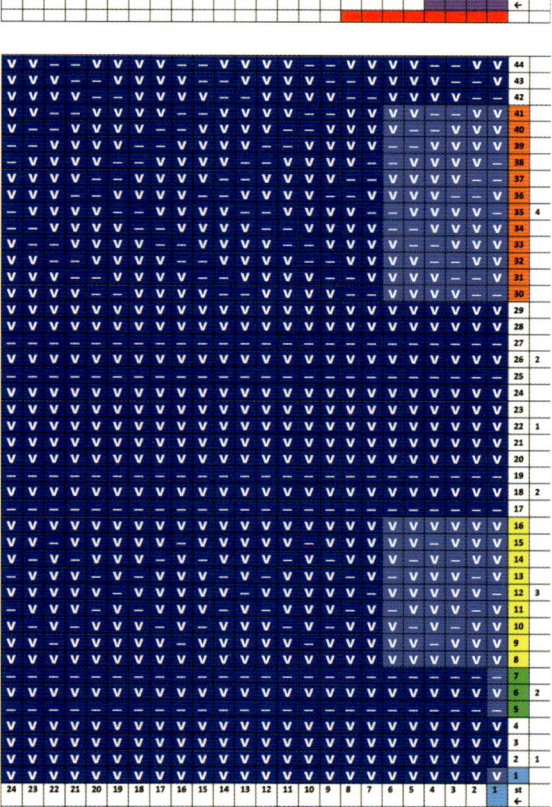

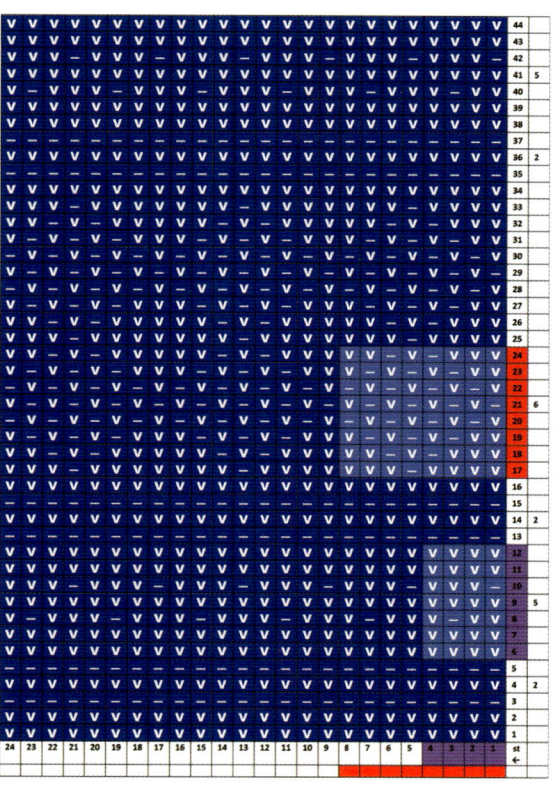

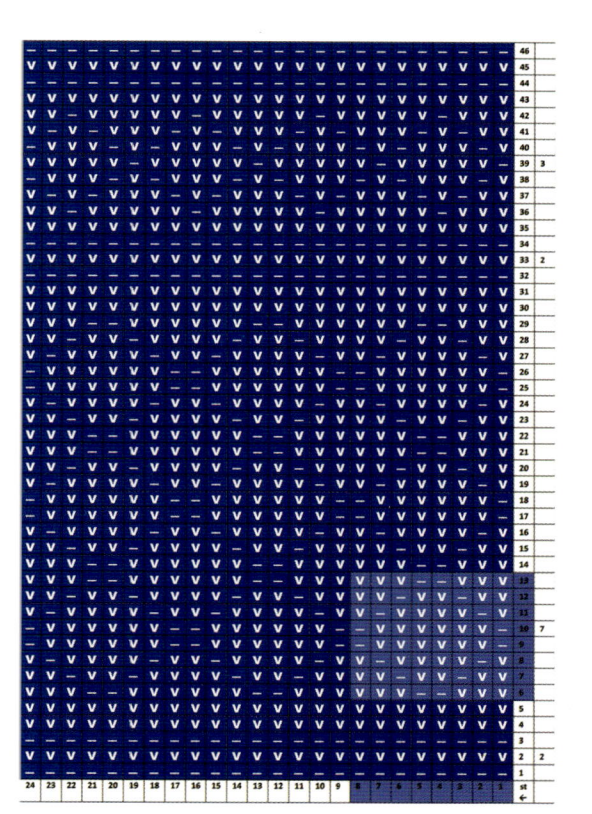

FISHERMEN WITH THEIR CATCH IN THE PORT OF LEMMER

7 ZUIDERZEE COAST

Around 1900, the Zuiderzee ports earned most of their money from fishing for Zuiderzee herring and anchovy. Anchovy or sardel (*Engraulis encrasicholus*) originate in the Mediterranean, but during the mating season hundreds of thousands of them swim up the Atlantic Ocean in large schools to spawn in the coves. The Zuiderzee was one of these spawning areas, before it was closed off from the sea in 1932 by the construction of the Afsluitdijk and renamed IJsselmeer. The anchovy was preceded by garfish, a much larger fish. If that fish was caught, chances were that anchovy would follow. All the coastal towns would then exchange their herring nets for anchovy nets, which had smaller mesh. The herring season ran from February to April, and the anchovy season from the end of April to July. In contrast to the North Sea herring, the Zuiderzee herring was unsuitable for gutting and salting, but it was very suitable for smoking (see page 27). After 1932, many smokehouses along the Zuiderzee would switch to smoking eel from the IJsselmeer and fish from the North Sea.

In the year before it was closed off, fishermen were allowed to 'empty' the Zuiderzee, because it would eventually be reclaimed. This meant a record number of catches. After the completion of the Afsluitdijk, the salinity in the water reduced over a period of 10 to 15 years. The result was that most of the species disappeared. Only eel, pike perch and smelt managed to stand ground. Thousands of fishermen lost their livelihood and had to turn to other sources of income. Initially, they would receive a small allowance from the Zuiderzee Fund. All the fishing ports along the former Zuiderzee disappeared and became marinas for pleasure yachting, with the exception of Urk.

From Workum, a lot of eel – not only caught in the Netherlands, but also imported from Denmark – was exported to England by so-called eel barges. Most of the pictures that were found there show fishermen in machine-knit English jerseys.

NORTH HOLLAND
WERVERSHOOF & MEDEMBLIK

In May and June, many towns in North Holland would fish for anchovy: Schermerhorn, Hoogwoud, Broek op Langedijk, Zuid-Scharwoude, Venhuizen, Bovenkarspel, Andijk, Wervershoof, Medemblik, Nieuwe Niedorp, Winkel and Callantsoog. Not only fishermen, but also gardeners, lockkeepers, hotelkeepers, fairground workers, sea carriers, and those with various other occupations went out fishing. Andijk had 40 flatboats, which were used on inland waterways for the rest of the year. The boats used for anchovy fishing were seaworthy rowing boats, 5 to 7.5 metres (5½ to 8¼ yards) long. The fishermen would put the nets out at night and haul them in the next morning. A new anchovy net would cost around 7 Dutch guilders, just for the netting. Ropes and anchors would cost a similar amount. A float line of four nets cost 40 to 45 guilders, and a longliner (page 26) from 300 up to 500 guilders. Around 30 to 50 nets were required, which meant that apart from the money to buy a ship, fishermen would need to invest another 500 to 700 guilders. If the catch was poor, these 'occasional' fishermen would lose quite a lot of money. In addition, they might lose around 300 guilders worth in nets because of natural tearing, storms or because they sailed over them.

Medemblik is the oldest city of West-Friesland. Since the opening of the Noord-Holland Canal in 1824, Medemblik was no longer on the sailing route to Amsterdam and the port fell into disuse. Only after 1880 did activity in the port pick up again, because of the emergence of anchovy fishing. The catches from, for example, Wervershoof and Andijk were sold at the fish auction in Medemblik.

157 (BOTTOM LEFT) BARRELS OF ANCHOVY NEAR THE FISH AUCTION OF MEDEMBLIK AT THE EASTERN PORT. THIRD FROM THE RIGHT IS KLAAS MOL JNZ.

158 DORUS BERKHOUT ON HIS SMACK WF 19 IN ITS HOME PORT OF MEDEMBLIK, CA. 1955. OUD WERVERSHOOF

WERVERSHOOF GANSEY

CHEST: 102CM + 6CM = 108CM (42½IN). TOTAL HEIGHT: 70CM (27½IN).

Knit a swatch first, with different sized needles if necessary. A gansey should not be too loosely knit. Follow the chart for the motif and adjust the width and/or height to your size, the yarn used and your tension/gauge. Follow the general instructions for the gansey on pages 54–55 and adjust where necessary.

Measurements

WIDTH: 2 × 54 = 108cm (42½in)
SHOULDERS: 17.5cm (6⅝in)
NECK: 19cm (7½in)
NECKLINE DEPTH: 6–7cm (2⅜–2¾in)
ARMHOLE HEIGHT: 23–24cm (9–9½in)
HEIGHT UP TO ARMHOLE, EXCL. RIBBING: 41cm (16⅛in)
SLEEVE LENGTH, EXCL. RIBBING: 43cm (17in)
WRIST CIRCUMFERENCE: approx. 23cm (9in)
RIBBING: according to preference, 6–8cm (2⅜–3⅛in)

159 MEINDERT SCHUITEMAKER WITH A WF 1 DINGHY FROM STAVEREN, UNLOADING ITS ANCHOVY AT THE FISH AUCTION IN MEDEMBLIK. FROM LEFT TO RIGHT: JAPIE DEKKER (CRUBUS), MEINDERT SCHUITEMAKER AND HIS SON AB. OUD WERVERSHOOF

Materials

- Approx. 800g (28¼oz) Lang Merino 150, dark blue 0035; or 100% merino yarn (50g (1¾oz) = approx. 150m (164yds))
- Circular needles, 3 and 3.5mm (US 2 and 4)
- Straight knitting needles, 3.5mm (US 4)

TENSION/GAUGE: 27 st in 37 rows on 3.5mm (US 4) needles = 10 × 10cm (4 × 4in)

RIBBING: k2, p2

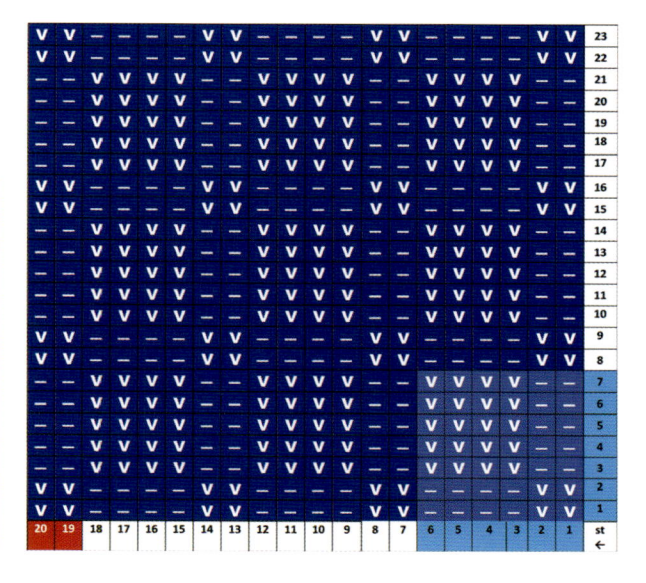

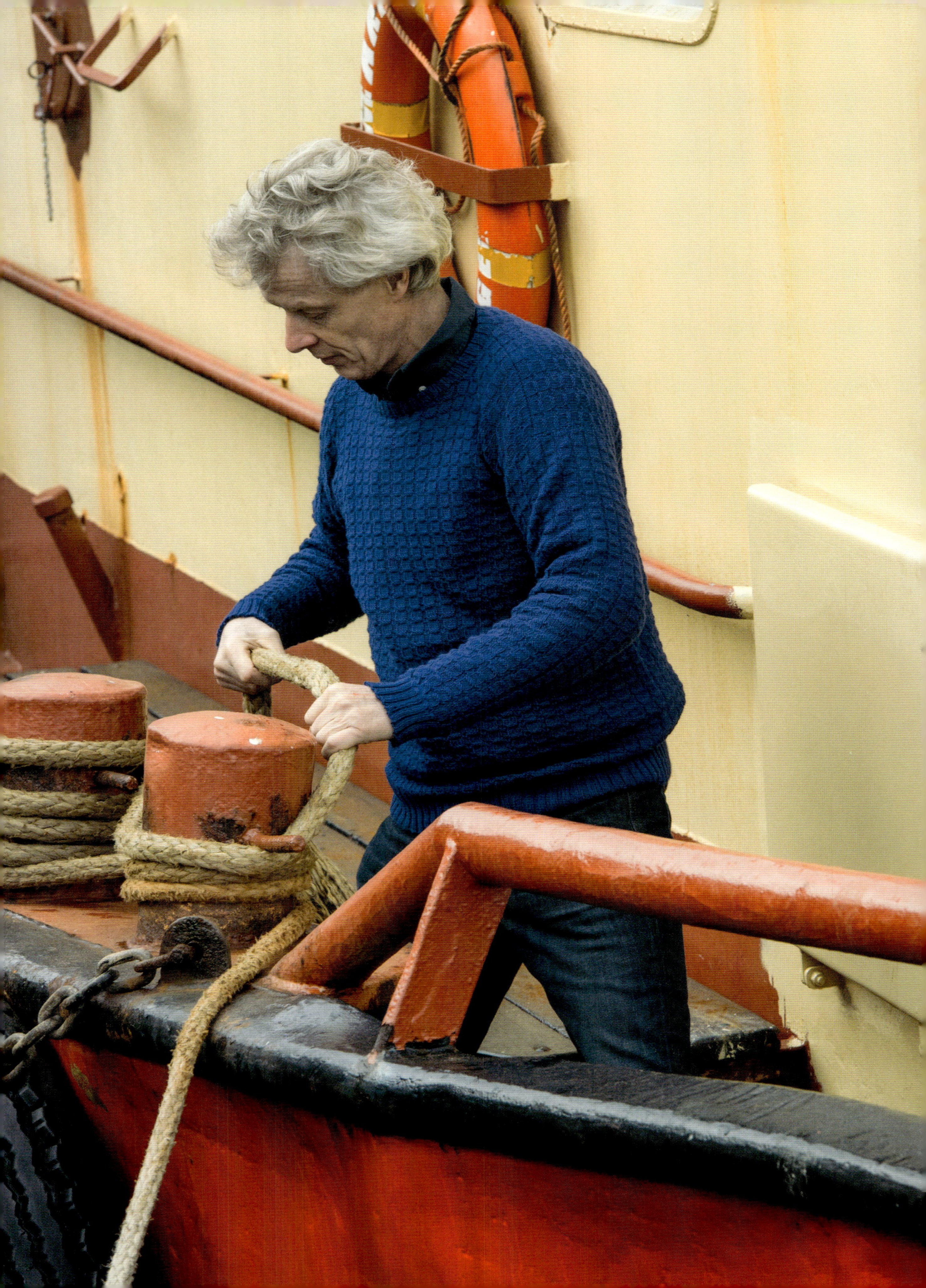

NORTH HOLLAND
ENKHUIZEN

160 FISHERMEN FROM ENKHUIZEN, CA. 1900.
STICHTING ZUIDERZEEAMBACHTEN, ENKHUIZEN

161 THE NETS ARE MADE SEA-PROOF IN A TANNERY IN ENKHUIZEN, CA. 1930. STICHTING ZUIDERZEEAMBACHTEN ENKHUIZEN

Enkhuizen was the main fishing town on the Zuiderzee; it had a huge fleet of herring buses, which were burnt in the bay of Lerwick on the Shetland Islands in 1704 by French privateers. It meant the end of herring fishing for Enkhuizen, which changed to fishing for anchovy in the Zuiderzee. In 1930, as a farewell to the Zuiderzee – which, after the completion of the Afsluitdijk in 1932, turned from an open, salt-water sea into the sweet-water IJsselmeer – the large Zuiderzee Fisheries Exhibition was held. Almost all of the Zuiderzee fishermen were forced to find other jobs. In 1948, the Zuiderzee Museum was opened in Enkhuizen, as a testament to the Zuiderzee fishing culture in the period 1880–1932. The open-air museum was added in 1983.

THE GANSEY, ENKHUIZEN 1, AND THE SKETCH AND CHART FOR ENKHUIZEN 2, CAN BE FOUND ON PAGES 142–143 OF *DUTCH TRADITIONAL GANSEYS*.

ENKHUIZEN 3 GANSEY

CHEST: 94CM + 6CM = 100CM (39⅜IN). TOTAL HEIGHT: 68CM (26¾IN).

Knit a swatch first, with different sized needles if necessary. A gansey should not be too loosely knit. Follow the chart for the motif and adjust the width and/or height to your size, the yarn used and your tension/gauge. Follow the general instructions for the gansey on pages 54–55 and adjust where necessary.

Measurements

- WIDTH: 2 x 50 = 100cm (39³⁄₈in)
- SHOULDERS: 16.5cm (6½in)
- NECK: 17cm (6¾in)
- NECKLINE DEPTH: 5–6cm (2–2³⁄₈in)
- ARMHOLE HEIGHT: 21–22cm (8¼–8¾in)
- HEIGHT UP TO ARMHOLE, EXCL. RIBBING: 41cm (16⅛in)
- SLEEVE LENGTH, EXCL. RIBBING: 43cm (17in)
- WRIST CIRCUMFERENCE: approx. 22cm (8¾in)
- RIBBING: according to preference, 5–8cm (2–3⅛in)

Materials

- 900g (31¾oz) Hjertegarn Vital, 6500; or 100% pure superwash wool yarn (50g (1¾oz) = approx. 150m (164yds))
- Circular needles, 3 and 3.5mm (US 2 and 4)
- Straight knitting needles, 3.5mm (US 4)
- Cable needle

TENSION/GAUGE: 24 st x 30 rows on 3.5mm (US 4) needles = 10 x 10cm (4 x 4in)

RIBBING: K2, p2

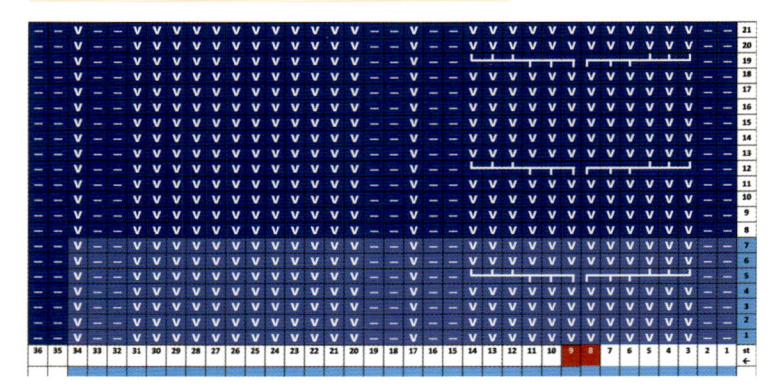

162 PIETER JOHANNES VAN DER MOLEN, A FISHERMAN FROM ENKHUIZEN, CA. 1950. ZUIDERZEEMUSEUM, ENKHUIZEN

Calculating the saddle shoulder

Work the sweater as indicated in the book, up to where you split the front and back. You have already calculated the armhole height. Measure the width of the saddle shoulder. In this case, this is the width of the middle cable of the sweater (sts 3 to 19, plus sts 15 to 19 of the pattern). In this case, the saddle is 9cm (3½in). Divide the result by two (9cm/2 = 4.5cm (1¾in)). Deduct the result from the armhole height. Here, the armhole height is 21cm (8¼in). This means: 21 – 4.5cm = 16.5cm (6½in).

Work until you reach the armhole height calculated (in this case: 16.5cm (6½in)), for both the back and the front pieces. Don't forget to decrease for the neckline on the front piece. Work the last row of both the back and the front pieces with a smaller-size needles.

Knitting the saddle shoulder

Use circular needles in the size used for the gansey. Pick up the shoulder stitches from the back and the front pieces, on the same circular needle, as follows: start at the neckline, work along the back towards the armhole and work along the front to the neckline. The tips of the needles both point towards the neck opening and the cable is at the armhole side. On the left needle, cast on the number of stitches you need for the saddle shoulder plus 2 sts. Note: Because you are now working top-down, you will be knitting a mirror image of the cable.

1. *K1, work the sts of the saddle shoulder in pattern and knit the last st of the saddle shoulder together with the first st of the sweater piece, through the back loop.
2. Turn the work, slip the first st k-wise, work in pattern until the last st of the saddle shoulder and purl the last st of the saddle shoulder together with the first st of the sweater piece.
3. Turn the work, slip the first st k-wise, work in pattern until the last st of the saddle shoulder and knit the last st of the saddle shoulder together with the first 2 sts of the sweater piece through the back loop.
4. Turn the work, slip the first st k-wise, work in pattern until the last st of the saddle shoulder and **purl** the last st of the saddle shoulder together with the first 2 sts of the sweater piece. Turn the work and slip the first st k-wise.* Repeat these four rows until you have no sts left of the sweater pieces.

Cut the yarn and leave the sts on the needle. Knit the second saddle shoulder in the same way.

You can now pick up the sts for the sleeve and knit the sleeve top-down. Start the sleeve pattern from the row that follows on from the last saddle shoulder row.

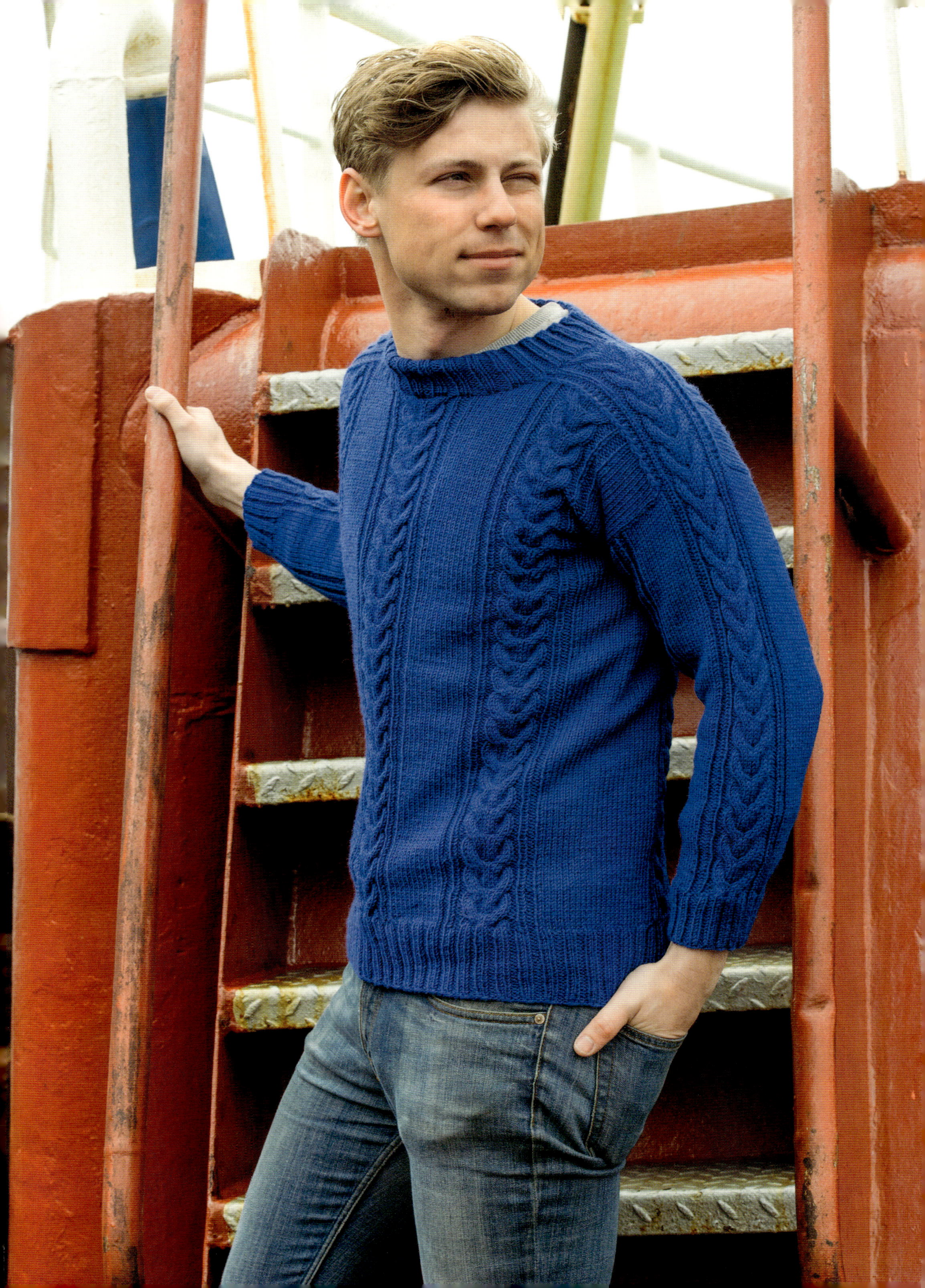

163 KLAAS BLOKKER, ONE OF THE LAST FISHERMEN FROM HOORN, CA. 1950. STICHTING ZUIDERZEEAMBACHTEN ENKHUIZEN

NORTH HOLLAND
HOORN

Hoorn has a glorious past. In the sixteenth and seventeenth centuries, Hoorn was one of the cities that was represented in the Dutch East India Company (VOC). The headquarters of the West India Company (WIC), the Nordic Compagnie (or Compagnie Spitzbergen), the Admiralty of the Northern Quarters, the West Frisian Mint (alternating with Enkhuizen), the College of Delegated Councils of West-Friesland and the Northern Quarter were also found here. Hoorn was the formal capital of the region north of the river IJ, which is still visible in the monumental and historic buildings in the town centre. Jan Pieterszoon Coen came from Hoorn. Captains Jacob le Maire and Willem Cornelisz Schouten from Hoorn were the first captains to sail to the southernmost point of South America with their ships *Hoorn* and *Eendracht*. They called this point Cape Horn, after their hometown.

In the eighteenth century, the ports silted up. The ships sailed on to Amsterdam or Zaandam, where, as well as in the neighbouring town of Oostzaan, ships were built and repaired. Under the French, the city became run down. In the nineteenth century, Hoorn again became a trading city with a regional function.

The fishing industry around Hoorn was small in scale and limited to anchovy and eel in the Zuiderzee/IJsselmeer.

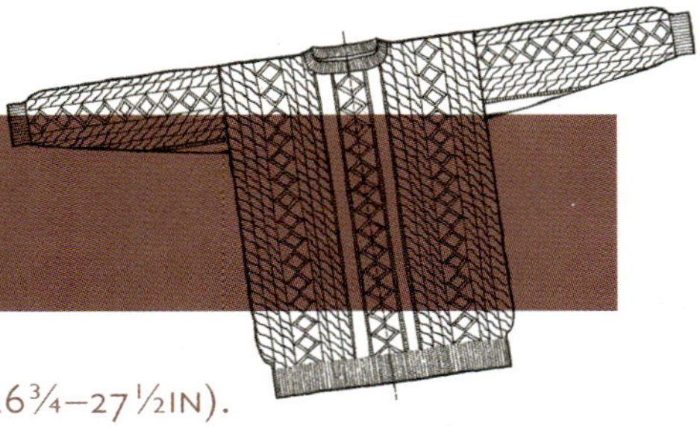

HOORN GANSEY

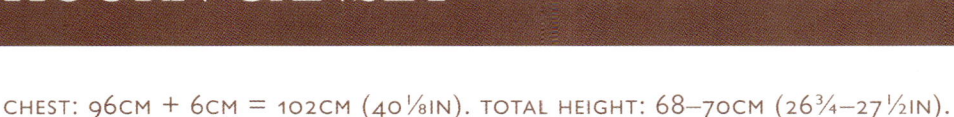

CHEST: 96CM + 6CM = 102CM (40⅛IN). TOTAL HEIGHT: 68–70CM (26¾–27½IN).

Knit a swatch first, with different sized needles if necessary. A gansey should not be too loosely knit. Follow the chart for the motif and adjust the width and/or height to your size, the yarn used and your tension/gauge. Follow the general instructions for the gansey on pages 54–55 and adjust where necessary.

Measurements

WIDTH: 2 × 51 = 102cm (40⅛in)
SHOULDERS: 16.5cm (6½in)
NECK: 17cm (6¾in)
NECKLINE DEPTH: 5–6cm (2–2⅜in)
ARMHOLE HEIGHT: 22–23cm (8¾–9in)
HEIGHT UP TO ARMHOLE, EXCL. RIBBING: 41cm (16⅛in)
SLEEVE LENGTH, EXCL. RIBBING: 43cm (17in)
WRIST CIRCUMFERENCE: approx. 22cm (8¾in)
RIBBING: according to preference, 5–8cm (2–3⅛in)

Materials

- Approx. 750g (26½oz) SMC Merino Extrafine 120, navy 0155; or 100% merino yarn (50g (1¾oz = approx. 120m (131¼oz))
- Circular needles, 3 and 3.5mm (US 2 and 4)
- Straight knitting needles, 3.5mm (US 4)
- Cable needle

TENSION/GAUGE: 26 st × 34 rows on 3.5mm (US 4) needles = 10 × 10cm (4 × 4in)
RIBBING: k2, p2

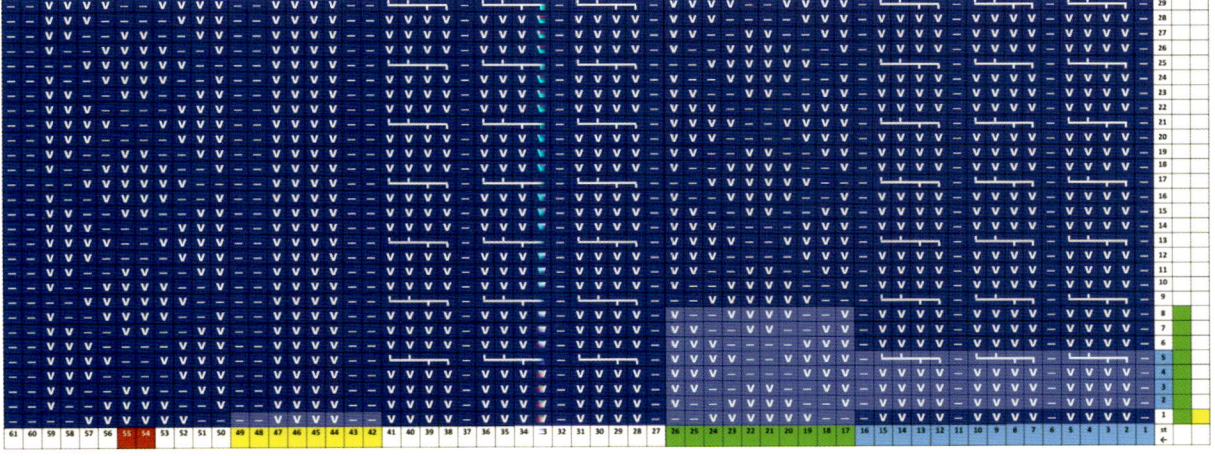

NORTH HOLLAND
VOLENDAM

164 FISHERMEN IN THE PORT OF VOLENDAM. STICHTING ZUIDERZEEAMBACHTEN ENKHUIZEN

165 FISHERMAN FROM VOLENDAM, CA. 1920. COURTESY OF LAU SOMBROEK

Volendam is one of the few fishing villages with a Catholic population. Only in Volendam did the gansey remain part of the traditional costume, as a result of which many authentic ganseys are preserved in the Volendam Museum. The Volendam traditional dress has become a national costume and is recognised all over the world as Dutch.

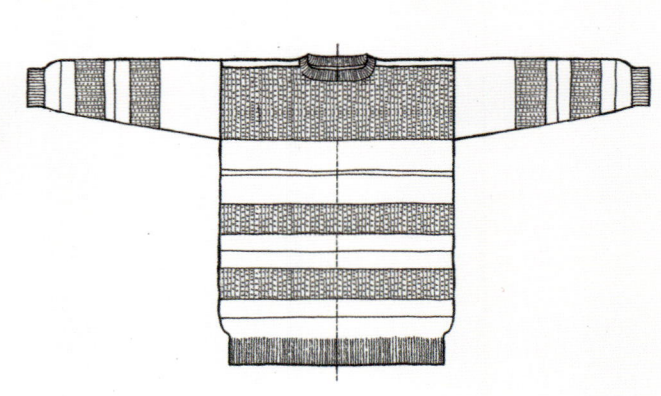

140

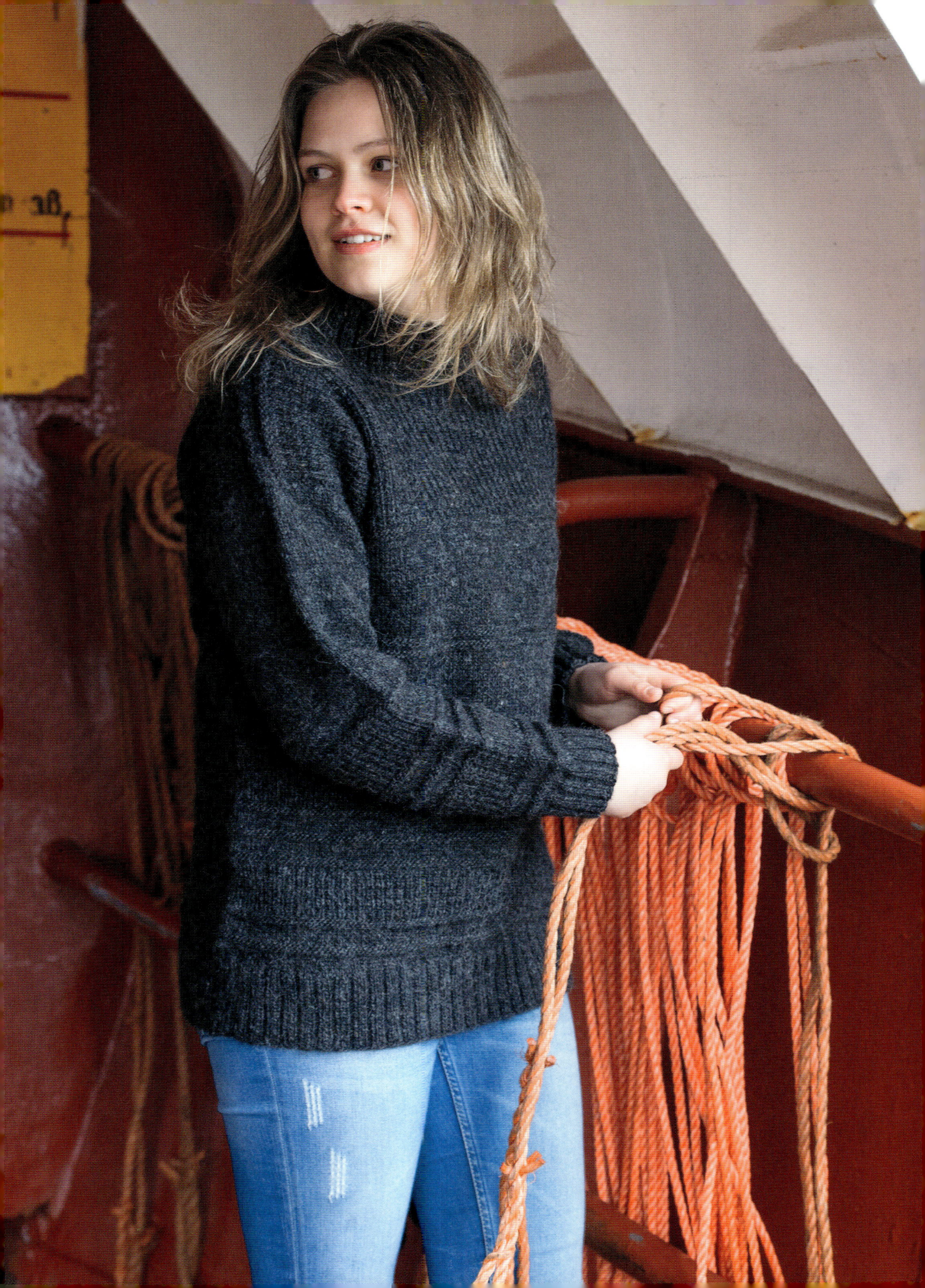

THE GANSEY, VOLENDAM 1, CAN BE FOUND ON PAGES 146–147 OF *DUTCH TRADITIONAL GANSEYS*.

VOLENDAM 2 GANSEY

CHEST: 94CM + 6CM = 100CM (39⅜IN). TOTAL HEIGHT: 68–70CM (26¾–27½IN).

Knit a swatch first, with different sized needles if necessary. A gansey should not be too loosely knit. Follow the chart for the motif and adjust the width and/or height to your size, the yarn used and your tension/gauge. Follow the general instructions for the gansey on pages 54–55 and adjust where necessary.

Measurements

WIDTH: 2 × 50 = 100cm (39⅜in)
SHOULDERS: 16.5cm (6½in)
NECK: 17cm (6¾in)
NECKLINE DEPTH: 5–6cm (2–2⅜in)
ARMHOLE HEIGHT: 21–22cm (8¼–8¾in)
HEIGHT UP TO ARMHOLE, EXCL. RIBBING: 41cm (16⅛in)
SLEEVE LENGTH, EXCL. RIBBING: 43cm (17in)
WRIST CIRCUMFERENCE: approx. 22cm (8¾in)
RIBBING: according to preference, 5–8cm (2–3⅛in)

Materials

∞ Approx. 650g (23oz) Léttlopi, dark grey heather 0058; or 100% pure wool yarn (50g (1¾oz) = 100m (110yds))
∞ Circular needles, 3 and 3.5mm (US 2 and 4)
∞ Straight knitting needles. 3.5mm

TENSION/GAUGE: 23 st × 32 rows on 3.5mm (US 4) needles = 10 × 10cm (4 × 4in)

RIBBING: k2, p2

166 GROUP OF MEN IN FOREGROUND, CLOCKWISE FROM LEFT: JAN SUL 'SULLETJE', FISHERMAN (1876–1937); KEES VAN DIRK DE BOER, FISHERMAN (1869–1925), WHO DIED UNEXPECTEDLY ON SEPTEMBER 4 1925 WHILE AT THE HELM OF THE BARGE; THAMES FLAT, ALIAS 'THAMES VET', BACHELOR; AND KEES BIEN, FISHING HAND (1872–1953), MARRIED TO AGIE VAN DE KOOLSNIJER. IN THE BACKGROUND: HUIBERTJE BOND ('HUIP VAN OUWE HEIN') (1878–1957). CA. 1920. WATERLANDS ARCHIEF, PURMEREND

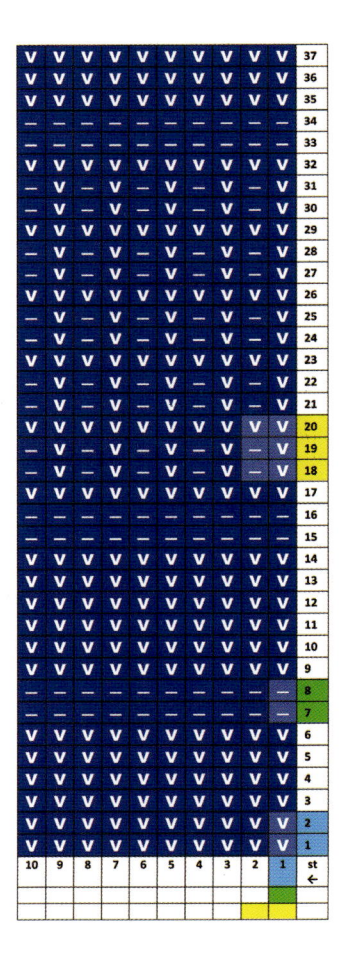

NORTH HOLLAND
MARKEN

167 COUPLE FROM MARKEN, CA. 1900.
ZUIDERZEEMUSEUM, ENKHUIZEN

Although the residents of Marken had been fishing for centuries – since the soil was unsuitable for farming, due to the number of floods in the area – the first port was not built until 1830. Many captains and chief mates of whalers came from Marken. On May 28, 1932, the last hole in the Afsluitdijk was closed. The new dyke stopped herring and anchovy on their way to their original spawning grounds in the Zuiderzee. Many fishermen from Marken joined the herring luggers in Vlaardingen and IJmuiden, but many others gave up on fishing altogether.

Marken had, and still has, a beautiful traditional costume. A special part of this costume is the Itse hat with multicoloured motifs, which is worn by the men in both summer and winter. The hats originally come from Fair Isle, one of the Shetland Islands; the fishermen from Marken called the Shetland Islands (H)itland – hence the Itse hat. When fishermen signed on with the North Sea luggers, they would go fishing north of Scotland, using Lerwick as a base port. From there they brought back mittens, stockings and hats. The winter hat consists of two pieces that are knitted together. The solid-colour part is folded to the inside, creating a double hat. The summer hat does not have the bottom half.

THE GANSEY, MARKEN 1, CAN BE FOUND ON PAGE 151 OF *DUTCH TRADITIONAL GANSEYS*.

MARKEN 2 GANSEY

CHEST: 90CM + 6CM = 96CM (37¾IN). TOTAL HEIGHT: 68CM (26¾IN).

This gansey is so special because of the name that has been worked on the chest, which cannot be seen clearly in the yarn used here. Knit a swatch first, with different sized needles if necessary. A gansey should not be too loosely knit. Follow the chart for the motif and adjust the width and/or height to your size, the yarn used and your tension/gauge. Follow the general instructions for the gansey on pages 54–55 and adjust where necessary

Measurements

WIDTH: 2 x 48 = 96cm (37¾in)
SHOULDERS: 15.5cm (6⅛in)
NECK: 17cm (6¾in)
NECKLINE DEPTH: 5–6cm (2–2⅜in)
ARMHOLE HEIGHT: 22cm (8¾in)
HEIGHT UP TO ARMHOLE, EXCL. RIBBING: 41cm (16⅛in)
SLEEVE LENGTH, EXCL. RIBBING: 43cm (approx. 17in)
WRIST CIRCUMFERENCE: approx. 22cm (8¾in)
RIBBING: according to preference, 5–8cm (2–3⅛in)

ALPHABET AND NUMBER. EXPERIMENT WITH OTHER TYPEFACES YOURSELF

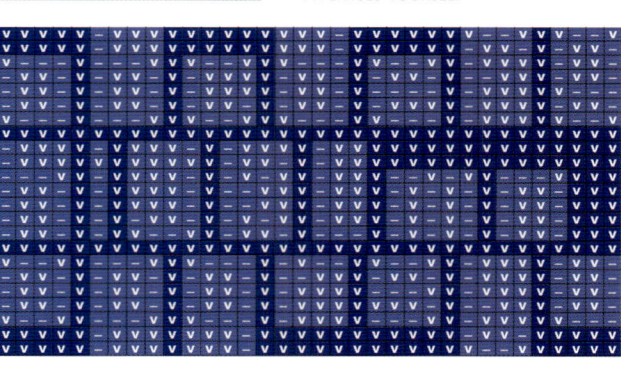

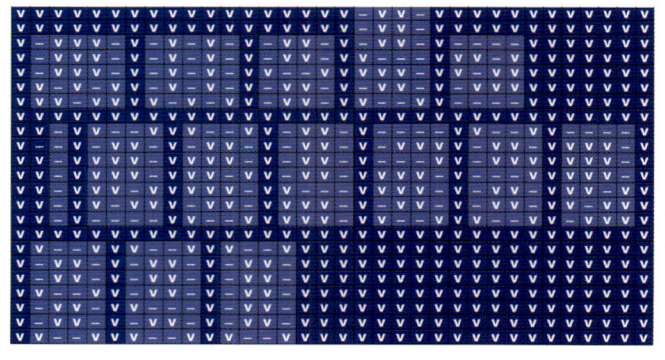

Materials

∞ Approx. 500g (17⅝oz) Lopi Einband, royal blue 9277; or 100% pure wool yarn (50g (1¾oz) = approx. 225m (246yds))
∞ Circular needles, 2 and 2.5mm (US 0 and 1)
∞ Straight knitting needles, 2.5mm (US 1)

TENSION/GAUGE: 33 st x 54 rows on 2.5mm (US 1) needles = 10 x 10cm (4 x 4in)

RIBBING: K2, p2

168 ITSE HAT. DUTCH OPEN AIR MUSEUM, ARNHEM

144

NORTH HOLLAND
HUIZEN

Huizen was one of the most important fishing towns on the Zuiderzee. The first port was built in 1854, which boosted the fisheries. The fleet consists of approximately 190 barges. The fishermen from Huizen mainly fished on the Zuiderzee and to a limited extent also on the North Sea. The fisheries created a flourishing fishing industry, also including related businesses such as preservation houses, shipyards, shipping companies, tanneries (preparation of the nets by boiling them in tan), basket makers, export firms, etc. In Huizen, there were 18 large fish smokehouses, or *hangens*, which mainly produced kippers for export to Germany. These hangens were run by *hangebazen* ('hang bosses'), who were not always very popular. Most workers were women who would, once the catch came in, work late into the night, for hours on end, to clean and spit the fish (this involved stringing the fish onto a wooden spit, 20 at a time, to be hung over a smouldering fire to smoke – see also Fig. 82 on page 43), for which they were paid per spit.

Characteristic for Huizen were the peddlers or porters, selling fish door to door. They were also employed by the kipper smokehouses and by fishermen from elsewhere.

At the start of the twentieth century, the fisheries were already in decline because Germany had banned the import of Dutch kippers, in an effort to become more autonomous. The construction of the Afsluitdijk was the nail in the coffin.

In Huizen, nobody remembers whether ganseys were worn, because they are not a part of the Huizer costume.

169 FISHERMEN ON A BARGE FROM HUIZEN. HUIZER MUSEUM, HUIZEN

HUIZEN 1 GANSEY

CHEST: 96CM + 6CM = 102CM (40⅛IN). TOTAL HEIGHT: 68–70CM (26¾–27½IN).

The gansey in the old photograph has short sleeves and was clearly a summer sweater. Here, it has been knit with long sleeves. Knit a swatch first, with different sized needles if necessary. A gansey should not be too loosely knit. Follow the chart for the motif and adjust the width and/or height to your size, the yarn used and your tension/gauge. Follow the general instructions for the gansey on pages 54-55 and adjust where necessary.

Measurements

WIDTH: 2 x 51 = 102cm (40⅛in)
SHOULDERS: 16.5cm (6½in)
NECK: 17cm (6¾in)
NECKLINE DEPTH: 5–6cm (2–2⅜in)
ARMHOLE HEIGHT: 22–23cm (8¾–9in)
HEIGHT UP TO ARMHOLE, EXCL. RIBBING: 41cm (16⅛in)
SLEEVE LENGTH, EXCL. RIBBING: 43cm (17in)
WRIST CIRCUMFERENCE: approx. 23cm (9in)
RIBBING: according to preference, 5–8cm (2–3⅛in)

Materials

∞ 750g (26½oz) Lang Merino 150, royal blue 0106; or 100% merino yarn (50g (1¾oz) = approx. 125m (137yds))
∞ Circular needles, 3 and 3.5mm (US 2 and 4)
∞ Straight knitting needles, 3.5mm (US 4)

TENSION/GAUGE: 27 st x 37 rows on 3.5mm (US 4) needles = 10 x 10cm (4 x 4in)

RIBBING: k2, p2

170 FISHERMAN, CA. 1950. ARCHIVE OF DRUKKERIJ BOUT/HUIZER COURANT, HUIZEN

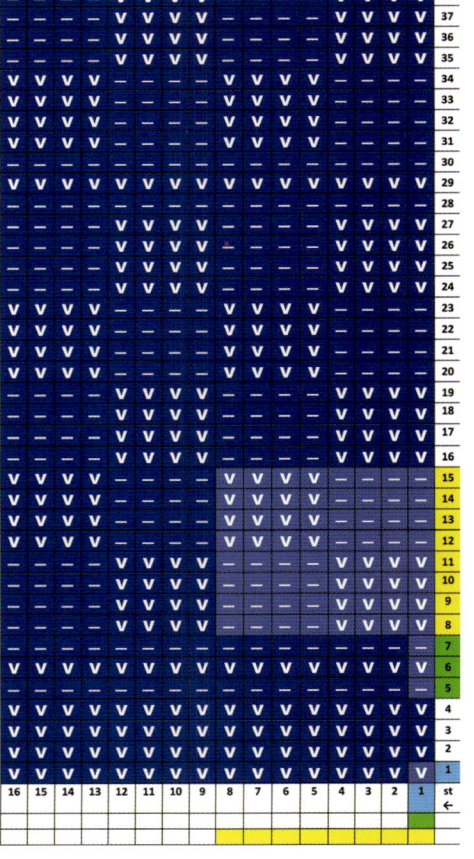

HUIZEN 2 GANSEY

CHEST: 74CM + 4CM = 78CM (30¾IN). TOTAL HEIGHT: APPROX. 55CM (21⅝IN).

Knit a swatch first, with different sized needles if necessary. A gansey should not be too loosely knit. Follow the chart for the motif and adjust the width and/or height to your size, the yarn used and your tension/gauge. Follow the general instructions for the gansey on pages 54–55 and adjust where necessary.

Measurements

WIDTH: 2 × 39 = 78cm (30¾in)
SHOULDERS: 12.5cm (5in)
NECK: 13cm (5⅛in)
NECKLINE DEPTH: 4–5cm (1½–2in)
ARMHOLE HEIGHT: 15cm (6in)
HEIGHT UP TO ARMHOLE, EXCL. RIBBING: 30cm (11¾in)
SLEEVE LENGTH, EXCL. RIBBING: 32cm (12⅝in)
WRIST CIRCUMFERENCE: approx. 14cm (5½in)
RIBBING: according to preference, 4–5cm (1½–2in)

Materials

- 400g (14oz) SMC Merino Extrafine 120, marine 0150; or 100% merino yarn (50g (1¾oz) = approx. 120m (131¼yds))
- Circular needles, 3 and 3.5mm (US 2 and 4)
- Straight knitting needles, 3.5mm (US 4)

TENSION/GAUGE: 24 st × 33 rows on 3.5mm (US 4) needles = 10 × 10cm (4 × 4in)

RIBBING: k2, p2

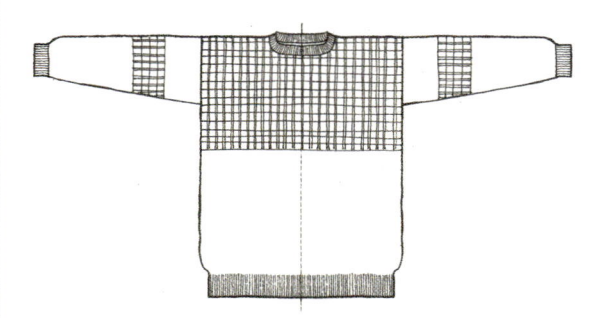

171 FISHERMEN FROM HUIZEN BUSY MENDING THEIR NETS, CA. 1950.
ARCHIVE OF DRUKKERIJ BOUT/HUIZER COURANT, HUIZEN

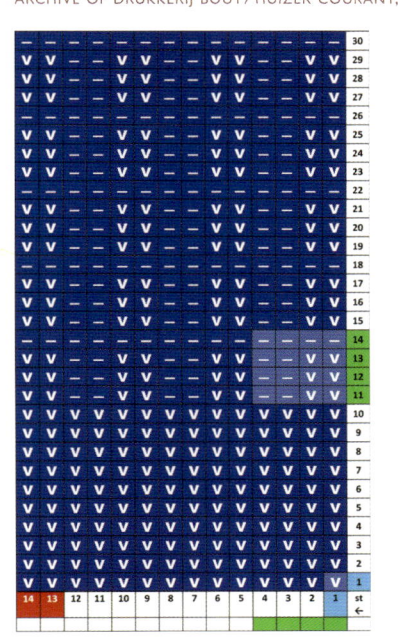

UTRECHT
BUNSCHOTEN-SPAKENBURG

Around 1900, there were around 200 barges in Spakenburg. This made the village one of the five biggest fishing towns on the Zuiderzee. In 1887 the new port was opened, and in 1899 the Fisheries Association De Eendracht was founded. The fisheries school did not open until 1911. Most families earned a living from fishing. For Spakenburg, the industrialisation that took hold in the Netherlands from 1870 never posed a real threat: fishing remained the main form of manual work.

However, the bad economic situation around 1900 meant that many people were forced to sign on with luggers from Vlaardingen and Katwijk. The closing off of the Zuiderzee in 1932 and the subsequent reclamation had a far greater impact on the lives of fishermen. Many fishermen had to find a different job.

The ganseys of Bunschoten-Spakenburg are characterised by vertical bands of cables, in countless variations, alternated with bands of stocking/stockinette. The child's gansey looks totally different; it has a rigging pattern (see page 52) on the chest, with horizontal bands with different motifs below.

172 CHILDREN IN THE PORT OF SPAKENBURG. STICHTING ZUIDERZEEAMBACHTEN ENKHUIZEN

173 FISHERWOMEN FROM SPAKENBURG ON THE MARKET IN AMERSFOORT, 1931. STICHTING ZUIDERZEEAMBACHTEN ENKHUIZEN

THE GANSEYS, BUNSCHOTEN-SPAKENBURG 1, 2 AND 3, CAN BE FOUND ON PAGES 155–157 OF *DUTCH TRADITIONAL GANSEYS*.

BUNSCHOTEN-SPAKENBURG 4 GANSEY

CHEST: 80CM + 2CM = 82CM (32¼IN). TOTAL HEIGHT: 49CM (19¼IN).

Knit a swatch first, with different sized needles if necessary. A gansey should not be too loosely knit. Follow the chart for the motif and adjust the width and/or height to your size, the yarn used and your tension/gauge. Follow the general instructions for the gansey on pages 54–55 and adjust where necessary.

Measurements

WIDTH: 2 × 41 = 82cm (32¼in)
SHOULDERS: 13cm (5⅛in)
NECK: 14cm (5½in)
NECKLINE DEPTH: 4–5cm (1½–2in)
ARMHOLE HEIGHT: 15cm (6in)
HEIGHT UP TO ARMHOLE, EXCL. RIBBING: 33cm (13in)
SLEEVE LENGTH, EXCL. RIBBING: 30cm (11¾in)
WRIST CIRCUMFERENCE: approx. 14cm (5½in)
RIBBING: according to preference, 4–5cm (1½–2in)

Materials

- 400g (14oz) SMC Merino Extrafine 120, royal blue; or 100% merino yarn 0151 (50g (1¾oz) = approx. 120m (131¼yds))
- Circular needles, 3 and 3.5mm (US 2 and 4)
- Straight knitting needles, 3.5mm (US 4)
- Cable needle

TENSION/GAUGE: 24 st × 33 rows on 3.5mm (US 4) needles = 10 × 10cm (4 × 4in)

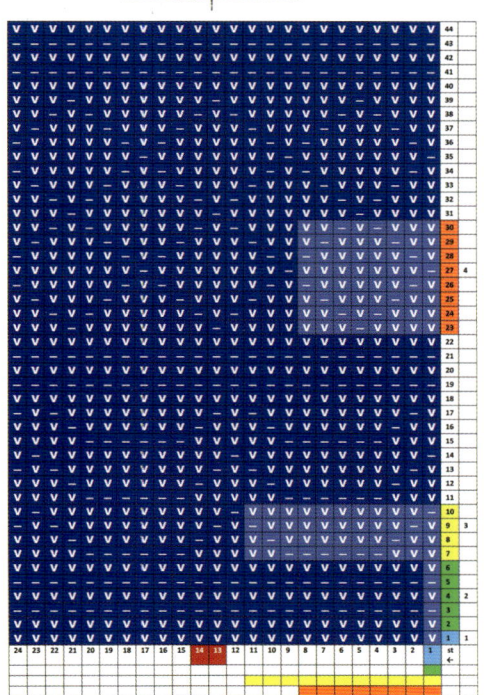

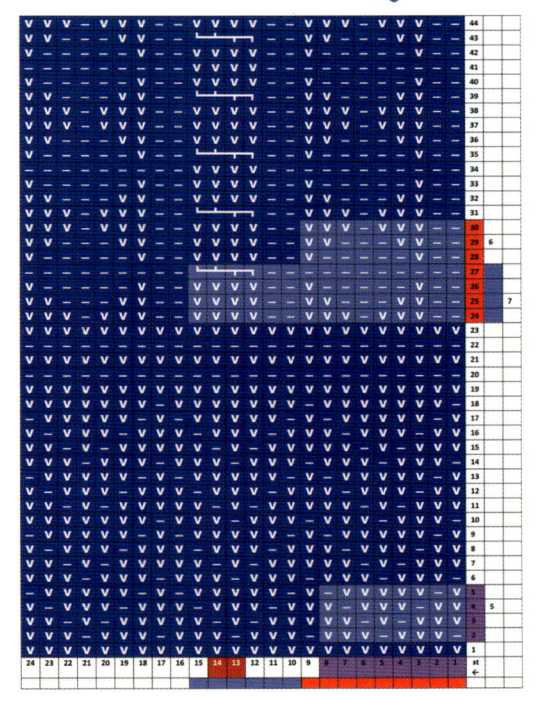

RIBBING: k2, p2

149

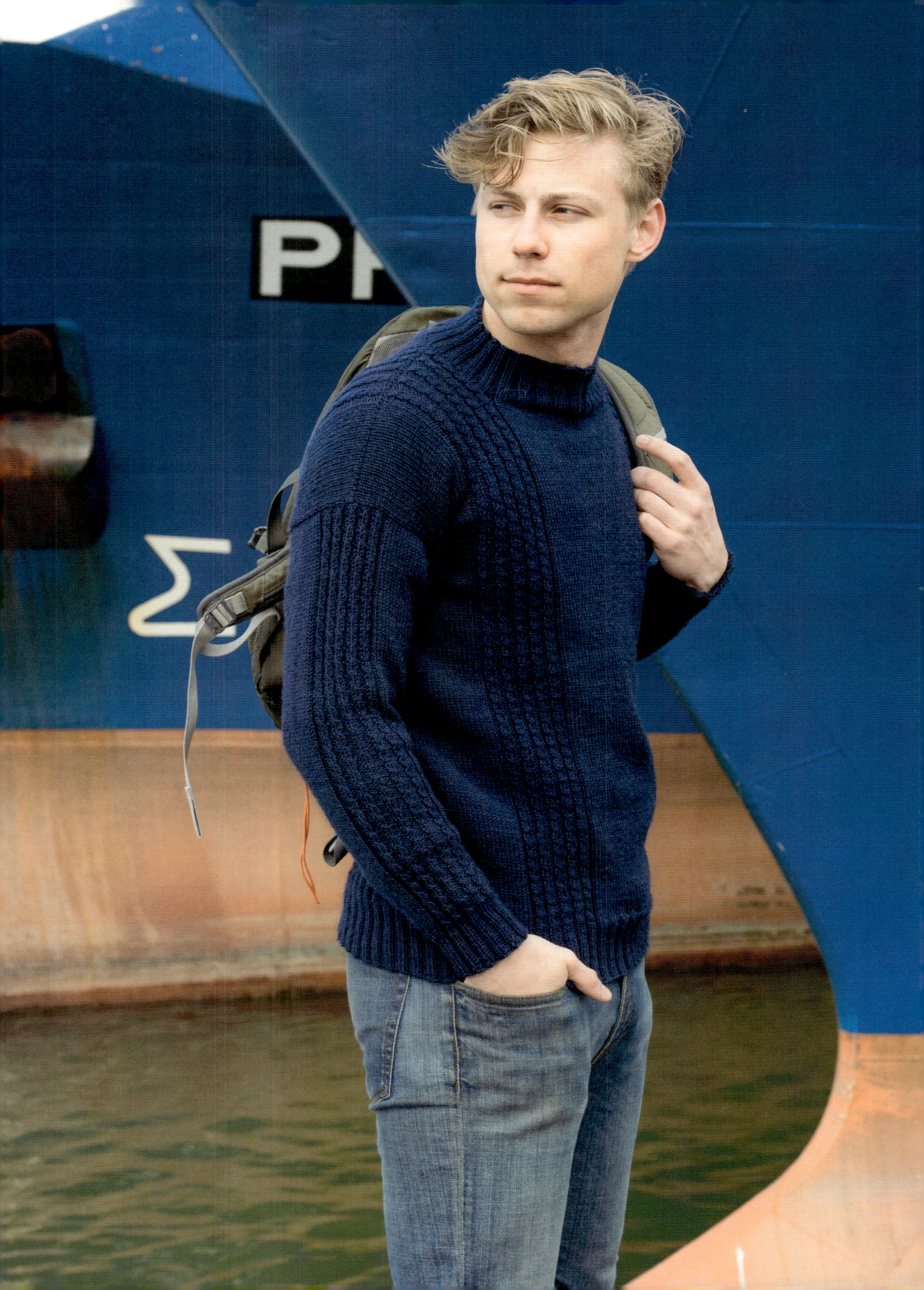

BUNSCHOTEN-SPAKENBURG 5 GANSEY

CHEST: 96CM + 6CM = 102CM (40⅛IN). TOTAL HEIGHT: 70CM (27½IN).

Knit a swatch first, with different sized needles if necessary. A gansey should not be too loosely knit. Follow the chart for the motif and adjust the width and/or height to your size, the yarn used and your tension/gauge. Follow the general instructions for the gansey on pages 54–55 and adjust where necessary.

Measurements

WIDTH: 2 × 51 = 102cm (40⅛in)
SHOULDERS: 16.5cm (6½in)
NECK: 18cm (7in)
NECKLINE DEPTH: 5–6cm (2–2⅜in)
ARMHOLE HEIGHT: 23–24cm (9–9½in)
HEIGHT UP TO ARMHOLE, EXCL. RIBBING: 41cm (16⅛in)
SLEEVE LENGTH, EXCL. RIBBING: 43cm (17in)
WRIST CIRCUMFERENCE: approx. 23cm (9in)
RIBBING: according to preference, 5–8cm (2–3⅛in)

Materials

∞ 800g (28¼oz) Hjertegarn Vital, 698; or 100% pure superwash wool yarn (50g (1¾oz) = approx. 115m (125¾yds))
∞ Circular needles, 3.5 and 4mm (US 4 and 6)
∞ Straight knitting needles, 4mm (US 6)
∞ Cable needle

TENSION/GAUGE: 22 st × 27 rows on 4mm (US 6) needles = 10 × 10cm (4 × 4in)

RIBBING: k2, p2

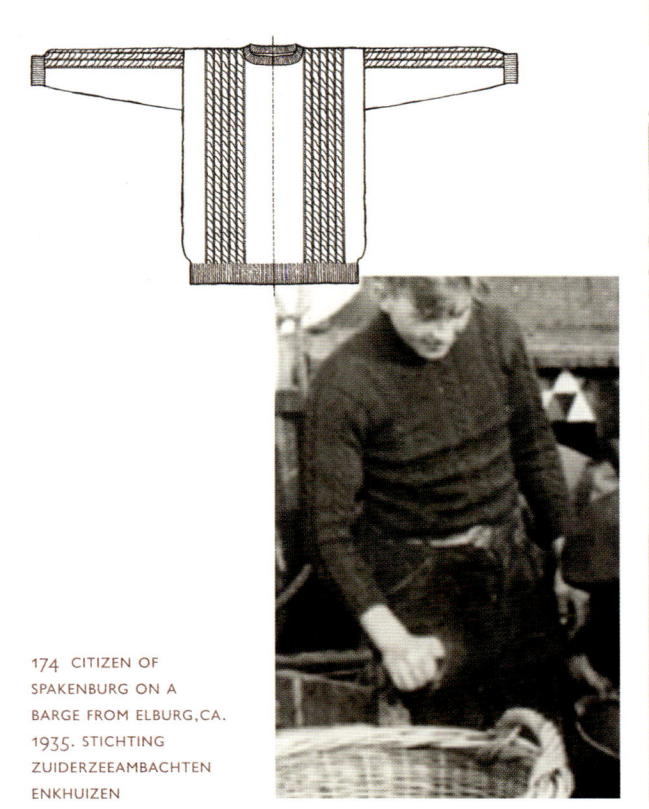

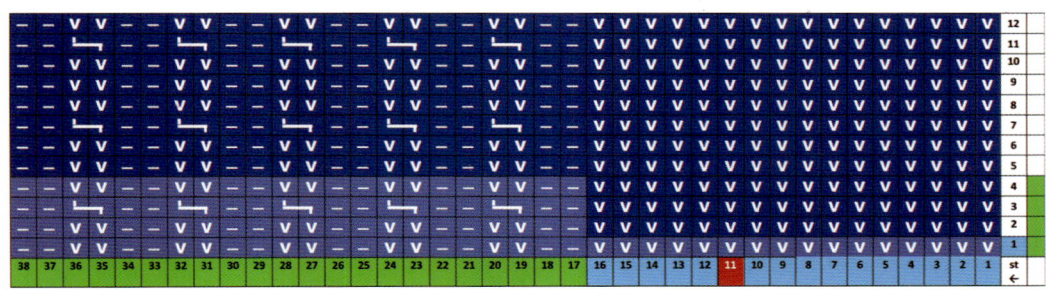

174 CITIZEN OF SPAKENBURG ON A BARGE FROM ELBURG, CA. 1935. STICHTING ZUIDERZEEAMBACHTEN ENKHUIZEN

GELDERLAND
HARDERWIJK

Once upon a time, the port of Harderwijk was home to more than 170 barges. There are only a few left now. The disappearance of the fishing fleet is the result of the closing off of the Zuiderzee, which the people from Harderwijk – entrepreneur Eibert den Herder in particular – protested vigorously against. Since he was an important manufacturer of fishmeal, he was elected as councillor. One of his first decisions was the construction of a channel: for centuries, the ships had had to moor just off the coast at Harderwijk. The port was not built until 1900. Queen Wilhelmina's speech of 1913 seemed to directly hit his companies and the interests of the fishermen: 'I deem the time has now come to start with the closing off and reclamation of the Zuiderzee.' Eibert was furious, held blazing speeches, and published outspoken pamphlets. The fishermen from Harderwijk refused to take part in the fleet review by Queen Wilhelmina during the Zuiderzee Fisheries Exhibition in Enkhuizen in 1930, to say farewell to the Zuiderzee. Den Herder was very creative in his protests. Amongst other things, he made a movie about the fisheries on the Zuiderzee, with a lot of filming on location. The result was a now priceless documentary about the fishing culture which, unfortunately, got partially damaged by fire. After the war, a documentary was made from the parts that had been saved, which can still be seen in the City Museum Harderwijk. The Afsluitdijk could not be stopped. What remained was the IJsselmeer eel, which is still caught and smoked by the fishermen from Harderwijk.

175 CHEERFUL FISHERMEN, 1921. CITY MUSEUM HARDERWIJK

THE GANSEYS, HARDERWIJK 1 AND 2, CAN BE FOUND ON PAGE 159 OF *DUTCH TRADITIONAL GANSEYS*.

HARDERWIJK 3 GANSEY

CHEST: 98CM + 6CM = 104CM (41IN). TOTAL HEIGHT: 68CM (26¾IN).

Knit a swatch first, with different sized needles if necessary. A gansey should not be too loosely knit. Follow the chart for the motif and adjust the width and/or height to your size, the yarn used and your tension/gauge. Follow the general instructions for the gansey on pages 54–55 and adjust where necessary.

Measurements

WIDTH: 2 × 52 = 104cm (41in)
SHOULDERS: 16.5cm (6½in)
NECK: 18cm (7in)
NECKLINE DEPTH: 6–7cm (2⅜–2¾in)
ARMHOLE HEIGHT: 22–23cm (8¾–9in)
HEIGHT UP TO ARMHOLE, EXCL. RIBBING: 41cm (16⅛in)
SLEEVE LENGTH, EXCL. RIBBING: 43cm (17in)
WRIST CIRCUMFERENCE: approx. 23cm (9in)
RIBBING: according to preference, 5–8cm (2–3⅛in)

Materials

- 850g (30oz) SMC Merino Extrafine 120, royal blue 0151; or 100% merino yarn (50g (1¾oz) = approx. 120m (131¼yds))
- Circular needles, 2.5 and 3mm (US 1 and 2)
- Straight knitting needles, 3mm (US 2)

TENSION/GAUGE: 27.5 st × 37 rows on 3mm (US 2) needles = 10 × 10cm (4 × 4in)

RIBBING: k2, p2

176 FISHERMAN FROM HARDERWIJK, CA. 1950. CITY MUSEUM, HARDERWIJK

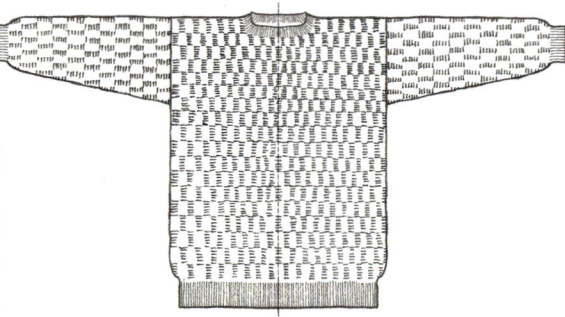

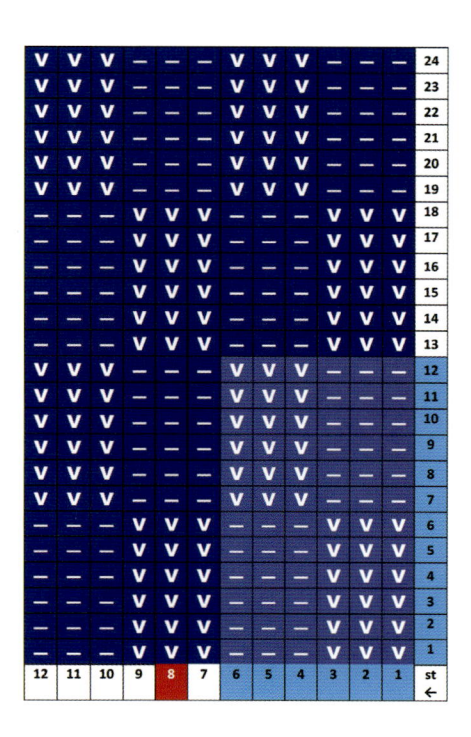

153

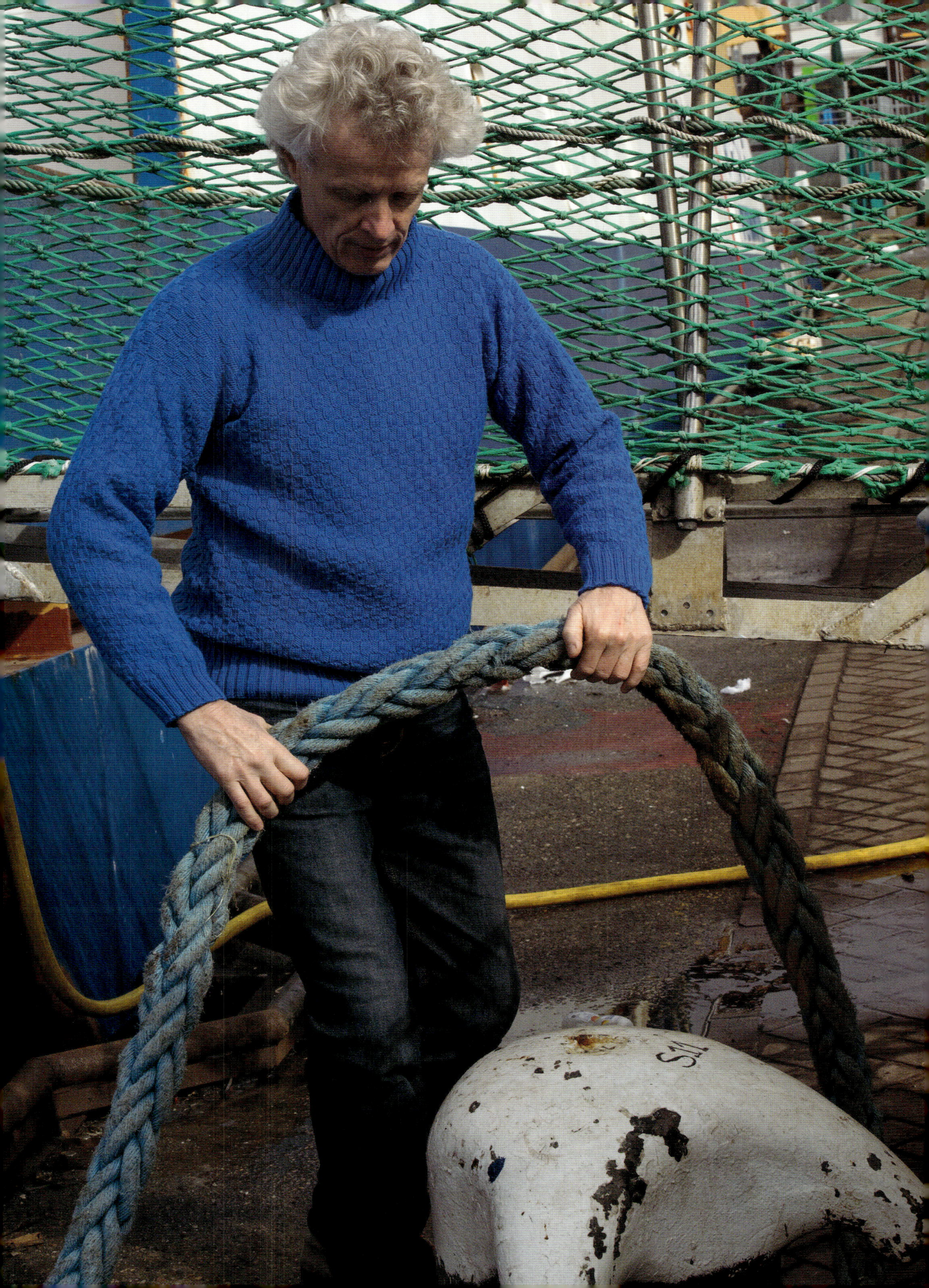

177 FISHERMEN 'FLODDERING' ON THE ICE, ELBURG, CA. 1930.
HISTORICAL ASSOCIATION ARENT THOE BOECOP, ELBURG

GELDERLAND
ELBURG

Only a small number of fishermen from Elburg managed to make a decent living. Like elsewhere, most lived on the breadline. In 1904, a quarter of the fishermen depended on alms support: the *bedeling*. The First World War years were fairly good: because of the meat shortage, prices for fish were high. In addition, the catch in the last war year, 1918, was extremely good. In 1919, the fleet of Elburg was at its largest. Gerrit Geusink (Gart de Luus) was registered under number EB 72 in the ship's register that year.

Until 1932, the Elburg fishermen mainly fished for herring, flounder, eel, smelt and shrimp. When the Zuiderzee froze over, a large number of vessels would use vertical nets and so-called *floddernetjes* ('wheedle nets') to fish for smelt under the ice. They would push the vertical smelt nets under the ice using long sticks and then pull them up again the next morning. *Flodderen* would be done in the twilight or dark, with a sled, long stick, compass, lantern, ice pick and six nets.

The fishermen would cut a triangular hole in the ice and push the nets under the ice in six different directions. The lantern would stand at the edge of the hole. After a while, the nets, with various catches, would be pulled up again (Fig. 177). However, fishing on the ice could be dangerous. If an offshore wind rose up suddenly, the ice floe the fishermen were standing on could break and drift away. This happened to three fishermen (a father and two sons) from Durgerdam, in the mid-nineteenth century. They were found alive two weeks later, but one of the two sons died shortly afterwards.

After the land reclamation of the eastern part of Flevoland in 1956 some fishermen would mainly fish for eel using fykes.

178 TANNERY AND PORT OF ELBURG.
STICHTING ZUIDERZEEAMBACHTEN ENKHUIZEN

THE GANSEY, ELBURG 1, CAN BE FOUND ON PAGE 161 IN *DUTCH TRADITIONAL GANSEYS*.

ELBURG 2 GANSEY

CHEST: 96CM + 6CM = 102CM (40⅛IN). TOTAL HEIGHT: 70CM (27½IN).

Knit a swatch first, with different sized needles if necessary. A gansey should not be too loosely knit. Follow the chart for the motif and adjust the width and/or height to your size, the yarn used and your tension/gauge. Follow the general instructions for the gansey on pages 54–55 and adjust where necessary. Note: The cables are mirrored left (cross along the back) and right (cross in front).

Measurements

WIDTH: 2 x 51 = 102cm (40⅛in)
SHOULDERS: 16.5cm (6½in)
NECK: 18cm (7in)
NECKLINE DEPTH: 5–6cm (2–2⅜in)
ARMHOLE HEIGHT: 22–23cm (8¾–9in)
HEIGHT UP TO ARMHOLE, EXCL. RIBBING: 41–42cm (16⅛–16½in)
SLEEVE LENGTH, EXCL. RIBBING: 43cm (17in)
WRIST CIRCUMFERENCE: approx. 23cm (9in)
RIBBING: according to preference, 5–8cm (2–3⅛in)

Materials

- ∞ Approx. 850g (30oz) Scheepjeswol Zuiderzee, cornflower blue; or 100% pure wool yarn (100g (3½oz) = aprox. 200m (218¾yds))
- ∞ Circular needles, 3 and 3.5mm (US 2 and 4)
- ∞ Straight knitting needles, 3.5mm (US 4)
- ∞ Cable needle

TENSION/GAUGE: 21 st x 30 rows on 3.5mm (US 4) needles = 10 x 10cm (4 x 4in)
RIBBING: k2, p2

179 FISHERMAN FROM ELBURG, CA. 1925.
STICHTING ZUIDERZEEAMBACHTEN ENKHUIZEN

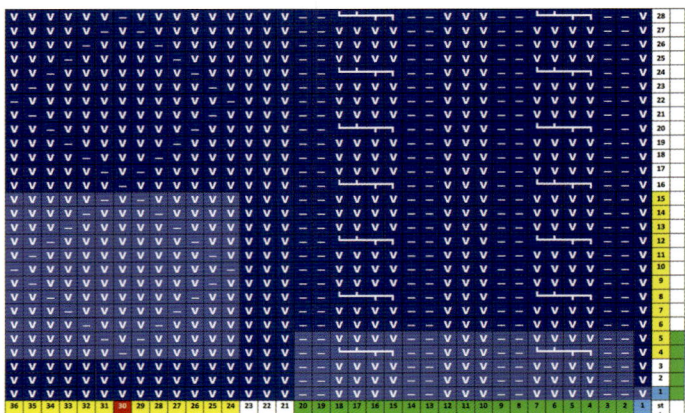

156

ELBURG 3 GANSEY

CHEST: 100CM + 6CM = 106CM (41¾IN). TOTAL HEIGHT: 70CM (27½IN).

Knit a swatch first, with different sized needles if necessary. A gansey should not be too loosely knit. Follow the chart for the motif and adjust the width and/or height to your size, the yarn used and your tension/gauge. Follow the general instructions for the gansey on pages 54–55 and adjust where necessary.

Measurements

WIDTH: 2 × 53 = 106cm (41¾in)
SHOULDERS: 17.5cm (6⅝in)
NECK: 18cm (7in)
NECKLINE DEPTH: 5–7cm (2–2¾in)
ARMHOLE HEIGHT: 23cm (9in)
HEIGHT UP TO ARMHOLE, EXCL. RIBBING: 41cm (16⅛in)
SLEEVE LENGTH, EXCL. RIBBING: 43cm (17in)
WRIST CIRCUMFERENCE: approx. 23cm (9in)
RIBBING: according to preference, 5–8cm (2–3⅛in)

180 SMACK BOAT FROM ELBURG IN THE PORT OF SPAKENBURG, 1941. STICHTING ZUIDERZEEAMBACHTEN ENKHUIZEN

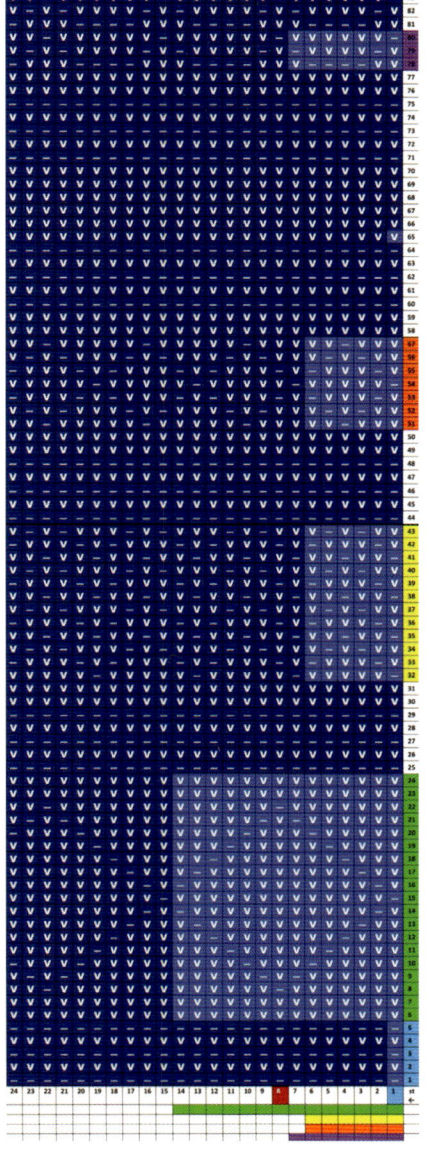

Materials

∞ Approx. 700g (24⅔oz) Loret Karman RAW Superwash, not-quite-white; or 100% pure superwash wool yarn (100g (3½oz)= approx. 250m (273½yds))
∞ Circular needles, 3 and 3.5mm (US 2 and 4)
∞ Straight knitting needles, 3.5mm (US 4)
∞ Cable needle

TENSION/GAUGE: 21 st × 26 rows on 3.5mm (US 4) needles = 10 × 10cm (4 × 4in)
RIBBING: k1, p1

157

OVERIJSSEL
GENEMUIDEN

Genemuiden is known for its rush cultivation and processing, an industry that goes back to the sixteenth century. In 1275, it got city rights from Jan van Nassau. It was then called 'Genemuden' – although the spelling 'Gelemuiden' is also found. Bishop Jan Van Arkel granted the city ferry rights over the Zwarte Water, at an annual delivery of 60 pounds of candle wax. In 1382, the right to hold three annual fairs was awarded, which made the city rich enough to be able to build a city hall.

The rush growers would use small boats to sail along the new plantings for cutting rushes, and often wore ganseys, like fishermen. The weaving of rush chair seats (chair-caners) was a big home industry.

On March 8, 1922, the ferry from Zwartsluis to Genemuiden sank just outside the town during bad weather. Eleven people drowned, including the mayor and his wife, and many people were injured. Today, there is still a ferry service between Genemuiden and Zwartsluis.

GENEMUIDEN GANSEY

CHEST: 98CM + 6CM = 104CM (41IN). TOTAL HEIGHT: 68–70CM (26¾–27½IN).

Knit a swatch first, with different sized needles if necessary. A gansey should not be too loosely knit. Follow the chart for the motif and adjust the width and/or height to your size, the yarn used and your tension/gauge. Follow the general instructions for the gansey on pages 54–55 and adjust where necessary.

Measurements

WIDTH: 2 × 52 = 104cm (41in)
SHOULDERS: 16.5cm (6½in)
NECK: 18cm (7in)
NECKLINE DEPTH: 6–7cm (2⅜–2¾in)
ARMHOLE HEIGHT: 22–23cm (8¾–9in)
HEIGHT UP TO ARMHOLE, EXCL. RIBBING: 41cm (16⅛in)
SLEEVE LENGTH, EXCL. RIBBING: 43cm (17in)
WRIST CIRCUMFERENCE: approx. 23cm (9in)
RIBBING: according to preference, 5–8cm (2–3⅛in)

Materials

- 850g (30oz) SMC Merino Extrafine 120, jeans 0154; or 100% merino yarn (50g (1¾oz) = approx. 120m (131¼yds))
- Circular needles, 3 and 3.5mm (US 2 and 4)
- Straight knitting needles, 3.5mm (US 4)

TENSION/GAUGE: 24 st × 35 rows on 3.5mm (US 4) needles = 10 × 10cm (4 × 4in)

RIBBING: k2, p2

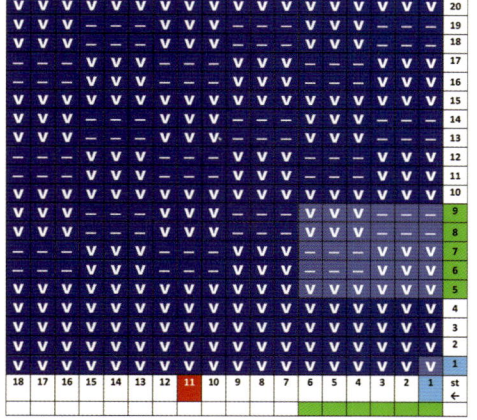

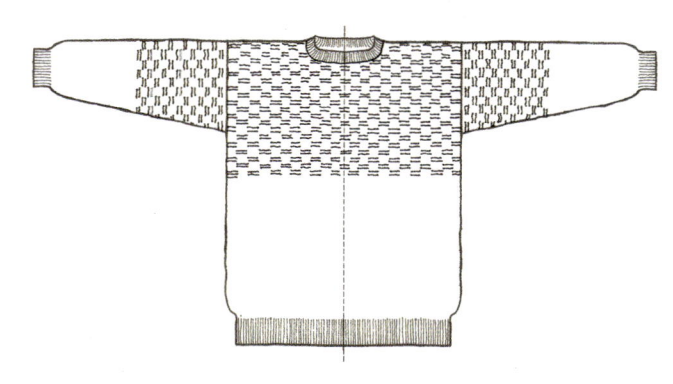

181 FROM LEFT TO RIGHT: ALBERT EENKHOORN AND GEUJE VAN DER HAAR, CA. 1935. FROM *SCHAKELS IN DE TIJD* BY HENK BEENS (SELF-PUBLISHED), GENEMUIDEN, 2000–2003

182 LACE STOCKINGS. MUSEUM HET OUDE RAADHUIS, URK

FLEVOLAND
URK

With the closing off of the Zuiderzee in 1932, it seemed that the days were numbered for the island of Urk and its fishing industry, because Urk is located almost in the heart of the Netherlands. Miraculously, this did not happened. The fishermen from Urk started fishing on the North Sea, built large barges and caught more fish. The fish auction also attracted a lot of fish-processing companies. Because Urk was a very insular community, the fishermen from the town would often be recognised by their distinctive ganseys (Fig. 183 and 185), making it possible to identify them if they drowned. The ganseys almost always featured cables, eyes of God – also called diamonds or flowers, Jacob's ladders, and sometimes flags. These elements always had to be included in the knitter's gansey design to show that they were united with God and to protect their loved ones. The knitter decided how the motifs were combined.

Early ganseys, like Urk 4 (on pages 162–163), had different motifs. The ganseys were often knit circularly on four needles, usually in cornflower or dark blue, and black in times of mourning, often a size too large, to be able to full the sweater in boiling water. Ganseys were worn on Sundays and public holidays, but also at work. For the Sunday sweaters, knitters from Urk used finer wool. The men on Urk would wear thick black knit stockings that went above the knee on weekdays, and lace stockings on Sundays (Fig. 182). The early ganseys look very different from the later ones (Fig. 183 and 186).

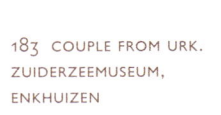

183 COUPLE FROM URK. ZUIDERZEEMUSEUM, ENKHUIZEN

184 CREW OF A SAILING LUGGER FROM VLAARDINGEN, OWNED BY REDERIJ DE EENDRACHT, CA. 1910. THE CREW MEMBERS CAME FROM ALL OVER THE COUNTRY, INCLUDING URK. VLAARDINGEN MUNICIPAL ARCHIVE

THE GANSEYS, URK 1 AND 2, CAN BE FOUND ON PAGES 163–164 IN *DUTCH TRADITIONAL GANSEYS*.

URK 3 GANSEY

CHEST: 98CM + 6CM = 104CM (41IN). TOTAL HEIGHT: 70CM (27½IN)

Knit a swatch first, with different sized needles if necessary. A gansey should not be too loosely knit. Follow the chart for the motif and adjust the width and/or height to your size, the yarn used and your tension/gauge. Follow the general instructions for the gansey on pages 54–55 and adjust where necessary.

Measurements

WIDTH: 2 x 52 = 104cm (41in)
SHOULDERS: 16.5cm (6½in)
NECK: 18cm (7in)
NECKLINE DEPTH: 6–7cm (2⅜–2¾in)
ARMHOLE HEIGHT: 22–23cm (8¾–9in)
HEIGHT UP TO ARMHOLE, EXCL. RIBBING: 41cm (16⅛in)
SLEEVE LENGTH, EXCL. RIBBING: 43cm (17in)
WRIST CIRCUMFERENCE: approx. 23cm (9in)
RIBBING: according to preference, 5–8cm (2–3⅛in)

Materials

∞ 850g (30oz) SMC Merino Extrafine 120, gentian blue 0153; or 100% merino yarn (50g (1¾oz) = approx. 120m (131¼yds))
∞ Circular needles, 3 and 3.5mm (US 2 and 4)
∞ Straight knitting needles, 3.5mm (US 4)
∞ Cable needle

TENSION/GAUGE: 24 st x 35 rows on 3.5mm (US 4) = 10 x 10cm (4 x 4in)

RIBBING: k2, p2

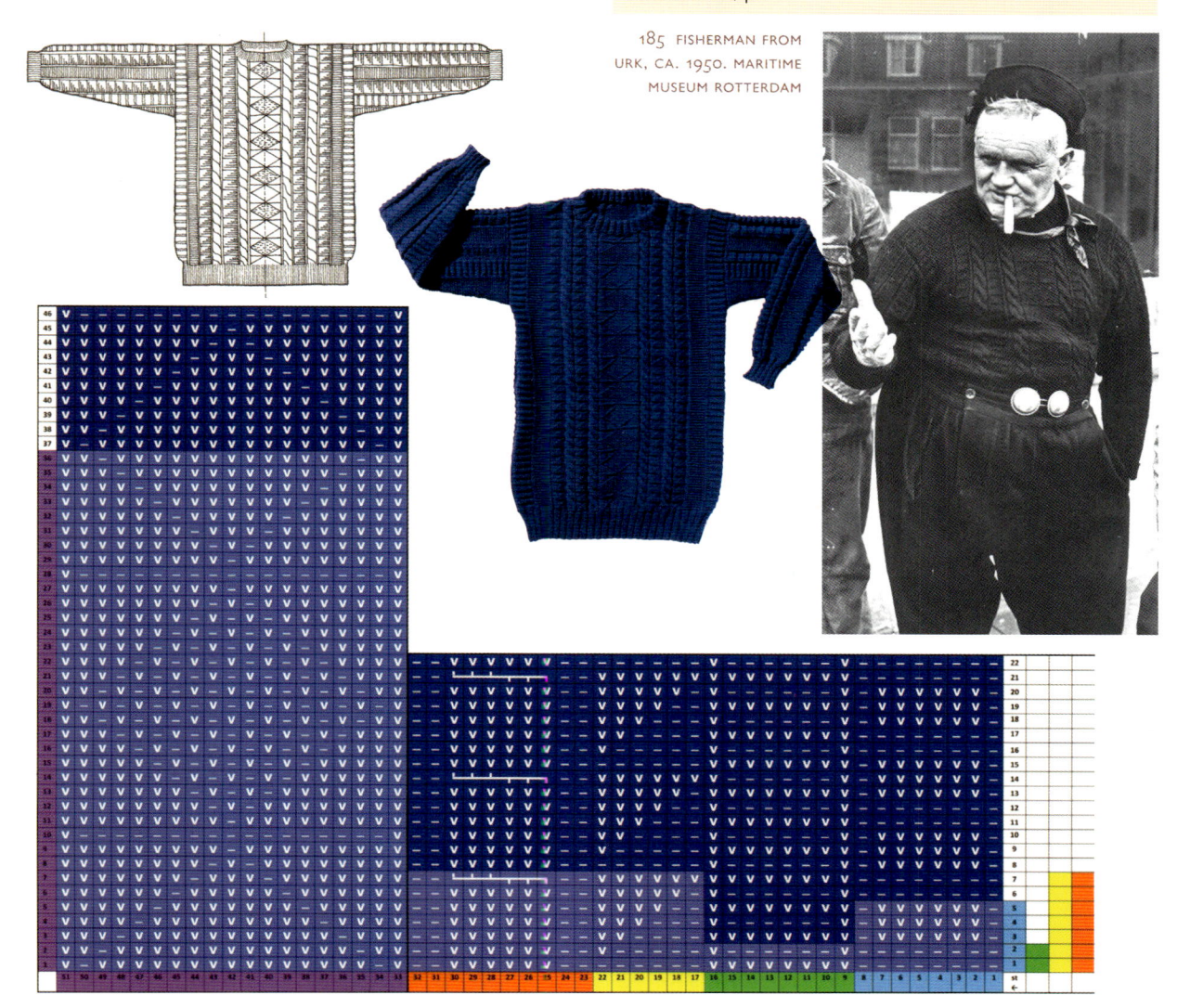

185 FISHERMAN FROM URK, CA. 1950. MARITIME MUSEUM ROTTERDAM

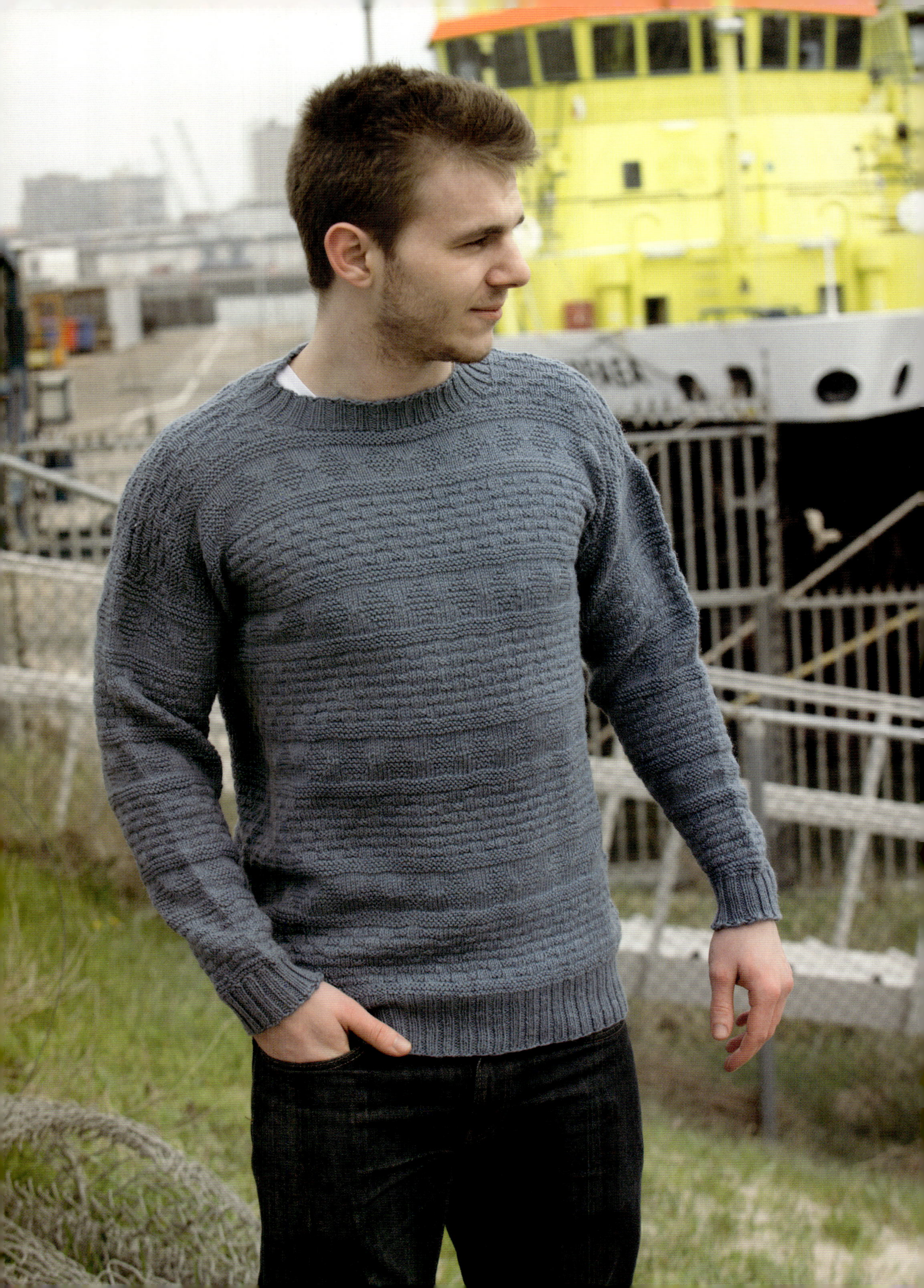

URK 4 GANSEY

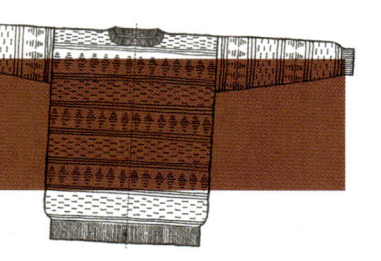

CHEST: 100CM + 6CM = 106CM (41¾IN). TOTAL HEIGHT: 70CM (27½IN).

Knit a swatch first, with different sized needles if necessary. A gansey should not be too loosely knit. Follow the chart for the motif and adjust the width and/or height to your size, the yarn used and your tension/gauge. Follow the general instructions for the gansey on pages 54–55 and adjust where necessary.

Measurements

WIDTH: 2 × 53 = 106cm (41¾in)
SHOULDERS: 17.5cm (6⅝in)
NECK: 18cm (7in)
NECKLINE DEPTH: 5–7cm (2–2¾in)
ARMHOLE HEIGHT: 23cm (9in)
HEIGHT UP TO ARMHOLE, EXCL. RIBBING: 41cm (16⅛in)
SLEEVE LENGTH, EXCL. RIBBING: 43cm (17in)
WRIST CIRCUMFERENCE: approx. 23cm (9in)
RIBBING: according to preference, 5–8cm (2–3⅛in)

Materials

- Approx. 700g (24⅔oz) Loret Karman RAW Superwash, denim; or 100% pure superwash wool yarn (100g (3½oz) = approx. 250m (273½yds))
- Circular needles, 3 and 3.5mm (US 2 and 4)
- Straight knitting needles, 3.5mm (US 4)

TENSION/GAUGE: 21 st × 26 rows on 3.5mm (US 4) needles = 10 × 10cm (4 × 4in)

RIBBING: k1, p1

186 GREETINGS FROM URK. POSTCARD WITH TWO FISHERMEN FROM URK, CA. 1884. CITY MUSEUM HARDERWIJK

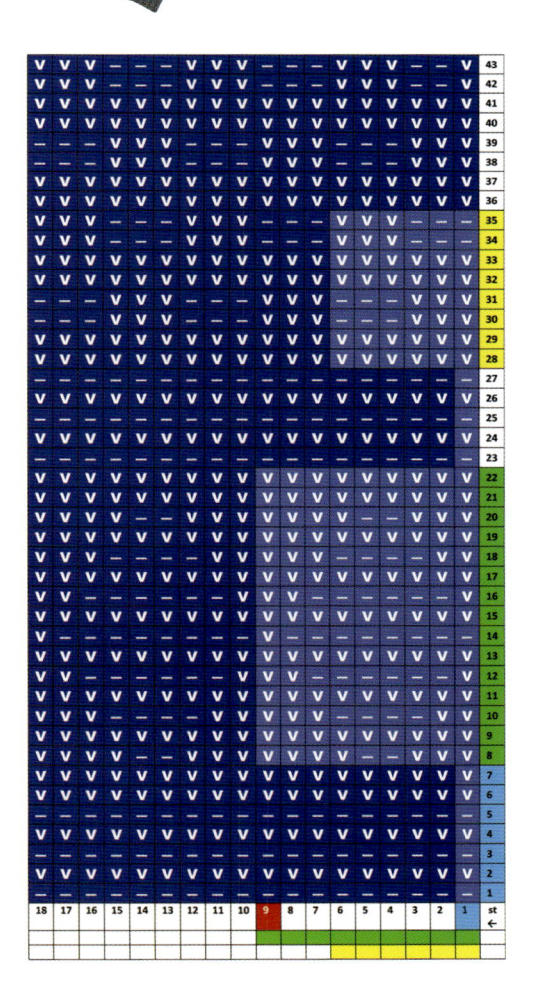

163

FRIESLAND
LEMMER

When the peat-processing industry in the area of Lemmer declined in the middle of the nineteenth century, peat workers started inland fishing to earn a bit of extra money. With the arrival of new, machine-knit nets at the end of the nineteenth century, which could also be used by relatively inexperienced fishermen, they set off to fish on the Zuiderzee. Fishing for anchovy was a good way to earn an income. However, nets were expensive and money was scarce. Because the smokers profited from large catches, they would often lend the fishermen money. In Lemmer, these smokers are also called *hangbazen*. They would demand the entire catch, on their conditions, meaning that the fishermen received a mere pittance. Shortly after 1900 the fishing fleet in Lemmer was at its largest, while the future of the fishing industry on the Zuiderzee was hanging on by a thread. Because Lemmer remains as a coastal town on the IJsselmeer, there is still a (very small) fishing industry today

The *Lemsteraken*, which are a type of barge, were built in Lemmer. *De Groene Draeck*, Princess Beatrix's sailing ship, is a *Lemsteraak*.

The ganseys found in Lemmer are all different. First, it was thought that only machine-knit English ganseys were worn in Lemmer, but after a lot of research we managed to find three ganseys from that were hand-knit there.

187 TEUN DE FLAPPER, CA. 1950.
COURTESY OF TRIX DE WAAL, EE

188 FISHING PORT OF LEMMER, CA. 1910.
STICHTING ZUIDERZEEAMBACHTEN ENKHUIZEN

189 ANCHOVY IN THE PORT OF LEMMER, CA. 1900.
ORIGIN UNKNOWN

LEMMER 1 GANSEY

CHEST: 98CM + 6CM = 104CM (41IN). TOTAL HEIGHT: 60–70CM (26¾–27½IN).

Knit a swatch first, with different sized needles if necessary. A gansey should not be too loosely knit. Follow the chart for the motif and adjust the width and/or height to your size, the yarn used and your tension/gauge. Follow the general instructions for the gansey on pages 54–55 and adjust where necessary.

Measurements
WIDTH: 2 × 52 = 104cm (41in)
SHOULDERS: 16.5cm (6½in)
NECK: 18cm (7in)
NECKLINE DEPTH: 6–7cm (2⅜–2¾in)
ARMHOLE HEIGHT: 22–23cm (8¾–9in)
HEIGHT UP TO ARMHOLE, EXCL. RIBBING: 41cm (16⅛in)
SLEEVE LENGTH, EXCL. RIBBING: 43cm (17in)
WRIST CIRCUMFERENCE: approx. 23cm (9in)
RIBBING: according to preference, 5–8cm (2–3⅛in)

Materials
- 850g (30oz) Hjertegarn Vital, 698; or 100% pure superwash wool yarn (50g (1¾oz) = approx. 115m (125¾yds))
- Circular needles, 3.5 and 4mm (US 4 and 6)
- Straight knitting needles, 4mm (US 6)
- Cable needle

TENSION/GAUGE: 22 st × 27 rows on 4mm (US 6) needles = 10 × 10cm (4 × 4in)

RIBBING: k2, p2

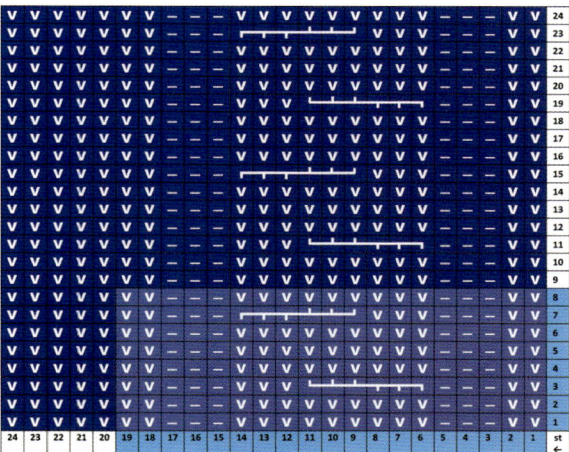

LEMMER 2 GANSEY

CHEST: 98CM + 6CM = 104CM (41IN). TOTAL HEIGHT: 60–70CM (26¾–27½IN).

Knit a swatch first, with different sized needles if necessary. A gansey should not be too loosely knit. Follow the chart for the motif and adjust the width and/or height to your size, the yarn used and your tension/gauge. Follow the general instructions for the gansey on pages 54–55 and adjust where necessary.

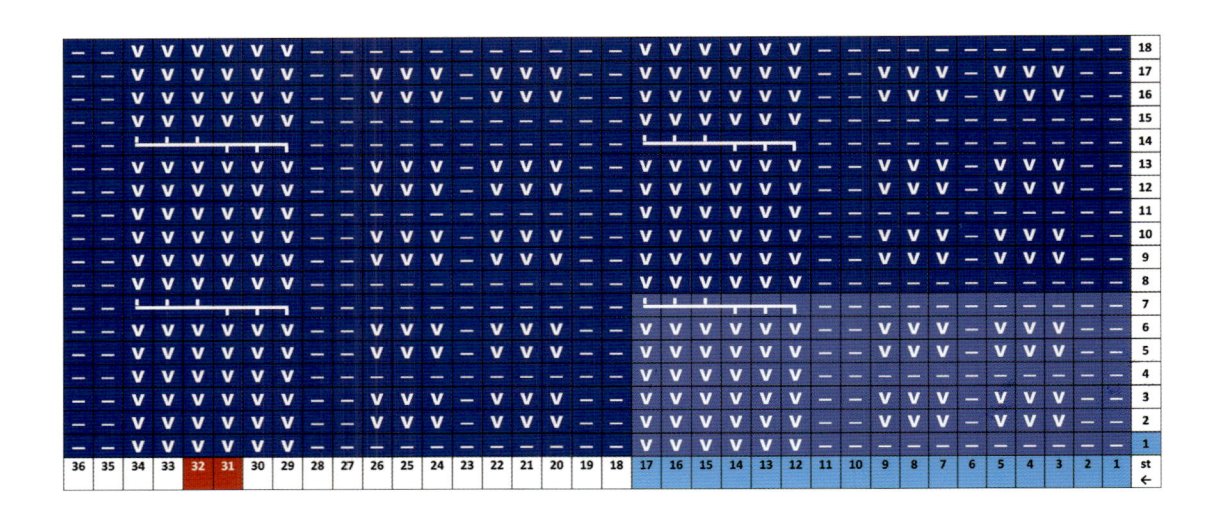

Measurements

WIDTH: 2 × 52 = 104cm (41in)
SHOULDERS: 16.5cm (6½in)
NECK: 18cm (7in)
NECKLINE DEPTH: 6–7cm (2⅜–2¾in)
ARMHOLE HEIGHT: 22–23cm (8¾–9in)
HEIGHT UP TO ARMHOLE, EXCL. RIBBING: 41–42cm (16⅛–16½in)
SLEEVE LENGTH, EXCL. RIBBING: 43cm (17in)
WRIST CIRCUMFERENCE: approx. 23cm (9in)
RIBBING: according to preference, 5–8cm (2–3⅛in)

Materials

∞ Approx. 850g (30oz) Scheepjeswol Zuiderzee, cornflower blue; or 100% pure wool yarn (100g (3½oz) = approx. 200m (218¾yds))
∞ Circular needles, 3 and 3.5mm (US 2 and 4)
∞ Straight knitting needles, 3.5mm (US 4)
∞ Cable needle

TENSION/GAUGE: 21 st × 30 on 3.5mm (US 4) needles = 10 × 10cm (4 × 4in)

RIBBING: k1, p1

DETAIL FROM FIG. 189

LEMMER 3 GANSEY

CHEST: 98cm + 6cm = 104cm (41in). TOTAL HEIGHT: 60–70cm (26¾–27½in).
Knit a swatch first, with different sized needles if necessary. A gansey should not be too loosely knit. Follow the chart for the motif and adjust the width and/or height to your size, the yarn used and your tension/gauge. Follow the general instructions for the gansey on pages 54–55 and adjust where necessary.

Measurements

WIDTH: 2 x 52 = 104cm (41in)
SHOULDERS: 16.5cm (6½in)
NECK: 18cm (7in)
NECKLINE DEPTH: 6–7cm (2⅜–2¾in)
ARMHOLE HEIGHT: 22–23cm (8¾–9in)
HEIGHT UP TO ARMHOLE, EXCL. RIBBING: 41–42cm (16⅛–16½in)
SLEEVE LENGTH, EXCL. RIBBING: 43cm (17in)
WRIST CIRCUMFERENCE: approx. 23cm (9in)
RIBBING: according to preference, 5–8cm (2–3⅛in)

Materials

∞ Approx. 800g (28¼oz) Lopi Einband double thread, blue 0942; or 100% pure wool yarn (50g (1¾oz) single thread = approx. 225m (246yds))
∞ Circular needles, 3 and 3.5mm (US 2 and 4)
∞ Straight knitting needles, 3.5mm (US 4)

TENSION/GAUGE: 21 st x 30 rows on 3.5mm (US 4) needles = 10 x 10cm

RIBBING: k1, p1

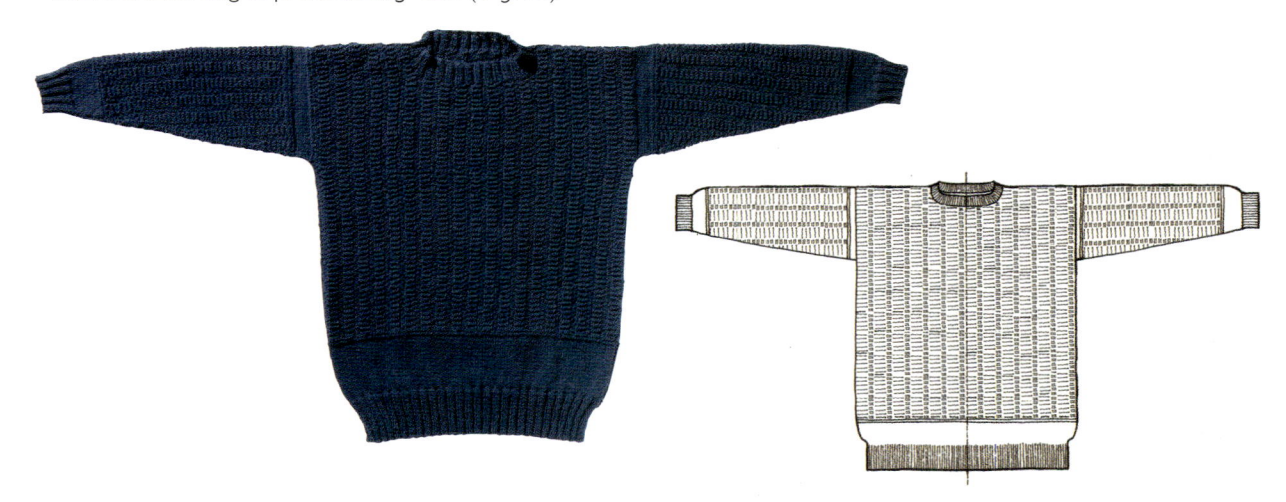

190 FISHERMEN FROM LEMMER SUPPORTING THE SOCIAL MOVEMENT AND SEEKING TO IMPROVE THEIR CONDITIONS. STICHTING ZUIDERZEEAMBACHTEN ENKHUIZEN

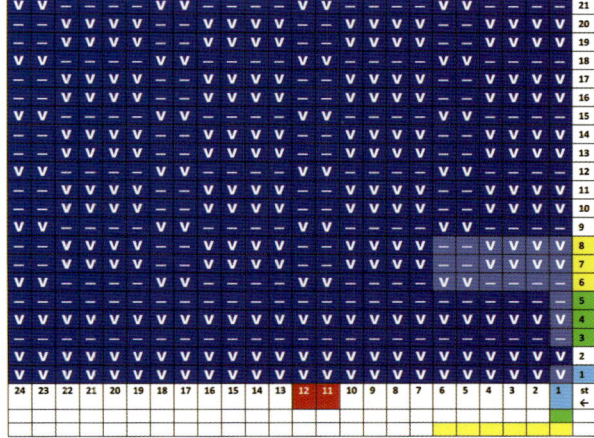

FRIESLAND
HINDELOOPEN

In 1880, Hindeloopen had a fleet of approximately eight vessels, with a total of 16 fishermen. In 1900, the fleet had grown to 75 vessels, with a crew of 192. The Zuiderzee herring and anchovy were the most important types of fish caught. The rest of the year, fishermen would work on the North Sea luggers sailing from Harlingen, on the fleets in Vlaardingen and IJmuiden or they would temporarily work as barge skippers. When the Afsluitdijk was built in 1932, the thriving fishing industry in Hindeloopen came to an end.

191 FISHERMEN ON THE QUAY OF HINDELOOPEN, CA. 1940.
STICHTING ZUIDERZEEAMBACHTEN ENKHUIZEN

THE GANSEYS, HINDELOOPEN 1 AND 2, CAN BE FOUND ON PAGES 169–170 IN *DUTCH TRADITIONAL GANSEYS*.

HINDELOOPEN 3 GANSEY

CHEST: 100CM + 6CM = 106CM (41¾IN). TOTAL HEIGHT: 68–70CM (26¾–27½IN).

Knit a swatch first, with different sized needles if necessary. A gansey should not be too loosely knit. Follow the chart for the motif and adjust the width and/or height to your size, the yarn used and your tension/gauge. Follow the general instructions for the gansey on pages 54–55 and adjust where necessary.

Measurements

WIDTH: 2 x 53 = 106cm (41¾in)
SHOULDERS: 15.5cm (6⅛in)
NECK: 18cm (7in)
NECKLINE DEPTH: 5–7cm (2–2¾in)
ARMHOLE HEIGHT: 23cm (9in)
HEIGHT UP TO ARMHOLE, EXCL. RIBBING: 41cm (16⅛in)
SLEEVE LENGTH, EXCL. RIBBING: 43cm (17in)
WRIST CIRCUMFERENCE: approx. 23cm (9in)
RIBBING: according to preference, 5–8cm (2–3⅛in)

Materials

∞ Approx. 800g (28¼oz) Hjertegarn Lima, royal blue 1690; or 100% pure wool yarn (50g (1¾oz) = approx. 100m (110yds)
∞ Circular needle, 4 and 4.5mm (US 6 and 7)
∞ Straight knitting needles, 4.5mm (US 7)

TENSION/GAUGE: 20 st x 26 rows 4mm (US 6) = 10 x 10cm (4 x 4in)

RIBBING: k2, p2

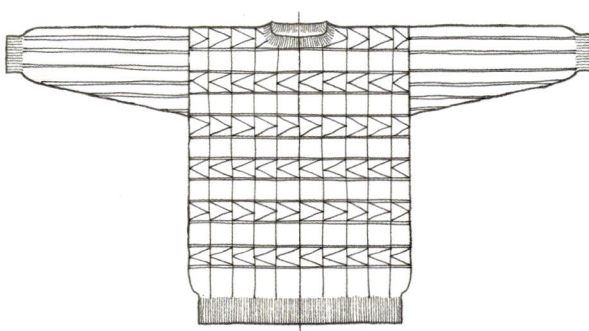

192 INDIVIDUAL FROM THE SEA RESCUE TEAM FROM HINDELOOPEN, CA. 1910. MUSEUM 'T FISKERSHÚSKE, PAESENS-MODDERGAT

SLEEVES

The beautiful motifs of the ganseys lend themselves really well to contemporary knits. This chapter gives you some examples to use as inspiration for your own creations. The easiest thing to do is find a good knitting pattern and use the motifs from the ganseys, as is done with the T-model sweater.

8 MODERN INTERPRETATIONS

MODERN GANSEY 'MADE BY MARGJE'

CHEST: 96CM + 6CM = 102CM (40⅛IN). TOTAL HEIGHT: 70CM (27½IN).

This sweater combines different motifs, blocks and cables, similar to Woudrichem 2 (page 117). The sleeves were set in and the shawl collar makes this design very contemporary.

Measurements

WIDTH: 2 × 54 = 108cm (42½in)
SLEEVE LENGTH, EXCL. RIBBING: 43cm (17in)
WRIST CIRCUMFERENCE: approx. 23cm (9in)
RIBBING: 7cm (2¾in)

193 SWEATER WITH SHAWL COLLAR, MARGJE ENTING, EEXT

Materials

∞ Approx. 800g (28¼oz) Lang Thema Nuova, 0054 royal blue; or 100% pure wool yarn (50g (1¾oz) = approx. 118m (129yds))
∞ Circular needles, 3.5 and 4mm (US 4 and 6)
∞ Straight knitting needles, 4mm (US 6)
∞ Cable needle

TENSION/GAUGE: 23 st × 32 rows on 4mm (US 6) needles = 10 × 10cm (4 × 4in)

RIBBING: k1, p1

BACK: Cast on as many sts as needed, based on your swatch, continue working in the round and work 7cm (2¾in) of ribbing. Divide the sts and place a cable in the middle on the front and back. Work 50cm (19¾in) in pattern up to the armholes. Divide up the work in a front and back piece and continue knitting back and forth. On both sides, cast off approx. 7 sts for the armhole, and decrease another 7 × 1 st, every right side row. Work the back piece in pattern until it measures 18cm (7in) from the armhole and cast off the middle 48 sts for the neck. Cast off the shoulders as follows: 3 × 8 sts, and 1 × 7 sts.

FRONT: Decrease for the armholes in the same way as you did on the back piece. Cast off the middle 48 sts for the neck when it measures 7cm (2¾in) up from the armhole. Continue working the shoulders until they are the same height as the back and then cast off as follows: 3 × 8 sts, and 1 × 7 sts.

SLEEVES: Cast on as many sts as needed, based on your swatch, continue working in the round, placing a marker to indicate the beginning of the round, and work 5cm (2in) of ribbing. After the cuffs, increase 15 × 1 st on both sides of the marker, evenly spaced in height. You now have 94 sts. Continue working in pattern until the sleeve measures 51cm (20in). Cast off 14 sts (start 7 sts before the marker) and continue working back and forth. Work another 24 rows. Now cast off 7 × 1 st on both sides of the sleeve cap, at the beginning of each row. Continue and cast off 2 sts at the beginning of each row. When 30 sts remain, cast off 3 × 10 sts. Close the shoulder seams.

SHAWL COLLAR: Pick up sts along the right-hand side of the neck opening, the back of the neck and the left-hand side. Work back and forth in ribbing, k1, p1, until the piece is as long as the width of the neck opening at the front. Loosely cast off all sts. Sew the collar onto the cast-off row at the front; let the pieces overlap each other. Sew the sleeves into the armholes

CARDIGAN

This cardigan with a chest of 100cm (39⅜in), was inspired by the ganseys from Scheveningen. Instead of ribbing, the cuffs and hem are worked in garter stitch. The 'skirt' of the cardigan is worked in stocking/stockinette. The cables on the bodice pull the fabric in a bit, which contrasts nicely with the wider skirt. This knitting technique with cables is a good way to tailor the waist. Fixate the desired waistline on the inside of the cardigan by crocheting chain stitches along the panels, to ensure they cannot be pulled open. The sleeves are raglan.

194 CARDIGAN WITH RAGLAN SLEEVES, KNIT ON 4MM (US 6)
NEEDLES WITH SCHEEPJESWOL ZUIDERZEE CORNFLOWER BLUE

TUNIC

The tunics on this page have a regular T-shape model, same as the ganseys. They fall approximately 12–14cm (4¾–5½in) over the shoulder and are knee-length. The motifs used are inspired by the cabled ganseys and the block gansey from Durgerdam, Marken etc.

195 CABLE SWEATER IN TWO COLOURS: LOPI EINBAND 1762 AND 1763, KNIT ON 3MM (US 2) NEEDLES

196 SWEATER WITH BLOCKS AND STOCKINETTE IN TWO COLOURS: LOPI EINBAND 9165 AND 9020, KNIT ON 3MM (US 2) NEEDLES

SWEATERS WITH GANSEY MOTIFS

197 GANSEY FROM ZEELAND BY SJAAK HULLEKES, WHO CONSTRUCTED THE DIAMONDS FROM ARNEMUIDEN, USING THE OPEN-WORK MOTIF IN THE HEARTS FROM THE THOLEN GANSEY, ON A BACKGROUND OF GARTER STITCH USED IN THE TERNEUZEN GANSEY

198 HADEWYCH V.D. WERF KNIT HARLINGEN 1 WITH RAGLAN SLEEVES, A FRONT PLACKET WITH ZIP AND A STRAIGHT COLLAR, IN SCHEEPJESWOL ZUIDERZEE OFF WHITE ON 4MM (US 6) NEEDLES

199 THE 'WEDDING BETWEEN WIERUM AND PAESENS-MODDERGAT' BY TRIX DE WAAL COMBINES VARIOUS MOTIFS FROM THOSE TOWNS IN A TAILORED GANSEY, MADE IN WADDENWOL, WHICH IS ONLY PRODUCED IN SMALL BATCHES. BY KNITTING CABLES AT THE WAIST, ONE CREATES NATURAL TAILORING, AS THE CABLES PULL IN THE FABRIC. FOR TIPS ON KNITTING THE SADDLE SHOULDER, SEE GANSEY ENKHUIZEN 3 ON PAGES 135–136.

WORD OF THANKS

Again, I am very grateful for all the help and cooperation I received from all the museums, historical associations, archives, knitter and wool suppliers, for their time and expertise, photographs and other material they showed me. Without their assistance, this book would still be nothing more than an idea. Particulary Kees van der Plas and Jan van Beelen of the Museum Katwijk, Ihno Dragt of the Admiraliteitshuis in Dokkum and Museum 't Fiskershúske in Paesens-Moddergat, Mrs Noordervliet-Jol of Muzee Scheveningen, Jacco Hooikammer of the Holland Open Air Museum in Arnhem, Erik Walsmit of the Zuiderzeemuseum in Enkhuizen, Peter Zuydgeest and Joke van Leeuwen-Zuidgeest of the Vlaardingen City Archive, Maarten Roeper of Museum Kaap Skil in Oudeschild and Berend Zwart of the Fisheries Museum in Zoutkamp, all of whom shared with me their extensive knowledge of the fishing industry, the customs, traditions and details of daily life of bygone times. I also want to thank all the others, such as Mrs and Mr de Weert-Doesburg from Hippolytushoef; Fons Grasveld from Hilversum; Jeanine Otten of the Hannemahuis in Harlingen; Corien van der Meulen, Peter Overeem and Gertjan Baron of the Harderwijk City Museum; Pieter Jan Klapwijk of the Maritime Museum in Rotterdam; Aaf Steur-Sombroek from Volendam; Peter van Kooij and Andre Groeneveld of the Zuiderzeemuseum in Enkhuizen; Gineke Arnolli of the Fries Museum; Maarten Noot of the KNRM Archive in Den Helder; Jan Sander of De Egmonder Pinck; Janny Stecher-van den Berg of the Oudheidkamer Pernis; Jankees Goud from Yerseke; Chris Feij of the Historical Association Arnemuiden; Henk Klaassen of the Stichting Zuiderzeeambachten in Enkhuizen; Henk de Jong from Willemstad; Joop Speulman of the Historical Archive Charlois; Ton Mooijer of the Waterlands Archive in Purmerend; Margriet van Seumeren of the Huizer Museum; Arjens van Gammeren and Joop van Straten from Woudrichem; Willem van Norel of the Historical Association Arent thoe Boecop in Elburg; Piet Koomen of Oud Werversfhoof in Werversfhoof; Piet Morsch of the Zijper Archive in Schagerbrug; Ad Tramper of the Municipal Archive in Vlissingen; Piet Glas from Petten; Punt Colenbrander, Sjaak Hullekeus, Arnhem and Alexander de Bruin of the Noord-Holland Archive in Haarlem; Adriana den Hertog, Desiree van Halewijn and the Kastelijn family from Goedereede; Bertine Ruizendaal-Baas and E. Ruizendaal-van Diermen from Bunschoten-Spakenburg; Irma de Jong from Huizen; Marja Bekendam-de Boer from Genemuiden; Carol Christiansen of the Shetland Museum in Lerwick, Shetland Islands; William Moore from Scalloway, Shetland Islands; Deb Gillanders from Whitby, England; Job de Bondt of De Bondt in Tynaarlo; Gerrit Brouwer and Erik van der Horst from Wilnis; Bianca Nagel of craft shop Het Spoeltje in Almere-Haven; Saskia Piferoen of Lang Yarns in Korschenbroich, Germany; Loret Karman from Amsterdam; Erica Tepper of Wolinhuis; Jan and Russ Stanland of Frangipani Guernsey Wool in Penzance, England; Jo An Luijken of Wolhalla in Ruurlo, who placed the 'call to yarn' on their website; Trix de Waal from Ee; Teuni Levering from Eelde; and Marianne Horsman-Wagener. All of whom, with their expertise and efforts, were a great help to me in the production of this book.

I also want to warmly thank all the knitters who were so enthusiastic about these new patterns and who, again, achieved great results; the wholesalers who provided the material for the ganseys; our models Marlon, Emiel, Maarten, Kees, Reidunn, Irene, Ollie, Sabine, Esther and Daniel, who patiently put on one gansey after another; Gerhard Witteveen for his photographs; Ingrid van Roekel of Studio Jan de Boer, who again made this book a visual dream; my husband, family and friends for their endless support; and – last but not least – Els Neele and the team at Forte, who worked so hard to make this book possible.

If I have forgotten someone somewhere, my warmest thanks!

ACKNOWLEDGEMENTS

Museums

City Museum / Stadsmuseum Harderwijk, Harderwijk
Corien van der Meulen
Peter Overeem
Gertjan Baron

Dutch Open Air Museum / Nederlands Openluchtmuseum, Arnhem
Hanneke van Zuthem
Jacco Hooikammer

Fisheries Museum / Visserijmuseum Aike van Sien, West-Terschelling
Aike en Geesje Lettinga

Fisheries Museum / Visserijmuseum Breskens, Breskens
Jan Albregtse

Museum Katwijk / Katwijks Museum, Katwijk aan Zee
Kees van der Plas
Jan van Beelen

Fisheries Museum / Visserijmuseum Zoutkamp, Zoutkamp
Berend Zwart
Esther Toxopeus
Truus Nienhuis

Fries Museum, Leeuwarden
Gineke Arnolli

Het Behouden Huis, Terschelling
Richard van der Veen

Het Hannemahuis, Harlingen
Jeanine Otten

Huizer Museum
Margriet van Seumeren

Kaap Skil Museum, of beachcombers and sailors, Oudeschild, Texel
Maarten Roeper
Corina Hordijk
Esther Bánki
Ineke Vonk
Nieteke Roeper

Maritime Museum / Maritiem Museum, Rotterdam
Pieter-Jan Klapwijk
Patricia Mensinga

Marker Museum, Marken
Lijsbeth Visser-Schouten

Museum het Arsenaal, Woudrichem
Joop van Straaten

Museum 't Fiskershúske, Moddergat
Ihno Dragt
Trix de Waal

Museum Het Mauritshuis, Willemstad
Henk de Jong

Museum De Meestoof, Sint Annaland, Tholen
Bonnie Joosse

Museum Noordwijk Genootschap Oud Noordwijk
Sjaan and Eli van Kekeren-Brouwer

Museum Het Oude Raadhuis, Urk
Mevrouw A. Woord-Ras

Museum Spakenburg, Bunschoten-Spakenburg
Adriaantje de Jong

Museum De Turfschuur, Kolhorn
Puck de Groote

Museum Vlaardingen, Vlaardingen
Alexandra Poldervaart
Dr. J.P. van de Voort

Muzee Scheveningen, Scheveningen
Mevrouw Nel Noorder-Vliet-Jol

National Sea Rescue Museum / Nationaal Reddingmuseum Dorus Rijkers, Den Helder
Henk Stapel

Propagansey, Whitby, Yorkshire, England
Deb Gillanders

Scalloway Museum, Scalloway, Shetland Islands
William Moore

Sea and Port Museum / Zee- en Havenmuseum, IJmuiden
Thijs Zwart

Sheringham Museum, The Mo, Sheringham, Norfolk, England
Philip Miles
Wendy and Graham Austin

Shetland Museum, Lerwick, Shetland Islands
Carol Christiansen

Toankamer 't Ponthús, Stavoren
Andries Visser
Jan Visser

Volendams Museum
Lennie Posthumus-van Eijkelenburg
Betsie Pool-Plat
Griet Schokker-Zwarthoed

Wieringer Eilandmuseum Jan Lont, Stroe
Jeanne de Weert

Zijper Museum, Schagerbrug (NH)
Gerard van Nes

Zuiderzeemuseum, Enkhuizen
Erik Walsmit
Peter van Kooij
Andre Groeneveld

Archives & associations

Antiquities Room / Oudheidkamer Pernis
Janny Stecher-van den Berg

Archive / Archief Schouwen-Duiveland, Zierikzee
Aad Pattenier
Huib Uil

Archive / Archief Drukkerij Bout/ Huizer Courant, Huizen

Bomschuitclub, Zandvoort
Rob Bossink

City Archive / Stadsarchief Vlaardingen
Joke van Leeuwen-Zuidgeest
Peter Zuydgeest

Historical Archive / Historisch Archief Arnemuiden
Chris Feij

Historical Archive / Historisch Archief Charlois, Rotterdam
Joop Speulman

Historical Egmond / Historisch Egmond
Louis van der Zeijden
Martijn Mulder
Harry Harms

KNRM Archive / Archief KNRM, Den Helder
Maarten Noot

Meertens Institute / Meertens Instituut (KNAW), Amsterdam
Diedrik van der Wal
Tineke Tegelaers

Municipal Archive / Gemeentearchief Vlissingen
Ad Tramper

North Holland Archive / Noord-Hollands Archief, Haarlem
Alexander de Bruin

Stichting Brusea, Bruinisse
Barend van Lange

Stichting Zuiderzeeambachten, Enkhuizen
Henk Klaassen

Regional Archive / Streekarchief Goeree- Overflakkee, Middelharnis
Jan Both

West-Frisian Archive / Westfries Archief, Hoorn
Ronald Schilstra

Yarn wholesale companies
J. De Bondt, Tynaarlo
Job de Bondt

G. Brouwer, Wilnis
Gerrit Brouwer
Erik van der Horst

Lang Yarns, Switzerland
Saskia Piferoen

Hjertegarn, Denmark
Handwerkzaak 't Spoeltje, Almere
Bianca Nagel

Frangipani Guernsey Wool, England
Jan and Russ Stanland, Penzance, Cornwall
www.guernseywool.co.uk

Loret Karman RAW
Loret Karman, Amsterdam
www.loretkarman.nl

Drops Garn Studio, Groningen
Tine Jensen

Rauma, Noorwegen
Erica Tepper
www.wolinhuis.nl

Knitted Knots, Rolde
Teuni Levering, Riek Siertsema
www.knittedknots.nl

De Noordkroon, Texel
Renske v.d. Tempel

Waddenwol
Museum 't Fiskershúske, Paesens-Moddergat

Coats
Schachenmayer, Germany
Foula Wool
Magnus
www.foulawool.co.uk

Jamieson's of Shetland
www.jamiesonsofshetland.co.uk

Jamieson & Smith
www.shetlandwoolbrokers.co.uk

Knitters
Ady Karsten-de Natris, Amsterdam
Scheveningen 2 and 3

Alie van Schouwenburg, Raalte
Middelharnis 2, Zwartewaal 3, Elburg 3

Anja de Groot, Drachten
Hindeloopen 2, Genemuiden, Stavoren 2

Antoinette Hendriks, Houten
Katwijk 1, Lemmer 2

Astrid Pereboom, Bloemendaal
Volendam, Goedereede-Havenhoofd 2

Bella Dekker, Rotterdam
Arnemuiden 2, Den Helder 3, Colijnsplaat, Enkhuizen 3, Stavoren 1

Bianca Boonstra, Bleiswijk
Vlaardingen 1, Pernis 2, Marken 2, Durgerdam

Danny Honig, Amsterdam
Katwijk 2

Dieuwertje Verbrugge, Groningen
Elburg 1, Harderwijk 2

Dineke Woldhek, Wijhe
Egmond 4

Ella Jonkman, Dongen
Tholen 1, Tholen 2

Elly Hagen, Zwolle
Stellendam 1

Froukje Fokkinga, Amersfoort
Den Helder 6

Gerdy Vrijhoef, Raalte
Urk 2, Zandvoort 2, Zwartewaal 4, Goedereede-Havenhoofd 3, Terschelling/Oostmahorn

Greta Galama, Vries
Katwijk 5, Lemmer 3

Hadewych van der Werf, Hoorn
Hindeloopen 1, Katwijk 4, Harlingen 1 with raglan sleeves (see Fig. 198)

Harma Boven, Musselkanaal
Woudrichem 2, Hindeloopen 3

Heleen Bierling, Groningen
Woudrichem 1

Hella Senf, Haarlem
Zwartewaal 2

Hennie Lubberdink, Deventer
Oudeschild/Texel, Vlaardingen 3, Arnemuiden 3

Hieke Pereboom, Jirnsum
Hoorn

Hilda van Dijk, Tzum
Wierum 1, Zandvoort 3, Pernis 3, Vlaardingen 6, Oosterend 1, Huizen 2, Harderwijk 1

Ina Ribbers, Roden
Zandvoort 1

Ina Stoel, Bergen op Zoom
Maassluis, Volendam 2, Harderwijk 3

Jacqueline Jansen, Alphen aann den Rijn
Zwartewaal 1, Bunschoten-Spakenburg 4

Jannie Gelling, Gieten
Egmond 4, Ouddorp 2

Jannie Woldhuis, Eelderwolde
Huizen 1

Jenny de Boer, Tolbert
Wervershoof/Medemblik, Harderwijk 4

José van der Kooij, Purmerend
Egmond 3

Kitty Neijssel, Groningen
Scheveningen 1, Brouwershaven, Breskens 2, Bunschoten-Spakenburg 5

Lenie Tensen, Lambertschaag
Egmond 2, Ouddorp 1, Kolhorn boek 2, Petten

Leslie Eisinger, Delft
Vlaardingen 2

Liesbeth Boekhorst, Oosterbeek
Ouddorp/Middelharnis 2, Den Helder 2, Scheveningen 5, Yerseke 3

Lina Redeker, Annen
Harlingen, Yerseke 1, Oosterend 2

Margje Enting, Eext
Den Helder 1, Zoutkamp, Hindeloopen 2a, Yerseke 4, Modern Gansey (see Fig. 193)

Marian Smolders, New Zealand
Goedereede-Havenhoofd 1

Marja van Hout, Haarlem
Pernis, Katwijk 3

Marjoke Hoenderdos, Utrecht
Marken, Vlaardingen 5, Willemstad

Marthy van der Kamp, Buren
Den Helder 4, Middelharnis 4

Mirjam Korfage, Hoorn
Den Helder 5, Vlaardingen 7

Monique Dreef, Nieuw-Vennep
Bunschoten-Spakenburg 2

Nanette Drijfhout-de Graaff, Langbroek
Arnemuiden 1, Terneuzen

Netty Groen, Helvoirt
Bunschoten-Spakenburg 1, Charlois, Vlaardingen 4, Arnemuiden 2

Nienke Koedam-de Boer, Losser
Urk 1, Harlingen 2, Elburg 2

Rennie Knoop, St Nicolaasga
Stellendam 2, Breskens 1

Renske Dijkstra, Wierum
Wierum 4

Rianne Nota, Drunen
Enkhuizen

Rien Kaal, Nijkerk
Bunschoten/Spakenburg 3

Saskia Kleinsma, Groningen
Egmond 1, Paesens-Moddergat 3, Enkhuizen 2, Urk 3

Saskia Vogel, Duiven
Wieringen, Yerseke 2

Sjaan van Kekeren-Brouwer, Noordwijk
Noordwijk (see first book)

Sonja Klein, Leiden
Kolhorn (see first book)

Trix de Waal, Ee
Wierum 3, Paesens-Moddergat 1, 2, 3, Lemmer 1, Wedding Gansey (see Fig. 199)

Will Tol-Krabbendam, Lemmer
Wierum 2, Scheveningen 4, Middelharnis 3

Literature

Guernsey and Jersey Patterns
Gladys Thompson
B.T. Batsford Ltd., London, 1955

Patterns for Guernseys, Jerseys & Arans: Fishermen's Sweaters from the British Isles
Gladys Thompson
Dover Publications, New York, 1969/79

Fishermen's Sweaters
Alice Starmore
Anaya Publishers Ltd, London, 1993

Fishing for Ganseys
The Moray Firth Gansey Project
Kathryn Logan, Moray Firth Partnership, Great Glen House, Inverness

Heirloom Knitting
Rita Taylor
Search Press, Kent, 2013

Traditional Knitting: Aran, Fair Isle & Fisher Ganseys
Michael Pearson
William Collins Sons & Co Ltd, London – Glasgow – Sydney – Auckland – Johannesburg, 1984

Knitting from the Netherlands
Henriëtte van der Klift-Tellegen
Lark Books, Asheville, North Carolina, 1985

Photography credits

For all photos in this book, we have provided the source. We have made our best efforts to find and credit copyright holders. If you feel you have the unacknowledged copyright of an image in this book, please contact the publisher.

First published in Great Britain in 2017
Search Press Limited
Wellwood, North Farm Road,
Tunbridge Wells, Kent, TN2 3DR

Original Dutch edition published as *Vissers Truien 2*
Copyright © 2015 Forte Uitgevers BV, Baarn, the Netherlands
Text copyright © Stella Ruhe 2015

Illustrations, patterns, and charts: © Stella Ruhe, Amsterdam
Photography: Gerhard Witteveen Fotografie, Apeldoorn, and Stella Ruhe, Amsterdam
Design cover and interior pages: Studio Jan de Boer, Amsterdam
English translation by Ammerins Moss-de Boer, for Vitataal Tekst and Redactie, Feerwerd

All rights reserved. No part of this book, text, photographs or illustrations may be reproduced or transmitted in any form or by any means by print, photoprint, microfilm, microfiche, photocopier, internet or in any way known or as yet unknown, or stored in a retrieval system, without written permission obtained beforehand from Search Press.

The publishers and author can accept no responsibility for any consequences arising from the information, advice or instructions given in this publication.

ISBN: 978-1-78221-508-0

For more information about the books of Forte Uitgevers, go to: www.forteuitgevers.nl and www.fortecreatief.nl
For more information about ganseys, go to: www.visserstruien.nl or www.facebook.com/visserstruien

Suppliers
If you have any difficulty in obtaining any of the materials and equipment mentioned in this book, then please visit the Search Press website for details of suppliers: www.searchpress.com

Printed in China by 1010 Printing International Ltd

North Sea Coast

NOORDWIJK GANSEY

MAASSLUIS GANSEY

BROUWERSHAVEN GANSEY

THOLEN 2 GANSEY
SCHEEPJESWOL ZUIDERZEE 2

YERSEKE 1 GANSEY
LANG, THEMA NUOVA 0034

YERSEKE 2 GANSEY
SCHEEPJESWOL ZUIDERZEE 1

YERSEKE 3 GANSEY
LANG DONEGAL MERINO 0035

YERSEKE 4 GANSEY
LANG MERINO 150 0025

ARNEMUIDEN 2/4 GANSEY
SCHEEPJESWOL ZUIDERZEE 1

Wadden Coast

TERNEUZEN GANSEY
SCHEEPJESWOL ZUIDERZEE 2

TERSCHELLING/OOSTMAHORN GANSEY
LANG, YAK 0032

HARLINGEN 1 GANSEY

HARLINGEN 2 GANSEY
SCHEEPJES SUBTILE 405

PAESENS-MODDERGAT 1 GANSEY

PAESENS-MODDERGAT 2 GANSEY